FILM REVIEW 1968-9

FILM REVIEW
1968-9

edited by F. Maurice Speed

South Brunswick and New York:
A. S. Barnes and Company

Library of Congress Catalogue Card No: 67–21491
American edition published by
A. S. Barnes and Co., Inc.
Cranbury, N. J. 08512

Printed in Great Britain

Book designed by Ken Reilly

CONTENTS

In order to marshal and check the facts for these introductory notes to this review of the 1967–8 cinema year, I've been toiling through the year's trade papers, both American and British, and at the end I've come to the conclusion that it has been a somewhat uneventful period! By that I don't intend to suggest that *nothing* interesting has been happening – such a suggestion would be ludicrous at any time in the film industry anyway – but that the year has passed without any tremendous financial crisis, any great technical advance or anything else important enough to be likely to make it stand out as a milestone in the modern history of the movies.

Trends have continued much as last year (and the year before that). The number of people going regularly to the cinema continues to decline, if gently, but with the increased price of the seats the cinema owners have been able to hold their own – and in some cases do a little better than that. Overall the "take" by the (British) cinemas in 1967 was much the same as in the previous year – around £60 million. And this in spite of an attendance drop of some 17 million (down to 272 million). But if the owners have been asking more for their seats they have also been prepared in most cases to re-invest a great deal of their money in making moviegoing more comfortable. For instance, in the autumn of '67 the Rank Group announced they would be spending £2 million during the year on major renovation and redecoration of their cinemas (this including a complete modernisation of their West End shop windows, the Odeon in Leicester Square, and the Leicester Square Dominion Theatre). Their main rivals, the ABC circuit, similarly announced in the spring of this year a big programme along the same lines, to run into some £3 million and including expenditure of anything between £75,000 and £300,000 per cinema (this expenditure to include the building of new cinemas where it was thought they could be a profitable proposition). Both the two smaller but important circuits, Granada and Essoldo, also announced plans during the year, to modernise and renovate some of their cinemas.

However, the small individual and independent cinema owner could hardly have gained a great deal of satisfaction from the news; for a long time he has felt that he is getting a pretty poor deal generally and as his numbers decrease and the financial hurdles he has to face become stiffer a very real possibility arises that a time may come when such independently run and owned cinemas may well be a thing of the past and the whole business will be shared by a few major circuits. The trend is there, as it is of course with nearly every other business – from farming to shipbuilding!

But if the profits of such cinemas have sunk lower and lower (until in many cases the owner-manager finds he would almost be as well, if not actually better off on the dole!), the Big Boys with their rationalisation and advanced management techniques have been able to hold their own or even in some cases show improvement. The Rank group, for instance, followed up a record year (the profit announced in September 1967, rose above that of the previous year by 18.9 per cent to £22,437,000!) by this year's April announcement that there had been a further rise on the first (financial) half-year of some £4 million above the corresponding six months – though in this case the Group's interests are so varied and well spread that the cinemas no longer provide the major profit yields. But Associated British and Granada were also well up profitably above anything previously achieved.

In America the research lads came up with the somewhat astonishing conclusion that 25 per cent of the cinema's potential patrons there take 75 per cent of the admission tickets: posing the headache that if this were right it would be fair to conclude that a substantial number of Americans, possibly even a majority, never – or at least hardly ever – go out to see a film! And then comes the inevitable question: Why so? Where have the moviemakers and the men who show the films gone wrong?

What are the main grumbles likely to be for the exhibitors this coming year – apart, of course, from the ever-rising costs and tax demands? Almost certainly Pay TV will be a bone of contention; so, increasingly, is likely to be the question of the non-cinema showing of films on 16 mm. Certainly the exhibitors in both America and Britain are worried by potentially unfair competition from the small-size film. And the possibility of sales of modern film features to the TV networks is a constant nightmare to the exhibitor, again especially to the smaller, independent ones.

* * *

But whatever the general state of mind of the exhibiting side of the business there is certainly no depression among the movie-makers. In Hollywood the young men have been taking over at the studios and a historic moment came earlier this year when the last of the great old-style movie moguls, Jack Warner, sold his share of Warner

Brothers to Seven Arts and the names were combined in a new production company headed by 39-year-old Kenneth Hyman, reportedly an Anglophile (certainly he's married to an English girl!) and son of the company's chairman. He comes into the hot seat with sound recommendations: two of his own, prior, independent productions were *The Hill* and *The Dirty Dozen* – the latter movie having already reputedly made him a millionaire!

At Fox, Richard Zanuck at 33 has now fully taken over production responsibility from daddy Darryl, and is making a great success of things at the studio, with profits rising steadily from those dreadful (red) *Cleopatra* days to last year's soaring profit figure of $15,420,000.

At Paramount the man in charge is 37-year-old Robert Evans, former clothing manufacturer and (not particularly successful) actor, who used the profits from his firm's sell-out to become an independent producer at Fox under Richard Zanuck, from where he was lured by Paramount's new management board to his present job a couple of years back.

At Columbia they have been able to boast of of the most successful year in their history and are at present in the midst of a £15 million production programme. Having announced a more-than $15 million profit for the past year, U.A. are also involved in one of the largest production programmes in their history. And so the story continues; bigger profits last year, bigger plans for this. It all adds up to a bustling scene, bursting with optimism and promise, and one can only hope that the films now in the production line will justify all the faith that is being shown in them!

1967 will probably go down in cinema history as Takeover Year for during it both Paramount and United Artists were swallowed by American commercial giants and it was only after a pretty desperate struggle that Columbia and M-G-M- fought off determined efforts to do the same. As a result of this upheaval there have been convulsions at the top in the companies, both in the board-rooms and at the points of production (see my previous notes about the young men taking over) but things appear to have settled down reasonably well.

Toward the end of the period, the scene suddenly switched to Britain with the shock announcement that EMI (the Electrical and Mechanical Industries record giant) were taking over ABPC (the cinema-chain-owning Associate British Picture Corporation). The complication here was the ABPC were also involved with TV and this raised a number of tricky issues which I don't think it is necessary to go into here, but the final result of which was that after a few weeks EMI announced they would not endeavour to raise the 25 per cent stake they already had in ABC, and so to all intents and purposes retired from the fray.

What could, incidentally, be a significant move by the TV giants was the announcement, made by America's Columbia Broadcasting System, that they were going into feature-film production with a programme of some ten or a dozen films annually on a budget of something between 40 and 50 million dollars! And of this amount $3 million are initially to be spent in Britain, the first film, *Angel*, due to start production this summer.

This helped to swell the rumblings in some quarters about the British production scene being dominated by the American dollar. Actually the annual investment in this country by the American companies is now apparently running at something like £40 million sterling and however unpalatable the fact may be to some the hard facts are that without this influx of foreign capital the British film industry would be a very minor affair. Perhaps the most reasonably realistic attitude to the problem was that of the Film Production Association of Great Britain who said last year, in effect, Let's encourage British Finance – but don't *discourage* American!

* * *

The considerable amount of talk over a long period about Anglo-French co-operation plans has so far been the case of the mountain producing the proverbial mouse, for the best of my knowledge it has resulted in only two such feature films so far.[1] In these circumstances one must accept with certain reservations the current trumpet blasts now being made about a two-year co-production deal (signed last October) between England and Italy.

* * *

What of the year's technical advances? Well the shop window for the majority of these was, initially, the Expo '67 Exhibition at Montreal, where a number of original and, apparently, fairly revolutionary methods of film presentation were on show. I wasn't able to get to Canada myself so I can only refer you to an extremely able review of the situation there made by the veteran

[1] But to be honest, it must be admitted that many short films like Peter Graham's *Edith Piaf* have been genuinely co-produced.

American film showman and writer Arthur Mayer, who, writing in *The Motion Picture Herald* last September said:
"But two-dimensional pictures look dated and dreary in the dazzling, mad movie world of Expo '67. A few of the shows utilize only three screens (par for the Expo course is surely six) and the Czech 'Diapolyecran', although it looks like an ordinary screen, actually consists of 112 two-foot cubes, each of which contains one or more projectors equipped with innumerable slides. Never was an insatiable public bombarded by so endless an assortment of stimuli. Mirrors, globes and prisms multiply, distort, unite and emphasize the images they convey. Lights flash on and off – a cacophony of sound varies from laudatory comments concerning the joys of life in Ontario and the perfidies of the United States (disclosed in the Cuban pavilion) to some musical scores of remarkable merit.
"Possibly all of this hooplah is one of the reasons why the new films appear to me more like sugar-coated pills conceived over rapid consumption than for careful analysis. Most of the new devices are thoroughly delightful but their net effect is to create emotion rather than sober judgement. Never have I seen Mr McLuhan's thesis that 'the medium is the message' so convincingly and so perilously demonstrated."
We here in Britain were subsequently given an opportunity to check up on at least some of these novelties at the British Multiscreen Festival held this April at the Odeon, Leicester Square, when we were shown examples of both multi-screen and multi-image movies. In the first the screen is of "strip" proportions (far more like an elongated letter-box than Cinema-Scope, which was originally labelled as such) and when three different or varying images are shown side-by-side on this it is good enough, but when the one image spreads across the three screens the irritations of two "jerky joins" is exactly the same as in the original Cinerama. The significant thing about the multi-image films is that, at least to me, they are at their most impressive when they are showing one large, overall image! As novelties both ideas are interesting and worthy of further exploration because at some point they might well be able to expand the technical horizons of the normal film.
But whatever promise these new forms of cinema may hold for the – surely distant? – future, one thing is certain: colour today is triumphant. Perhaps spurred on by the advent of colour TV, more and more films are being made in various colour processes and already the black-and-white movie is becoming the exception in the British and American studios.
During the year Associated British came up with a new method of production in the studios which they have called Add-a-Vision and which, they claim, will, by borrowing in some ways from television technicalities, reduce production costs by saving at least 10 per cent in the time needed to make a movie in the studios.
On the exhibiting side, the Rank Group produced D–150, a system installed in the new Odeon at Marble Arch. For the technically minded, D–150 is "a deeply curved single-screen mounted in the normal manner on a 120° frame, with motorised, programmed masking to permit rapid and positive change from one aspect to another. Its patented surface has a gain factor of approximately 2. The design of the screen eliminates cross-reflection while increasing contrast and colour saturation. When being used for D–150 presentations the screen is 70 feet in width and has a curvature of 120° (or an average of 20 feet rise on the 'chord').
"Lenses for D–150 are specially designed to eliminate distortion that would result from projection with a standard lens on to a screen the size of the D–150 deeply curved screen. The lenses weigh 16½ lb. each and incorporate a backing lens of 5¼ in. f/1.9 and an adjustable front component which can be set to vary the size of the picture by about 6 feet.
"D–150 offers all of the advantages of instant, automatic change to ALL screen formats at the push of a button on the deeply curved screen."
A small but certainly not insignificant achievement was carried out by M-G-M- by which their everlasting classic *Gone With the Wind* was transformed from the old size of film to the more spectacular 70 mm. To solve the changeover from a ratio of 1.33 in width to 1 high, to a ratio of 2.2 to 1, the laboratory technicians developed a scanner-printer and viewing device which allowed movement of the lens of the viewing device from one side of the frame to the other – in effect, reshooting the film to make certain all essential action was included in the new print.
"The shutters on the printing devices used in making the new 70 mm negative clicked 1,280,000 times. In every step of this complicated laboratory feat, wherever one strip of film was being transferred to another, a liquid film gate was used to reduce the grain and eliminate scratches. This was necessary because in 1939 film emulsions

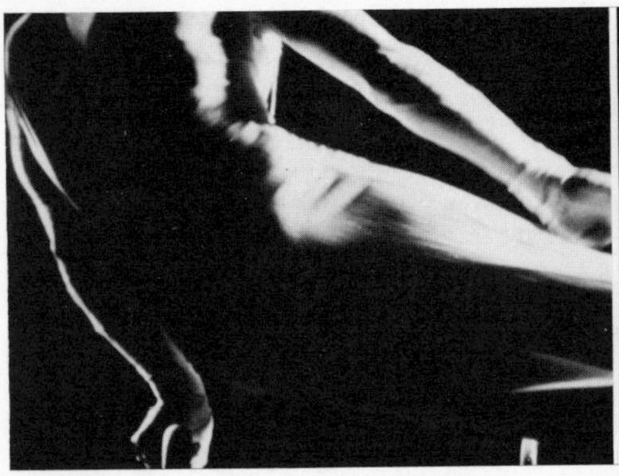

Multiscreen and Multi-Image Films: the most interesting new technical cinematic innovation went on – experimental – view at TVC's Multiscreen Festival, held in London (the Leicester Square Odeon) this spring. Already seen at "Expo '67" these Multiscreen and Multi-Image films presented several linked, or sometimes separate, images on the one screen at the same time. Though now just a novelty, it was obvious that they held great promise at some future time as an extension of normal film technique. Stills shown are from *Sources of Power*, a Lion Pacesetter Production sponsored by the Central Office of Information for the British Pavilion at "Expo '67": with three images screened adjacent to each other.

A Place to Stand, a dynamic multi-image optical sponsored by the Province of Ontario for their National Pavilion at "Expo '67" and awarded the "Oscar" for the best short film of 1967.

A film which became the centre of a quite considerable censorship argument was Dusan Makavejev's *The Switchboard Operator* which, refused a certificate for showing in the cinema presumably because of certain scenes centred on the dissection of the body of a beautiful young girl, was subsequently seen in part – the part being these actual scenes! – by the far wider TV audience.

Among all the new films, one of the most important and interesting historical revivals of the year was that by Gala Films of the original, 1931, Fritz Lang thriller "*M*", in which Peter Lorre as the child killer gave the greatest performance of his career.

Still the most popular – voted so by the cinema managers – of the short cartoon films is M-G-M's Academy Award-Winning *Tom and Jerry* series, now being seen on both the small (TV) and large (cinema) screen.

were inherently more grainy than the products of today.
"Once the 70 mm print problem was solved, it was up to M-G-M's sound department to bring the sound up to modern-day standards. By separating the voice tracks, music and effects on to separate magnetic tapes, it was possible through use of the newest electronic devices to equalise these sounds and put them on the release prints for directional dialogue and effects in stereo". Altogether it was quite an achievement.

* * *

Finally we come to the films themselves and the trends for the year. My own personal view here is that in many ways the movie-makers have been moving too fast in the wrong directions. For instance it has sometimes seemed that each director has tried to outdo his fellows in his daring treatment of sex, with the result that the film has been going further and further in its detailed examination of physical love-making so that not even the picturing of the final act itself is left unshown (it is in fact followed quite rigorously to the bitter end in the Swedish version of Vilgot Sjoman's *I Am Curious!*). Nudity, too, has become the norm: not only female but now male nudity is creeping into films without any real excuse for their inclusion.
The new freedom given to the moviemakers by this more permissive age has been in many cases grossly abused; the constant use of foul language, four-letter words, nudity and physical love-making in films has not made them any greater works of art or more entertaining: sensational, yes, but that's hardly a firm foundation in the long term. More recently it has begun to dawn on the exhibitors that the sensational and the sensationalised X certificated film may not be a permanent answer to their problems and that these Exy films might, indeed, be driving more patrons away than those they are luring into the cinemas. Nudity and sex have their rightful, honest places on the screen. They are an integral part of some stories, but it is crucial for artistic and other reasons that they are not just thrown into every film for the sake of cheap sensationalism, for the moment this happens they will attract the pornographically minded and drive away the great, sane majority of moviegoers whose support alone can keep the movies as a major form of entertainment. Let us never confuse permissiveness with viciousness – and during the past year this seems to me to be what has happened all too often.

* * *

Finally, a word of welcome to the American Film Institute, established in June 1967 with a distinguished board of trustees headed by Gregory Peck, a minimum three-year initial budget of $5 million and a worthy aim: "To promote the progress of the film arts and greater public understanding, appreciation and enjoyment of film", this to include film fellowships, the commissioning of textbooks, cataloguing of film resources, the establishment of film libraries and advanced study centres, and the subsidizing of new moviemakers.
I said initially in these notes that this has been an uneventful year in the cinema, and having completed them I would still repeat the statement, though anxious to qualify that judgement by saying that even so, this being the world of movies, quite a lot has been happening, as I'm sure, if you have read this far, you are now very well aware!

IN MEMORIAM

BASIL RATHBONE, who died on July 21, 1967 in New York at the age of 75, will inevitably always be associated with the part of Sherlock Holmes, which he created and played in a series of films featuring the famous Conan Doyle sleuth. But in fact this essentially English actor, with his impeccable accent and clipped delivery, had a very wide acting experience. Born in Johannesburg, South Africa, and educated at Repton College, England, Rathbone went into the Liverpool Scottish Regiment in World War I, winning the Military Cross. After trying insurance as a career he turned to acting, making his first appearance at Ipswich's Theatre Royal in 1911, subsequently touring with Sir Frank Benson's No. 2 company. He made his London stage début in 1914. His screen début, in 1925, was in an American film, *The Masked Bride*, but a number of British films followed and in 1939 he began his famous Holmes series. He was one of the most polished performers on the screen.

CHARLES BICKFORD, who died in hospital in Los Angeles on November 10 last year, was one of the screen's craggiest heroes and toughest villains, making the transition gradually through his screen career, completing it by ending up as a much sought-after character player. Bickford, who was in his 78th year, was appearing in TV shows (*The Virginian* series) almost until the end. Born in Cambridge, Mass., he was a U.S. Naval stoker during World War I, turning to acting when demobbed. It was not until ten years after his initial stage appearance that he made his first film, de Mille's *Dynamite,* in 1929. His screen reputation was made with his part opposite Garbo in *Anna Christie*. Some of his finest work was in Westerns (*The Plainsman*, *Red Wagon*, *The Big Country,* etc.) but he appeared and made a success in all sorts of roles in all sorts of films. He survived, only just, a lion mauling on the set in the mid-thirties, an accident which took him out of films for about a year. Off-screen he was as salty as on, never hesitating to give his opinion on any subject in no uncertain manner.

SMILEY BURNETTE will always be associated with the name of Gene Autry, for it was while he was operating a one-man radio station that he was invited to join Autry in the latter's stage show. Subsequently, starting in 1934, he appeared as Autry's increasingly familiar "side-kick" in a whole series of Autry movies. He was only 55 when he died in California last summer.

PAUL MUNI's real name was Muni Weisenfreund, and he was born in Lemberg, Austria, on September 22, 1895: so he was 71 when he died in August 1967, in California. His wide range brought him a great variety of roles but he will perhaps be best recalled by moviegoers for his outstanding character performance in *Scarface, I am a Fugitive from a Chain Gang, Story of Louis Pasteur, Juarez* and *Life of Emile Zola*. Muni was trained in the Yiddish theatre in New York, joining when still a lad and remaining with it until 1926; it was with this company that he made his first British stage appearance, at the Scala Theatre, London, in 1924. Of late his screen parts had been less rewarding.

JANE DARWELL, who died in California in August last year at the age of 87, had a career on stage, screen and TV which had spanned more than sixty years. She had initially studied music before turning to drama and – silent – films. Latterly plump, usually smiling and happy (there were very few of Shirley Temple's films in which she did not have a featured role) it was in that stark film *The Grapes of Wrath* in 1939 that she gave what was probably her greatest performance – one which brought her an Oscar. She continued to play in films until well over 80: indeed, her last part was in *Mary Poppins*.

When on the night of July 8, 1967, VIVIEN LEIGH was found dead in bed at the early age of 53, she was studying for a new role and her future was full of promise and plans. Miss Leigh's real name was Vivien Mary Hartley and she was born at Darjeeling, India, on November 5, 1913. She came to London in 1920, entered RADA, and married, at the age of 18. Her beauty, revealed in her first professional part in Ashley Duke's *The Mask of Virtue* brought her a contract from Korda. She had but little screen experience when Selznick cast her in the role of Scarlet O'Hara in his gargantuan *Gone With the Wind,* but her performance in this was memorable enough to bring her an Oscar and world-wide critical acclaim. On the stage two of her greatest successes were in Wilder's *Skin of our Teeth* and Williams's *A Streetcar Named Desire* (winning a second Oscar when the later was filmed in Hollywood). But these were only the highlights in a succession of fine stage and screen performances, both in classical and modern roles. Divorced from her first husband in 1940, she married Laurence Olivier that same year, subsequently divorcing him in 1961. Miss Leigh was always dogged by poor health and never appeared to get completely rid of the TB which she suffered from when young.

16

The son of a well-known Austrian clown, ANTON WALBROOK – real name Adolph Anton Wilhelm Wholbruck – was born in Vienna in November 1900, commencing his stage career there when he was in his twenties. With the advent of the Nazi régime Walbrook became a refugee, and came here to carve a new career for himself. In Britain, Walbrook made an instant success as Queen Victoria's German husband in *Victoria the Great*, and was a hit in the stage production of Coward's *Design for Living*. During the war he appeared with success in a number of British films, including *Gaslight*, *The Life and Death of Colonel Blimp* and, most popularly memorable, as the pianist-pilot in *Dangerous Moonlight*. He was one of the first non-singing actors to tackle a singing part in a musical: succeeding in both *Call Me Madam* and *Wedding in Paris*. During the last few years he had made a return to Europe to play in his own language and it was, in fact, while he was on the stage in Munich that he suffered the heart attack which presaged his death at the beginning of October last year.

Someone who knew FRANCOISE DORLEAC well said that she was generally late and usually in a hurry, and it was probably this characteristic which led to her tragic car smash one night last August just ten miles out of Nice as she was on her delayed way to start a new film! Miss Dorleac made her first impact outside her own country – where she already had a number of small parts to her credit – in 1964 in Truffaut's *La Peau Douce*. This led to international interest in her and, as she spoke English, she was soon making British-made movies, notably *Where the Spies Are* and *Cul de Sac*. She was also in *Ghengis Khan*. In one of her last films, *Les Demoiselles de Rochefort*, she co-starred as a sister to her real-life sister, Catherine Deneuve.

With the death of SPENCER TRACY, in Hollywood on June 11 last, at the age of 67, went one of the last of the great film-stars of the twenties–thirties period. *The Times* obituary, indeed, quoted Tracy as himself saying: "When I go a whole epoch will have ended", and he said this without any conceit: it was a statement of fact. He was one of the outstanding players in the era in which the stars dominated Hollywood and the screen, one of the many "greats" which Louis B. Mayer created for M-G-M. Obstinate in the studios, he was at the same time the complete professional and extremely proud of it. His list of films are a shining string of celluloid jewels: *San Francisco, Fury, Captains Courageous* (in spite of the fact that the role did not really suit him), *Boys' Town, Bad Day at Black Rock,* and, more recently, *Judgement at Nuremberg*. Though ill for several years and in fact quite aware he was under sentence of death, he never refused a good part and he had only just completed *Guess Who's Coming to Dinner,* opposite one of his favourite co-stars Katharine Hepburn, when he died. Tracy was unique, a man of his time and place: and, to complete the necessary cliché, "there'll never be another like him".

JAYNE MANSFIELD was an outsized character in many ways; plump, bosomy, she happily lived in the old Hollywood star tradition, her private life put her screen roles to shame on occasion as she hit headline after headline.
And, tragically, she died in the same way, in a terrible car crash in August 1967 at the early age of 33. Born Joyce Palmer in the Pennsylvania town of Bryn Maw she made her stage début in *Will Success Spoil Rock Hunter?*, playing the sort of Hollywood siren which she was in fact to become. Various small roles came her way, in some of which she showed that she had a real sense of comedy, being quite happy to satirise herself as a sex symbol. Before her death she had slipped into a series of less happy sex movies and had become primarily a cabaret star in night-clubs. One of her best movies was the British Western, *The Sheriff of Fractured Jaw*.

One of Hollywood's perfect Englishmen, REGINALD DENNY, educated at St Francis Xavier College, Sussex, died in June 1967, at the age of 72, having been acting since a child and in films since 1919. Son of an actor, he was only eight when he made his first London appearance at the old Court Theatre in *A Royal Family*. In 1911 he made his initial trip to America, on a tour of *The Quaker Girl* and after the war, in which he served in the R.F.C., (predecessor of the R.A.F.), he returned there to begin his long succession of film and stage roles.

Mr Denny, who died in a nursing home at Teddington, Surrey (close to Richmond where he was born) was particularly successful in the role of Sapper's hero Bulldog Drummond and he made eight movies as this character.

MAURICE ELVEY, who died August, 1967 at Brighton at the age of 79, was one of Britain's cinematic veterans, making something like three hundred films during his forty-five-year career. Elvey's real name was William Seward Folkard and he was born in Darlington on November 11, 1887. He started out as an actor but quickly switched to stage direction and became established for his work both in London and New York before, in 1912, switching again to the cinema. His first movie, he would happily recall, was *Maria Marten* after which he went on to make a long line of popular silent movies. When the talkies came, Elvey quickly began to re-make some of his silent successes in the new medium. He was always forthrightly commercial, though *Beware of Pity* was an artistic success. Latterly he had turned to broad British farce with films like *Dry Rot*. In his retirement he was always ready to reminisce in public on TV or elsewhere of his experiences and for a time wrote regularly about Good Food in London.

CLAUDE RAINS was never ashamed of the fact that he started out as a theatrical call-boy at London's His Majesty's Theatre, subsequently moving up to prompter and then assistant stage-manager. Born in London in 1890 (some sources say 1889), it was only after some thirty-three years of stage acting and managing, interrupted by the war, that he made his screen début, taking a leading role but never in fact being seen in *The Invisible Man*. But this was followed by a long line of more conventional roles, notably in *The Constant Nymph*, *The Devil's Disciple*, *They Won't Forget*, *Juarez* and, in lighter vein, *The Lost World*. Another of his best performances was in Pascal's contentious *Caesar and Cleopatra*. One of his last screen appearances was in *Lawrence of Arabia*. He died, in Laconia in New Hampshire.

ALBERT WARNER, who died on November 26, 1967 was one of the four brothers who built the fabulous Warner Brother's celluloid empire. Beginning as an exhibitor, he moved into production with his brothers in 1912: it was they who made *The Jazz Singer* in the van of the talkie revolution. Third of the four brothers to pass from the scene, he was 84 when he died at the Miami Beach home to which he had retired some years previously.

Anyone who saw *The Wizard of Oz* will recall BERT LAHR, with his crab-apple face, in it. Bert, whose real name was Irving Lashreim, had a long career as a comic in stage musicals and it wasn't until 1933 that he went into films. Latterly he had also been seen frequently on TV, and back in the thirties and forties he was a star radio performer. He was 72 when he died on December 3 last in a New York hospital, and at the time of becoming sick he was actually making a new film, *The Night They Raided Minsky's*.

One of France's greatest film directors, JULIEN DUVIVIER, died in Paris this winter at the age of 71. Born in Lille on October 8, 1896, Duvivier started out as an actor and then became assistant stage director before turning to the films. He was responsible for some of the great pre-war French screen classics, *Pepe le Moko, Carnet de Bal, Poil de Carotte* among them. Going to Hollywood, he made a number of (commercially successful) movies including *The Great Waltz* and *Tales of Manhatten*. He was versatile; directing, producing and writing, and sometimes combining all three talents, notably in the *Don Camillo* movies.

BASIL SYDNEY, who died last January at the age of 73, was born at St Osyth, Essex, on April 23, 1894, and made his first appearance on the London stage in 1909. And it was primarily as a stage performer that he was known, with a tremendous list of extremely diverse roles to his credit in both the classics and modern plays. But he did appear in films in productions that ranged from Olivier's *Hamlet* to *The Dam Busters*. His ability was to always give a professional, convincing performance no matter what kind of role or what type of production.

G. W. PABST, the famous Austrian director who died in Vienna in the summer of 1967 at the age of 82, made many films during his long career but probably none more famous or memorable than *The White Hell of Piz Palu:* others include, *West Front 1916*, *Joyless Street* with Garbo and *The Beggar's Opera*.

HAROLD HUTH, who died last winter, was an actor and a director as well as producer. Retiring from acting because of ill-health, Huth became casting director for Gainsborough before becoming co-producer and producer. Born in Huddersfield in 1898, he will probably always be best remembered in the business by his *Love Story* and other melodramas made at the old Gaumont-British studios at Lime Grove in the forties. In 1957 be became managing-director of Warwick Television Films.

London-born (1906) BENITA HUME, who died on November 1, 1967, was a RADA graduate who made her initial London stage appearance in 1925 in *Kismet*. And she made her screen début the same year in *The Happy Ending*, thereafter appearing in a long succession of silent and then sound films. At the time of her death she was in private life Mrs George Sanders.

ANDY CLYDE was, as one might expect, from Scotland: born Blairgowrie, March 25, 1892, the son of a stage-manager. Going to America he began to appearing in some of Mack Sennett's comedies in 1929 and later was cast in a number of feature-films including *McFadden's Flats*, *Annie Oakley* and *This Above All*. But it is for his appearances in a long series of Westerns that he will be best remembered, especially as saddle pal to Bill Boyd in the *Hopalong Cassidy* series. He died in Hollywood last summer at the age of 75.

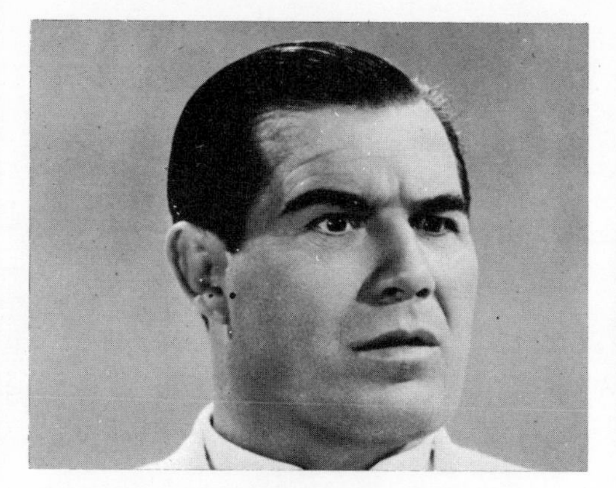

New Yorker born and bred, JAMES DUNN, who died last autumn in Santa Monica at the age of 66, had appeared in a great many movies since he made his screen début in 1931 in *Bad Girl*. His greatest film success, however, was in 1945, when he was awarded the Best Supporting Actor Oscar for his performance in *A Tree Grows in Brooklyn*.

Iowan born (August 9, 1899) NAT PENDLETON, who died on October 13, 1967, began his business career with the Standard Oil Company, for whom he went to Portugal. After a year there he opened his own General Importing Company. Returning to the U.S. in 1921, he founded and became General Manager of the True Story Film Corporation. After this he went into professional wrestling and it was as a wrestler that he made his acting début on the stage. Subsequently he made a great many screen appearances in character parts, often in tough and comedy roles.

DUNCAN MACRAE was a Scots actor who preferred working in Scotland. Born and educated in Glasgow, he came from Highland crofting stock and was actually a teacher until the last war, when he took up acting. A founder member of the Glasgow Citizen's Theatre he was also a great worker for the Edinburgh Festival over a period of twenty years. Famous for his panto "Dames" his last stage role south of the border was in Molière at the Mermaid Theatre, London; his last film *Thirty is a Dangerous Age Cynthia*. He appeared in *Casino Royale, Our Man in Havana, Tunes of Glory* and *The Kidnappers;* and many will recall his grand performance in *Whisky Galore*. TV fans will best recall him in the *Finlay* episodes and, more especially as the captain in the *Para Handy* series. Like another great comedian, Alastair Sim, Macrae's lugubrious and comic range was immense and his facial expressions could tell a whole story. He collapsed in November 1966 and died on March 23, 1967, in Glasgow's Victoria Infirmary: the cause of death being an inoperable brain tumour.

Director ANTHONY MANN was actually working on location in Berlin in the summer of 1967 on his new film *Dandy in Aspic* when he collapsed and died. Born in California in June 1906, Mann had been a stage actor and director before making his first film in 1942. Some of his best-known films include *Winchester '73, Bend of the River, Glen Miller Story, El Cid, The Heroes of Telemark* and *The Fall of the Roman Empire*.

Among other film personalities who died during the latter half of 1967 were TOTO, the famous Italian clown and comedy actor who had made more than a hundred films in his own country; LUDWIG DONARTH, who will be recalled as Al Jolson's father in the biographical films about the "Mammy" star; and JACK RAMSDEN, former editor of *British Movietone News*.

22 CARL DREYER, who died in Copenhagen at the end of March last, at the age of 79, was one of the "great" film directors. Born in Denmark, he did various jobs before becoming a journalist, which – at least indirectly – led to his shift into screen-play writing. His first film was made in 1917, and it was called *The President*. There followed several more films, and then in 1928 came the movie which was to bring him world renown, *La Passion de Jeanne d'Arc*, which, made in France, was stamped right the way through with his highly individual style and a sincerity which made this immediately a film classic. After his *Vampyre*, made in 1932, he left the film world and returned to writing, and apart from a small documentary he did nothing more until 1943, when he made *Day of Wrath*, which again was an immensely powerful film. His last movie, *Gertrud*, was one of the films selected for inclusion in the annual London Film Festival in November '67. At the time of his death, Carl Theodore Dreyer was actually at work on a screenplay about the life of Christ, which he hoped he would be able to film against the actual locations of the events in Israel.

STUART ERWIN, who died four days before the Christmas of 1967, was born in California. He won his first film role in rather amusing circumstances: this was by impressing a talent scout with his performance in a play in which he took five characters simultaneously! His first film was *Does Mother Know Best?*, and he went on to make a considerable number including *The Cock-Eyed World*, *Men Without Women*, *Going Hollywood*, etc. More recently he was the star in the TV series *Trouble With Father*.

DORETTA MORROW, who died from cancer in London in February last at the age of 41, was an American who for the last few years had made England her home. She made a number of films, including *Because You're Mine*, but she was best known for her stage work, including more than a thousand performances in *Kismet*. She also appeared in the 1959 Palladium pantom ime. Other work included cabaret and TV.

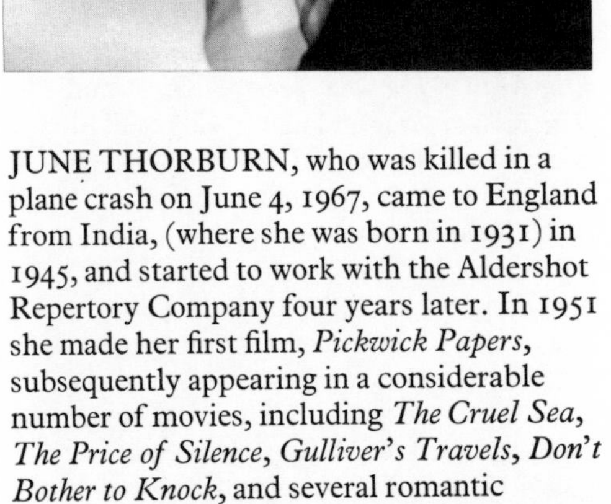

JUNE THORBURN, who was killed in a plane crash on June 4, 1967, came to England from India, (where she was born in 1931) in 1945, and started to work with the Aldershot Repertory Company four years later. In 1951 she made her first film, *Pickwick Papers*, subsequently appearing in a considerable number of movies, including *The Cruel Sea*, *The Price of Silence*, *Gulliver's Travels*, *Don't Bother to Knock*, and several romantic melodramas. She was also seen quite often on TV.

JUANITA HALL will best be recalled by filmgoers for her performance as the Tonkinese Mama in *South Pacific*, in the film of which she repeated her enormous stage success with the singing of the "Balli Ha'i" number. She died at the age of 66 in New York on February 28 last. Prior to her death, she had been unable to work for several years owing to continued illness.

Though primarily a stage actor, Sir DONALD WOLFIT did appear in a considerable number of films during his long and distinguished career, which ended in a London hospital on February 17 last at the age of 65. He started, during the 1914 war, as a boy singer and reciter of poems, later served seasons with the distinguished drama companies of Charles Doran, Matheson Lang, Barry Jackson and Harcourt Williams. At the outbreak of World War II he organised a company to tour Shakespeare and other classics for ENSA. Wolfit made his first movie in 1934, *Death at Broadcasting House*, and from then on appeared pretty regularly on the screen; in a series of horror movies like *Blood of the Vampire*, *Hands of Orlac* and *Dr Crippen*, also in other such contrasting films as *The Pickwick Papers*, *Room at the Top*, *Lawrence of Arabia*, and *The Sandwich Man*. But one of his most memorable screen roles was that of *Svengali* in a 1955 screen re-make of that famous story.

VIRGINIA MASKELL, who died tragically at the end of January last, soon after being found in a state of collapse not far from her home, was only 31, and she never quite fulfilled the promise of her early films (Judgement from a friend: "She was too *nice* a person ever to get on in the movies!"). She made her début in 1959 in the film *Virgin Island*, which was only completed after a great deal of background trouble, but which was to prove something of a personal triumph for this fresh and lovely young actress. Subsequently she was seen, perhaps a little less impressively (though always giving an interesting performance), in *The Man Upstairs*, *Jet Storm*, *Doctor in Love*, *Suspect*, and *Only Two Can Play*. She also appeared, occasionally, on the stage and on TV. Her last film, *Interlude*, is at the time of writing still awaiting its first showing.

MAE MARSH, who died early this year in California at the age of 72, was one of the most famous of the earliest stars of the silent screen. Born in Madrid, educated at the Convent of the Immaculate Heart in Hollywood, she was only 14 when, going to the studio to watch elder sister Lovey Marsh working in a slapstick comedy, she was "spotted" by the great D. W. Griffith, who immediately gave her parts in his epics *Birth of a Nation* and *Intolerance*. Later, as one of the silent era's foremost glamour stars, she became Samuel Goldwyn's first "Goldwyn Girl". In 1925 she came to England to appear in *The Rat*. A few years later she retired from the screen for a period of some 12 years, but returned to the studios soon after the advent of talkies and began to make a new career for herself as a small part player. One of her last pictures was *Two Rode Together*.

One of Britian's best, most sensitive directors, and a considerable figure in the British Film Industry in many other ways, the Hon. ANTHONY ASQUITH died in a London nursing home on February 21 at the age of 65. The son of the first Earl of Asquith, Anthony went to Winchester and Balliol and it was while at Oxford that he became a founder member of The Film Society. After University he went to Hollywood for six months to study movie-making methods there. Back home he started as a sort of man-of-all-work in the studios, but in 1928 was given his first movie to direct, *Shooting Stars*. From then on he was seldom not in the throes of making a movie; some of his more worthwhile later work was seen in *Pygmalion*, *French Without Tears*, *The Demi-Paradise*, *Way to the Stars*, *The Winslow Boy*, *The Browning Version*, *The Millionairess*, and his last picture, *The Yellow Rolls Royce*. Always interested in the "other side" of the industry, he was President of the Association of Cinematograph, Television and Allied Technicians and was a Governor of the British Film Institute.

NICK ADAMS is probably better known for his TV work, especially in the series *Saints and Sinners*, than for his large screen work, though he had appeared in well over a score of pictures, including *Mr Roberts*, *Rebel Without a Cause*, *The F.B.I. Story*, *The Interns*, and his last (and yet to be seen), *Fever Heat*. At the time of his death he was due to start a new movie in Mexico.

EARL ST JOHN, who died this winter at the age of 76 (suddenly while on holiday in Spain) was one of the best kind of film showmen. Likeable, knowledgeable and efficient, he started out (he was born in Baton Rouge) selling films. These ranged from Chaplin's comedies to religious epics like *From Manger to Cross*. He first arrived in this country when he came here as an American soldier in the First World War. He stayed on after the end of hostilities to become a cinema manager in Manchester, later becoming Publicity Director of Paramount Pictures over here. It was Earl who opened the Plaza, the Carlton and the Paramount in Tottenham Court Road. When Rank bought out the Paramount circuit, St John became Executive Producer down at Pinewood Studios and as such began to turn out the long run of successful films, more than 140 in all, many of them real money-spinners like *The Card*, *The Million Pound Note*, *A Town Like Alice*, *Genevieve*, the *Doctor* films and *A Tale of Two Cities*.

CHARLES CHAPLIN Junior, at 42 the eldest son of Chaplin Senior, died last March in Hollywood after a heart attack. Though an actor, he never reached any great heights in his profession, and he always felt that his name was against him: he is on record as once saying that he wished he had been called James! His most notable achievement was his 1960 book, *My Father, Charlie Chaplin*, with its sometimes illuminating account of Life with dad!

FAY BAINTER, who died last April in Hollywood at the age of 74, had not been seen very much on the screen during the past few years, although she did make an occasional appearance on TV. In fact she had been ill for a considerable period. The high-spot of her screen career was the winning of an Oscar in 1938 for her supporting performance in *Jezebel*. Her career spanned some 25 years and included in addition to her 35 movies a number of Broadway stage productions.

FINLAY CURRIE, who died on May 10, 1968, at the age of 90 was still working until a week or so before his death: although not well, as late as last March he was gathering critical praise for his TV work. From Edinburgh, he was trained as organist, but appeared on the stage there as early as 1898. His first appearance down South was in vaudeville (his act was billed as "Harry Calvo, the double-voice vocalist"), later as a comedian he toured both in America and Australia. In the 30's he started appearing in straight plays in the West End and started to work in movies about the same time. He subsequently appeared in an enormous number of films including *Rome Express, Great Expectations, The Mudlark, Ben Hur* and *The Fall of the Roman Empire*.

WORLD ROUND-UP

PETER COWIE is the much-travelled Editor and Publisher of the "International Film Guide", a film critic and an authority on the movies and moviemakers of all countries.

"Hollywood is dead. Long live American films!" a cynical observer might note in 1968 as the pattern of world film production, once a prey to every trend in the Los Angeles suburb, shifts distinctly away from the concept of a "film factory". Paradoxically, American film-makers are learning from their European counterparts more than at any stage since the twenties, when foreign talents like Lubitsch, Mamoulian, Dieterle, Stiller, and Sjöström were "imported" by Hollywood to raise artistic standards. Now John Frankenheimer, busy filming *The Fixer* in Budapest and *The Homecoming* in London, can say with relish from his house in Beverly Hills: "Europe is where the action is: Godard, Antonioni. I want to be part of that, if I can." Arthur Penn, everybody's director of the moment, made *Bonnie and Clyde* in Texas just as he had shot *Mickey One* in Chicago. Sidney Lumet's last three films have been created in London (*The Deadly Affair*), New York (*Bye, Bye, Braverman*), and Stockholm (*The Seagull*).
This respect for the European way of cinema is reflected in the enterprising policy of United Artists, one of the mightiest of U.S. distributors. Not only did U.A. buy Ingmar Bergman's *Persona* and *The Hour of the Wolf* for a million dollars, they purchased the Swede's latest picture, *The Shame*, almost before a camera was turned. The same company released Claude Lelouch's *Vivre pour Vivre*, while Universal snapped up Volker Schlöndorff's *Mord und Totschlag* (*A Degree of Murder*) before it was even shown at Cannes.
All this has led to an intense cross-fertilisation of ideas and money at every level of the industry. In the late fifties, the leaders of the French *nouvelle vague* were constantly writing about their adulation for Hawks, Ray, Losey, Walsh and the rest. Now it is Arthur Penn who tells an interviewer that he has been influenced by Godard and Truffaut, Frankenheimer who enthusiastically admires the technique of Kurosawa, and Lee Marvin who, so delighted with the fanciful style of John Boorman in *Point Blank*, has insisted on working with the British director on future films.
More and more of the heads of production in Hollywood are in their thirties. The major studios are more receptive to new ideas, to a new climate of, if you like, permissiveness. Once again *Bonnie and Clyde* and *Point Blank* offer themselves as examples: both pierced with a vivid brand of violence that has offended some and excited many people. Not surprisingly there has been a hectic revival in gangster pictures. The wheel turns full circle, leap-frogging a generation back to the thirties, when national policies and paper money seemed as precarious as they do today.

FRANCE

Only one matter has united the sympathies of every French *cinéaste* this past year – the dismissal of Henri Langlois, co-founder of the Cinémathèque Française and its dominant spirit for over thirty years.
"Could they (the Centre National) not have realised that the Cinémathèque was the real heart of French cinema?" queried *Cahiers du Cinéma* in a special supplement on the rumpus. Langlois became in February a martyr in the larger struggle against the "colonisation" of the cinema by the French Government. The Centre National is held in almost slavish esteem by exhibitors and industry men all over France, because it

controls the purse strings and holds a whip-hand over the tax system whereby certain classes of cinema can qualify for relief. There is an air of desperation among film men in Paris. Even the specialised art houses are finding business poor because too many people have tried to enter the market, and because the ever-increasing revival of old films on television is more menacing than before.

It is clear that the French film industry urgently needs an overhaul if the achievements of the *Nouvelle Vague* are to be consolidated. It needs, in short, a man with the energy and skill of Harry Schein in Sweden. There is a surfeit of co-productions lacking in character and sincerity, and many of the major directors – Chabrol, Malle, Enrico—have moved into the glossy production belt, losing much of their talent *en route*.

Truffaut has shot two new films of considerable interest, *The Bride Wore Black* and *Stolen Kisses*, and Jean-Pierre Melville has made *Le Samurai* and *La Chienne*. This latter is a remake of Renoir's 1931 film of the same title, and the old master himself has been in Paris preparing for a new picture with Jeanne Moreau. Alain Resnais's *Je t'aime, je t'aime* was received with much enthusiasm and Jacques Tati's *Playtime* was a slow but immensely effective comedy filmed in 70 mm and colour in a "town" specially constructed in the suburbs of Paris. It is ten years since his last picture, *My Uncle*, appeared, but the wait has been more than justified. Buñuel continues to work in France, following *Belle de Jour* with *The Milky Way*. Finally, Eric Rohmer, a director who in 1960 one would have thought unlikely to survive the euphoria surrounding the *Nouvelle Vague*, proved himself an astute and discriminating film-maker with *La Collectionneuse*. This is a sensual description of a *ménage à trois* in Provence, where two dandies down from Paris on a reading holiday are tantalised by a long-legged creature named Haydée Politoff. Their rather literary conversations in the balmy countryside suddenly seem delightfully sophisticated after the inane and pretentious concoctions served up by Jean-Luc Godard.

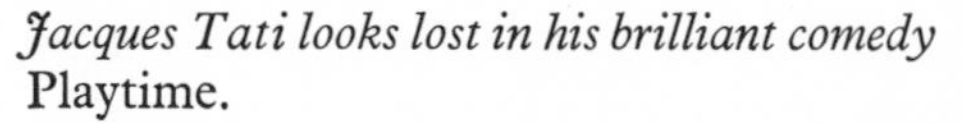

Jacques Tati looks lost in his brilliant comedy Playtime.

U.S.A.

With the arrival in Europe this year of P. Adams Sitney's "travelling circus" of underground films from America, one can begin to gauge the extent of the revolt against Hollywood. Are these underground pieces, ranging from a few minutes to hours in length, sometimes projected on two screens simultaneously, sometimes shot originally on 8 mm – are they the authentic image of American cinema today? They are certainly more indigenous than the epics and large-budget films made by American directors in Europe, and at least they do not pander to television like so many Hollywood studios. But as the festival of experimental cinema at Knokke-le-Zoute emphasised last Christmas, there are underground film-makers in every country, Holland, Sweden, Germany, etc. The most recognisably American films these past eighteen months have been off-beat comedies like *A Thousand Clowns*, *A Fine Madness*, *Funnyman*, and *The Tiger Makes Out*. These all exploit the unique urban landscape in which most Americans live, using this background to point up the humour rather in the manner of W. C. Fields and Laurel and Hardy in the thirties. Mayor John V. Lindsay has encouraged location shooting in New York by relaxing various restrictions and ordinances that formerly prevented film companies from choosing sites freely in the metropolis.

An important event this year has been the launching of the American Film Institute, under the leadership of George Stevens, Jr. He plans to make film preservation a vital part of the Institute's activity, and there is also a system of grants for budding film-makers and probably for student research as well. A complete catalogue of all American films past and present is one of the most ambitious undertakings of the Institute, which has its headquarters in Washington.

CANADA

The language division in Canada extends to film production. Parisians are fed exclusively on a diet of movies from Quebec and Montreal, by directors like Lefebvre, Perrault, Groulx and others. But here in Britain and in the United States, it is the English-speaking cinema of Toronto and Ottawa that prevails. Furthermore, there are very few pure-bred Canadian films. Raymond Stross's production of *The Fox*, starring Anne Heywood and Keir Dullea, was shot around Toronto but is no more a Canadian movie than *The Luck of Ginger Coffey*. Several native directors have moved south of the border, among them Sidney Furie, Silvio Narizzano, and Norman Jewison (who made the Academy-Award winning film *In the Heat of the Night*). But one figure whose best work has strong Canadian associations is Allan King. His documentary, *Warrendale*, about a children's asylum, moved and shocked audiences wherever it was screened during 1967. Among the fictional films mention should be made of *Waiting for Caroline*, Ron Kelly's vision of love between French and English-speaking Canadians, and *The Ernie Game*, Don Owen's over-fragmented study of a nihilistic youth in Montreal.

SWEDEN

The Swedes are proud that theirs is virtually the only European film industry not used as an investment pool by the Americans (although United Artists have paid large sums for Bergman's last three films, and Bo Widerberg is filming *Ådalen*, about a strike that took place with bloody consequences in northern Sweden in 1931, with American backing company). The two big firms, Sandrews and Svensk Filmindustri, still predominate, and both have given a free hand to energetic young producers.

At Sandrews, Göran Lindgren's main achievements have been Cornell's cool and wry comedy, *Hugs and Kisses*, and Vilgot Sjöman's controversial and (to foreign audiences) sexually startling study, *I am Curious*. Lena Nyman, the chubby blonde star of Sjoman's two-part film, is "curious" about everything on a line between sex and socialism. Much of the action consists of *cinéma-vérité* interviews, questions and answer sessions that sometimes involve even the director himself. The fundamental danger of this brand of cinema is that its arbitary selection of interviews and incidents flies in the face of the objectivity that such an ultra-realistic approach would suggest. In the cinema of the late sixties, it is becoming increasingly hard to distinguish between fact and fabrication.

At Svensk Filmindustri, Bengt Forslund has produced another excellent film by Jan Troell, and a romantic colour film called *Ola and Julia* about a pop singer and a stage actress, directed by young Jan Halldoff. Troell's second feature, *Eeny Meeny Miny Moe*, centres on a schoolmaster (Per Oscarsson), who feels himself persecuted and inadequate to cope with what appears to be a thoroughly normal and healthy set of pupils. Troell has photographed and edited the picture so dramatically and so lyrically that what could easily be a rather solemn and didactic piece has emerged as a vigorous

Max von Sydow struggles with Mikael Rindquist in Ingmar Bergman's The Hour of the Wolf.

analysis of a human problem endemic in today's world.
Ingmar Bergman has completed his twenty-ninth feature, *The Shame*, during the past few months, but his most recent work released in Stockholm has been *The Hour of the Wolf*, an intermittently brilliant and diabolical variation on the director's recurrent theme of the artist at the mercy of a hostile society. Bergman shows that he is still the cinema's number one sorcerer, but *The Hour of the Wolf*, which was scripted as long as 1965, leaves an impression of muddle and indulgence.
With the aid of the Swedish Film Institute, other films are being made independently. Stig Bjorkman's *I Love You Love* stars Evabritt Strandberg and Sven Wollter, and Jan Lindqvist's *They Call us Mods* would probably not exist if it were not for the enlightened patronage of Harry Schein's Institute. Nordisk Tonefilm, a company which left the production field three years ago, has returned with two films by Torbjörn Axelman, *Summer of the Lion*, a shallow but delightfully unpretentious sex comedy, and *Hot Snow*.

DENMARK
The death of Carl Dreyer this year is a loss to world cinema, and it perhaps also marks the end of an era in Danish film production. For the first time in decades there is a school of talented directors in Denmark, willing and able to regenerate their national cinema with the help of the Film Foundation there. Henning Carlsen, though, has disappointed many with his latest film, *People Meet and Sweet Music Fills the Heart*. This is a wild excursion into fantasy, a film in which all semblance of plot is discarded. Harriet Andersson is the blonde dancer who leads the romp, from Copenhagen to New York via Rio de Janeiro. *People Meet . . .* is a frustrating and almost perversely undisciplined film, but Harriet Andersson has not looked so attractive in years.
The Red Mantle, the most expensive film ever produced by the Danes, makes splendid use of the barren landscape of Iceland, where it was largely shot. It is a saga, constructed along "Western" lines, with some dazzling camerawork and a palpable sense of the medieval horror of death. The dialogue is too archaic, and the ritual compositions are a shade too deliberate, but in terms of sheer spectacle *The Red Mantle* matches anything Hollywood can do. Palle Kjaerulff-Schmidt and his habitual scriptwriter Klaus Rifbjerg look through the eyes of a young actress (Yvonne Ingdal) in *The Story of Barbara*.

Oleg Vidov in a scene from the Danish film The Red Mantle.

A typically vigorous shot from Tattooing, *the West German film directed by Johannes Schaaf.*

GERMANY

The young generation has taken over with a vengeance in West Germany. Last year, with films like *Es* and *Yesterday Girl*, the future seemed bright. Now, several of the new director's films have proved to be flops, and it's difficult to single out the really talented figures, as it was when the *Nouvelle Vague* was in full spate in France around 1960. Jean-Marie Straub clearly has exceptional gifts, and his *Die Chronik der Anna Magdalena Bach* was a fascinating follow-up to his first feature, *Nicht Versöhnt*. Hans-Jürgen Pohland's *Katz und Maus*, adapted from Günter Grass's novel, was generally considered a failure, and Ulrich Schamoni's *Alle Jahre wieder* was rather blunt and unimaginative in its picture of middle-aged melancholia. A more stimulating, if less original work was *Tattooing*, directed by a young television film-maker, Johannes Schaaf. The very style – all vigorous camerawork and unexpected instants of fury and protest – charts the hazardous moral approach to life of a boy sent home from reform school who rejects his foster-father's efforts at conciliation. *Tattooing* is also inhabited by an ebullient little girl called Helga Anders, who has the self-confident sophistication of Julie Christie.

An enormous number of young directors have been securing financial grants from the Kuratorium "Junger Deutscher Film". If a picture is successful, then the director himself is responsible for paying back the sum originally advanced – with interest. Alexander Kluge, the spokesman for the new generation, and director of the world's most advanced film school (at Ulm), says that "It's necessary for a young director to consider the economic factors involved. Of course one needs a good production assistant and administrator of accounts. Freedom needs more responsibility, and you enjoy sufficient freedom if you also have economic control. The *cinéma des auteurs* is not merely a question of new style and content – it may also be a different economic approach to the making of films."

ITALY

There has not been a "school" of directors working in harmony in Italy for at least twenty years now. Italian cinema in the 60's thus depends on its "giants", celebrated names like Antonioni, Fellini, and, to a lesser extent, Visconti and Rosi. Antonioni is now making *Zabriskie Point* in the United States, while Fellini, although he has contributed one episode (starring Terence Stamp) to the portmanteau film *Histoires Extraordinaires*, has been trying in vain to set up *The Journey of G. Mastorna* after a dispute with Dino De Laurentiis.

One of the most impressive pictures has been Elio Petri's *To Each his Own*, about a series of sinister murders in Sicily. The Mafia is never explicitly discussed, but it is *there*, like a fish lurking in turgid waters, and one shares the mounting fear and confusion of the young professor who is drawn into the clutches of the organisation. Petri's virtuoso editing and command of colour combine to grip an audience while at the same time the film provides a sardonic social commentary on Sicily today.

From the younger generation a few hopefuls have emerged: Giovanni Vento (with *Il Nero*), Romano Scavolini (with *La Prova Generale*), and of course Marco Bellocchio, whose *La Cina e Vicina* is a remarkable extension of the talent revealed in *Fists in the Pocket*. But there is not much more of quality among the 250 feature films completed annually in Italy. Most of them are Westerns, second-rate historical epics, *exposés à la* Jacopetti, and spy thrillers. Cinema is still very much a *spectacle* in Italy (and television has so far made few inroads on the industry's profits). Thus the only films easily financed are those appealing to the taste of millions.

Irene Papas as the widow in To Each his Own.

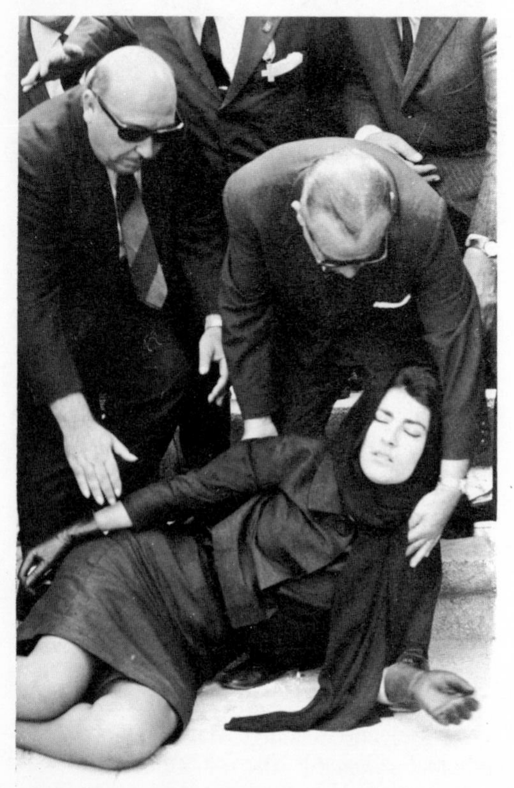

CZECHOSLOVAKIA

The foundation of the success of Czech cinema these past few years has been the sovereign power of the director. Miloš Forman, Jan Němec, Vera Chytilová, Jaromil Jires, Karel Kachyna, Pavel Juracek, Antonin Maša, Jirí Menzel, Evald Schorm, Ivan Passer, Jan Kadar and Elmar Klos: what country can boast an array of talent such as this? Each of these film-makers has succeeded in implanting his personality deeply and vividly in his work, so that Forman's wry humour, for example, or Němec's fluent interplay of fantasy and reality, have become immediately recognisable and renowned. Now, with the relaxation of political censorship in Czechoslovakia, new masterpieces are coming to light, such as Němec's *The Party and the Guests*, in which the director shows, in his now familiar staccato style, how easily people can be led, how gladly they settle for the easy path through life, and how the non-conformist is hounded down.

Evald Schorm's films to date have concentrated on the anti-heroes of the sixties, the angry young factory worker in *Courage for Every Day*, and the architect frustrated by the temptation to compromise with modern moral standards in *The Return of the Prodigal Son*. Each of his figures fights against resignation, the creeping malaise of our time, but each hates to be alone, to be given time to reflect. Schorm has now completed two more films, *Five Girls to Cope With* and *The End of the Priest*. Forman has made another comedy with quietly serious overtones, *Like a House on Fire*, which tries to reason how good, decent people can cause themselves so much misery and humiliation without in the least meaning to.

The Czechs have also produced an excellent two-part historical epic, *Marketa Lazarová*, and their annual production is running at about 38 features a year. Probably no other national cinema is so eager to analyse contemporary problems; certainly no other set of film-makers manages to do so with such wit and candour.

YUGOSLAVIA

Facts and figures concerning the cinema usually tell a sorry tale nowadays. But in the period July 1966 to July 1967, Yugoslav feature film production increased by 50 per cent (from 21 to 31 pictures), a sure indication of the dynamic enthusiasm among directors in Belgrade, Zagreb and Ljubjlana. Dušan Makavejev's *Love Dossier* has been acclaimed everywhere, by the public as well as by the critics. Zivojin Pavlović's *The Rats Awake* won a Silver Bear at Berlin, and Aleksandar Petrović's only slightly less (to my mind) impressive film, *Happy Gipsies . . .*, shared a Grand Prix at Cannes and was nominated for an Oscar. Add to this the wealth of shorts and cartoons that have made the Zagreb Studios world famous, and there is the nucleus of a very flourishing film industry.

Among features seen since my last world round-up, Purisa Djordjević's *The Dream* stands out. This is successful in its blend of hopeful prognostication and bitter fighting as a young partisan girl dreams of a future with her lover that is snuffed out brutally by the war. Dragoslav Lazić's *The Hot Years*, first noticed at Pesaro and later at the London Film Festival, is a love story at once tender and violent, containing some of the most spontaneous and convincing scenes the Yugoslav cinema has offered in recent years – the young couple's visit to the boy's parents in the country, the end of an all-night orgy. Another interesting newcomer is Ante Babaja, whose *The Birch Tree* was screened at the Mar del Plata festival in 1968.

U.S.S.R.

The Soviet cinema has been particularly busy these past eighteen months, celebrating the 50th anniversary of the Revolution. A vast new version of *Anna Karenina*, starring Tatiana Samoilova, was entered but never screened at Cannes, and Bondarchuk's *War and Peace* is now touring the world in an abridged version. Part III (*Borodino*) is outstanding, full of panoramic action and moments of intimate contemplation. It is a film redolent of death and of partings, with the uselessness of war its predominant sentiment. More and more Soviet pictures are being shot in the 70 mm process, and among the new ones are *People on the Nile*, a co-production with Egypt, and *My Country*, a feature-length documentary. Julia Solntseva, widow of the great director Dovzhenko, has finished *Unforgettable*, based on her late husband's war stories written in 1942.
Over 400,000,000 people attend Soviet cinemas every year.

JAPAN

Film production, as in many countries, is diminishing in Japan, and now scarcely totals 400 pictures a year, compared with nearly 600 in the halcyon days of the early 60's. Furthermore its directors seem unable in many cases to tackle subjects with a bearing on contemporary events. Kurosawa is working on a big co-production with the Americans about Pearl Harbor, and Ichikawa has completed a combination puppet-live action film called *Topogigo and the Missile War*. Kaneto Shindo has released yet another erotic study, *The Origins of Sex*, and the immensely gifted Hiroshi Teshigahara has been engrossed in an hour-long documentary about the Indianapolis speed races held at the base of Mount Fuji. Of the younger directors, Yukio Aoshima is one of the most original. *The Bell*, his comedy about the antics of a group of youngsters during a hot weekend, was shown at the Critics' Week at Cannes in 1967. Masahiro Shinoda's *Punishment Island* has a powerful theme – that of the man who spends his entire life in pursuit of revenge, and finds it at last horribly unsatisfying – and also has the advantage of an extremely subtle script, finely acted. But it is clearly difficult to experiment in the highly traditional, commercialised world of Japanese cinema. Even Kobayashi's *Rebellion*, awarded the British Film Institute's Sutherland Trophy this year, is just another slow, formally beautiful examination of samurai problems.

BRAZIL

Although most Brazilian films are not shown in Britain or the United States, many of them appear with surprising success at European festivals. Some of the younger directors know Paris well, and as a result films like *The Black God and the Blond Devil* and *Land in Trance* have been exhibited in France. Even *Vidas Secas* has been given an airing by BBC 2 television. Directors are supported by the National Institute of Cinema in Rio de Janeiro. Among the most significant are Glauber Rocha, Nelson Pereira dos Santos, Joachim Pedro de Andrade, Carlos Diegues, Ruy Guerra and Roberto Santos. Brazil is probably the only underdeveloped country where the cinema is passionately directed towards the improvement of social, political, and educational conditions. This is "cinema nôvo" with a mission.

THE NETHERLANDS

For the past twenty years, Dutch cinema has been synonymous with craftsmanship and integrity in the documentary field. Artistic flair has combined with business acumen to search out the essence of a subject, whether it be magnetism, building or stained glass. Now there is something of a division in the industry. While Bert Haanstra, John Ferno, Herman van der Horst and Hattum Hoving continue to produce non-fiction films of superb skill, a new generation is springing forward in the persons of Frans Weisz, Adriaan Ditvoorst, Nikolai van der Heyde, Wim Verstappen, Harry Kümel, and even the novelist Hugo Claus.
But the way is not easy for these directors, who insist on expressing themselves and their views through the medium of feature films. There is no tradition of Dutch-speaking cinema, and most Dutchmen believe instinctively that films, like watches and cars, are best imported from abroad. The domestic market is just not large enough to sustain a feature film in any event, and as there is only a small amount (£110,000) at the disposal of the national production fund, these new pictures have to be shot on a shoestring budget (anything from $1,000 to $50,000). The result is that beside the immaculately polished documentaries the features look clumsy and technically immature. But if the will to

survive is there, then a feature film industry is bound to bloom sooner or later in the Netherlands. Harry Kümel's *Monsieur Hawarden*, a drama set in the 19th century, has inspired comparisons with Bergman, and many columns have been devoted, in foreign film magazines, to Ditvoorst's *Paranoia* and Verstappen's *Joszef Katús*.

HUNGARY

After Poland and Czechoslovakia, it is the turn of Hungary to dominate the communist film world. As with Bergman in Sweden, one man has led the breakthough towards international recognition. Miklós Jancsó's *The Round Up* ran for months at the Academy in London; *Life* magazine devoted a feature to this extraordinarily ascetic director who, already in his mid-forties, was only now recognisable as a man of tremendous talent. His two recent pictures, *Under Red Stars* and *Silence and Cry*, are disturbing achievements, probing the fate of man in a hostile environment and giving the lie to the Magyar view of history as being full of courageous stands and roistering celebrations. As an experimenter with style, Jancsó is as revolutionary as Eisenstein was in the twenties. All his work is immediately distinguishable by its spare dialogue, its prowling camera movements, and its denial of human passion – men and women are ordered to strip by their guards, not for titillation's sake but for humilation.

At the other end of the scale, András Kovács cares little for flamboyant technique. Instead, he is keenly committed to the state of Hungary today; the predicament of its intellectuals and those in positions of responsibility. His latest film, *Walls*, revolves around a dilemma of conscience, and contemporary political conscience at that. Each of the many characters typifies a facet of opinion and morality in modern Hungary. István Szabó's brilliant Moscow prizewinner, *Father*, embraces the views and experiences of two generations. It is haunting and contemplative, never boring for an instant, and never afraid of passing ironical remarks about the imperfections of communism. This little masterpiece brims with compassion and the atmosphere of the forties and fifties is recreated with barely a hint of artifice. Other directors from Hungary to watch are István Gáal, Pál Sandor, and Peter Bacsó, all of whom manage to combine a "committed" approach to their subject-matter with a lissom style and a gift for handling players.

Above: Poison is administered in Miklos Jancsó's latest picture, Silence and Cry.

POLAND

The decline of Polish cinema in the last eight years is due to a variety of reasons. The death of Andrzej Munk in 1961 struck a profound psychological blow (as did Zbigniew Cybulski's, of course, early last year). The war themes that had sustained the great Polish films of the fifties were more or less exhausted. And then both Wajda, with *Ashes*, and Kawalerowicz, with *Pharaoh*, suffered two resounding international failures. In April 1968 Kawalerowicz was even officially accused of making "bad films", and, until the ferment in Warsaw subsides, it will be difficult to predict the future of Polish cinema.

Jerzy Skolimoski made *Hands Up*, (but ran into governmental opposition with this oblique analysis of communist society) and other promising young film-makers include Witold Leszczynski (*The Days of Matthew*), Witold Lesiewicz (*A Place for a Lonely Man*), Henryk Kluba (*The Thin Man and the Rest*), and Janusz Morgenstern (*Live Once More*). Increasing attention seems to be given to television productions these days in Poland, too.

A scene from Hands Up.
directed by Jerzy Skolimoski,

36 *Ripe for revival?*
Those delightful British Jack Hulbert films of the thirties.

BRITISH CINEMA OF THE 30's

As one who grew up in British cinemas of the 30's, I remember all too well the lack of pride – and lack of interest – that most of us took in our own home-grown product.
Oh, the latest Jack Hulbert or Will Hay comedy was very much of an event to look forward to, especially for the youngsters, and the oldsters were loyal to George Arliss.
But Alexander Korda's lavish budgets notwithstanding, there was a tendency to regard British pictures then as poor relations to Hollywood, and when the critics did sincerely urge us to see a new British film, their pride was usually prompted by the fact that "at last" we'd beaten Hollywood at its own game, and done something as well as – or better than – M-G-M or Warner Brothers. The "genuine" British films, thoroughly British in theme and thought, whether they be comedy or drama, were usually shunted to the wayside, as being necessary fodder for the theatres, but not of any lasting importance.
In a way, this attitude was partially understandable. The quota laws, which provided that every British distributing wing of an American production company make a certain percentage of British films each year, and that every cinema show a given percentage of British films, did naturally promote the production of uninspired cheapies that were made *only* to fill those legal requirements. M-G-M, for example, sponsored cheap westerns in Canada (which were legally British) and made such lurid little second features as *Dr. Syn Fang*, but made little attempt to sell them. Just having *made* them got them off the legal hook. But of course the independent cinemas, which couldn't afford the bigger and better British films – or couldn't acquire them until the better-class cinemas had milked them dry – had to fall back a great deal on these lesser quickies. And in the whole history of the cinema, there has probably never been a less attractive or more unentertaining breed of film than the *really* cheap British second feature. Even the lowest-grade American western could at least offer action, pleasing scenery and splendid horses – but the only possible virtue one can point to in a film like *Tiger Bay* (the old Anna May Wong melodrama, not the more recent Hayley Mills film) is that two decades hence it would prove an academic stepping-stone for students of the career of Thorold Dickinson, who, like David Lean and other top British directors, got his start as an editor on early cheapies.
As for the accusation that British films tried to copy Hollywood, it was of course partly true. *Rhodes of Africa* proudly proclaimed itself a great epic in the tradition of *The Covered Wagon* and *Cimarron*, but was only a monumental bore. In an effort to lend Hollywoodian glamour and know-how to British films, many Hollywood stars were imported – but usually they were personalities like Laura La Plante, Harry Langdon or Jimmy Durante who (often through no lessening of their own talents) had slipped badly at their native box offices. Their arbitrary injection into quite unsuitable roles neither helped the British reception, nor did their presence prove an open sesame to U.S. box-offices. Of course, not all of the imitations were doomed to failure. The Jessie Matthews musicals, big box-office at home, were also very successful in the States. Patterned somewhat on the Astaire–Rogers formula, they were slick, glossy, often surprisingly elaborate musicals, helped by American co-stars who had *not* slipped (Robert Young was one of the more frequently used) and American song-writers like Rodgers and Hart. But their one major asset – Jessie Matthews herself – was definitely an original, and no imitation. Her combination of grace and sauciness, sexiness mixed with innocence, made her a unique and charming star. Her personality is as fresh and appealing today, as are most of her films.
But the quota quickies and the imitation-Hollywood films formed but a small part of the great British output of the 30's, and despite the frequent revivals of highlight films at England's National Film Theatre, and the very occasional vintage revival on British TV, it seems to me that this great wealth of material is lying fallow and unappreciated. It's no surprise to find that the best of Jack Hulbert and Will Hay stand the test of time supremely well. Hulbert's *Bulldog Jack* is not only a delightful spoof, but an excellent thriller in its own right, and I think a widespread theatrical revival today would so enchant audiences and surprise its distributors that a whole new Hulbert following could be created, to sustain periodic revivals of his best films just as has been done with the Marx Brothers and W. C. Fields. Similarly, it is no revelation that the best of Hitchcock's British films – and especially *Saboteur* and *The Lady Vanishes* – are his best from *any* period. But what is surprising is that the 30's seems to be emerging as one of the major periods of the British film, in many ways eclipsing the big Rank and Korda prestige years of the 40's. British films certainly came into their own as a major box-office factor in the 40's, and we were justly proud that we could turn out

stars, directors and films that could finally invade foreign (and specifically American) markets and get results. For perhaps the first time we went to British films *because* they were British, and with a new-found fervent patriotism, critics were not content just to praise, but had to stress Hollywood's inferiority at the same time. Yet the majority of British films from the 40's proved to be not too durable. *A Matter of Life and Death*, Powell and Pressburger's big Technicolor prestige feature, today seems trivial and self-indulgent, and spectacularly inferior to America's more serious but thematically related *All That Money Can Buy*, which has endured as a permanent classic. Carol Reed's *Odd Man Out*, in its day considered perhaps the supreme achievement of the British cinema, now seems quite cold, artificial and hopelessly pretentious, a film for students and aspiring directors, but not for audiences. "Pretentious" is perhaps the key word, for it takes a genius to make a deliberately pretentious film that somehow does survive as a work of great and permanent art. Murnau pulled off that trick with *Sunrise*; so did Welles with *Citizen Kane*, but I can think of no other comparable examples.

I suspect that *Odd Man Out*, understandably a hit with the critics, was a hit with the public too because it somehow reflected the gloomy defeatism which the nation was plunged into – momentarily – when the end of war did not bring with it the expected return to normalcy and plenty. Both British and American films of the immediate post-war period were filled with gloomy themes of psychological problems, madness, suicide, tragedy often quite arbitrarily supplanting the expected happy ending. But as the mood passed, so did the impact of the films. The films that survive best from this period are those that do not strive *consciously* for artistry or are tied to a transient period, but those that best combine good story-telling with genuine (and thus unobtrusive) craftsmanship. David Lean's two Dickens films – *Great Expectations* and *Oliver Twist* – are perfect examples of this. They get better with each passing year, and there isn't a pretentious frame in either of them.

It is this lack of pretension that characterises so much of the British film output of the 30's. Though hit by the depression less drastically than America, Britain was still in serious straits. On the one hand, their films reflected the times and – both in comedy and drama – tried to be helpfully optimistic. On the other hand, they tried to help audiences forget their troubles by offering as much cheerful escapism as possible. To a large degree, pretension was out of place in such a climate. In Hollywood, the rugged social melodramas of Warner Brothers, the cheerful musicals and the sophisticated comedies by Lubitsch, quite outweighed the sporadic art-for-art's-sake film of a von Sternberg. The pattern in Britain was much the same, the occasional arty film like Korda's *Knight Without Armour* – expensive, lushly photographed, edited *à la* Eisenstein, grand fun in a superficial way but no more – quite submerged beneath the so-called "run of the mill" films which had far more honesty and vigour. The Gracie Fields vehicles, with Gracie as a kind of spokeswoman for the unemployed, sported such "prosperity is just around the corner" titles as *Look Up and Laugh* and *Looking on the Bright Side*. Unpretentious in the extreme, many of them written (with one suspects no great literary sweat) by J. B. Priestley, they nevertheless represent the depression period with a striking degree of honesty, cure-all happy endings notwithstanding. Lack of funds forced many producers out of the studios into the streets for as much of their films as possible, and this too added a quality of unforced realism. *Sing As We Go*, a Gracie Fields vehicle of no great artistic value, may one day be invaluable as a record of a specific strata of life in those years – and its extensive and prolonged footage at the Blackpool fun-fair and beach likewise has historic documentary value.

British films of the period were rather unique in drawing upon many roots and many nationalities. European, and specifically German, talents had flocked to the British studios at the end of the silent era. Britain's 1929 silent version of *The Informer*, with a German/American director in Arthur Robison, and Swedish and German stars in Lars Hanson and Lya de Putti was, and is, a remarkable film – in many ways quite superior to John Ford's Hollywood remake, and containing scenes and compositions that Ford obviously copied intact. German talent stayed on in British films of the 30's, helping to produce such films as *The Tunnel*, which was justifiably retitled to the more showmanly *Transatlantic Tunnel* for U.S. release. With American stars Richard Dix, Walter Huston and Madge Evans backing up Britain's George Arliss and Leslie Banks, Britain's Maurice Elvey directing, and Curt Siodmak and Clemence Dane providing a bizarre writing team, the film emerged rather like *Metropolis* crossed with *A Bill of Divorcement*, but it was a major science-fiction effort, and its sets and big action sequences impress still. No print has survived in England, even within the vaults of the studio that made it, but one good print is still extant in New York – and was recently requested for a top-secret screening by Army brass at the Pentagon in Washington!

While British films were making the best use of German and other European directorial talent (Victor Seastrom, Erich Pommer, Jacques Feyder, E. A. Dupont) and bringing over such Hollywood top-liners as William K. Howard, Raoul Walsh and cameramen Harry Stradling and James Wong Howe, it was also busily training its own talent. Of the lesser British films of the 30's, one often comes across the names of Sidney Gilliat and Frank Launder, David Lean, Thorold Dickinson, David MacDonald (directing Tod Slaughter melodramas!), and, of course, writers who became better known *outside* the film field – Walter Greenwood, J. B. Priestley and others. If there were any common denominators in the good British films of this period, they were variety and literacy. Even comparatively minor films often offered extremely literate and well-spoken scripts, and despite some admittedly appallingly bad independent films (cheap musicals, comedies and crime dramas seemed to predominate), one also finds amazing quality and production values in some of these second features too. A now forgotten company called Phoenix Films, a subsidiary of Ealing Studios, turned out some really remarkable films which today hold up rather better than many more imposing and ambitious efforts. *Brief Ecstasy*, for example (in view of its title a curious but coincidental blending of the plot elements of *Extase* and *Brief Encounter*) – a sex drama that must have been considered quite daring in its day, though by today's standards tame in its content – is magnificently photographed by Ronald Neame. Linden Travers never looked more beautiful, and the whole film has a visual style that wouldn't be amiss in a much more ambitious Josef von Sternberg vehicle. Conversely, the same company's *The Silent Passenger* – a Peter Wimsey melodrama by Dorothy L. Sayers – is taut, brisk, workmanlike, moving along to a genuinely exciting Hitchcockian climax in a deserted railway siding. *Secret Lives*, a World War I spy tale, and *Calling the Tune* – an unusual melodrama built around the history of the record industry – were further notable Phoenix productions. Solidly mounted, unstinting in location work, they might even have been major releases had they been able to increase their budgets sufficiently to afford bigger star names. Presumably, though here I am guessing, it was their very quality (and expense) that caused their downfall, since as second features they could hardly have recouped their costs from England alone.

South Riding – a dishonest and romanticised 'social' film if you will, "Jane Eyre" in modern dress – still works well as a piece of literary hoke, and tells us as much about conditions and attitudes in England than by its *evasions* as it would have done had it been starkly realistic. The slick, second-string Hitchcock imitations such as *Non Stop New York* and *Strange Boarders*; the stage-derived farces with Stanley Lupino and Lupino Lane; the curiously old-fashioned yet elaborately romanticist films from Twickenham Studios; the rugged outdoor semi-documentaries such as *The Turn of the Tide* and *The End of the World* . . . and, of course, the comedies! I don't think any other film-producing country in the world had so many comics working at the same time as England did in the 30's, drawing as it did on the rich reservoir of radio and the music-halls. Some, like Leslie Fuller and Ernie Lottinga are admittedly of but passing interest, though the crudity of their films may have short-changed them for posterity. But the major comics, drawing as much on the silent American comedies as on British music-hall traditions, offer a wealth of still fresh and delightful material: George Formby, a reincarnation of Harry Langdon; Jack Hulbert, using Harold Lloyd's formula of comedy plus thrill, and Will Hay, welding a W. C. Fields character to Buster Keaton plot mechanics; how well the best of their films hold up! Jack Hulbert, relatively unknown in the United States, invariably wins over audiences *in toto* when one of his films is shown, not just because of his own sprightly personality and the fast-paced comic excitement of his films, but also because he is one thoroughly British comedian who can be understood without any difficulty by American audiences. I remember that through the 30's and 40's British writers were frequently up in arms at U.S. complaints at the inability to understand British speech. We had to put up with Edward G. Robinson and snarling gangsters, it was argued; why then should the Americans not accept our speech as gracefully? It seemed a valid point – but there is a difference between the slang content of dialogue, and the accented delivery of dialogue. As a New York resident for some eighteen years now, I can understand the American attitude rather better. Since many Americans can't understand *other* Americans, their shortcomings with certain British films is easier to accept. There is nothing more frustrating than showing a great Will Hay film to a group of Americans (intelligent, largely film students) who *want* to like it, can and *do* appreciate the visual gags, but are absolutely floored by the rapid-fire patter and totally different accents of Will Hay, Moore Marriott and Graham Moffat! Indeed, since my own associations with the British cinema are of the Clive Brook–Diana Wynyard–Ralph Richardson vintage and calibre, I find that – even as an Englishman – I share the average American's bewilderment at the dialogue and accents of such current British films as *Up the Junction.* Ironically though, the pop elements of music and sex are getting these new British films the widespread theatrical distribution in America that was denied the earlier films with impeccable diction but – alas – no sex! Just the other day I ran the creaky old Aldwych farce *Thark* – the Tom Walls–Ralph Lynn–Robertson Hare comedy of 1930 – to a thoroughly American audience, anticipating disaster and bewilderment. Astonishingly, it was a rousing success. The methodical pacing – allowing time for laughs before the next line came along – enabled a New York audience to understand both the dialogue and the plot, and somehow the mechanics still worked. I doubt if it would have received a better reception in Ealing or Deptford. When a New York audience can take a 1930 British antiquity so much to heart – and *Thark* is hardly the kind of film I had in mind when talking about the staying-power of so many British films of the 30's – then surely British audiences could be expected to react with equal delight to the Gainsborough and Wilcox films of that period – and should be given the opportunity to do so.

THE EVERYMAN

JIM FAIRFAX-JONES writes about his EVERYMAN at Hampstead

A snapshot of the staff of the Everyman taken in 1934. The only two survivors still on duty are Jim Fairfax-Jones (centre) and Chief Electrician-Projectionist Tom Robertson (centre back) who has probably shown to the public more famous films than any other living projectionist.

The Everyman was built in 1888 as the Hampstead Drill Hall and Assembly Rooms to provide a centre for the Hampstead Detachment of the 3rd Middlesex Rifle Volunteer Corps. For many years it was used not only for this purpose but also for less belligerent activities such as dances, concerts, and whist drives. In 1919 the Volunteers departed and the building was converted into a theatre by Mr Norman MacDermott, who named it The Everyman. Under his direction it became famous for the quality and variety of its productions. One recalls the wonderful seasons of Shaw given by the Macdona players, the production of plays by Ibsen, Chekhov, and Pirandello, as well as presentations of new plays, of which Noel Coward's "The Vortex" was a notable example. After MacDermott's reign the theatre passed through many hands and at the time we acquired it, it was derelict and down and out.

It seemed to me at the time that, following the success of the London Film Society which, giving its first performance on October 25, 1925 with a programme consisting of Leni's *Waxworks* and a collection of shorts by Ruttman, Chaplin, and Brunel, succeeded in creating a focal point in London for those interested in studying the best of cinema to be collected from the Studios of the World, followed by the founding of film societies in cities such as Edinburgh, Leicester, Glasgow, Birmingham, and Southampton, the kernel of an audience sufficiently large and interested to support a full-time professional cinema giving similar programmes had been established. Having carried out the necessary work of conversion, we opened the Everyman as a repertory cinema on Boxing Day, 1933.

Financially this had been made possible by a group of friends who thought the idea worthy of practical encouragement.

The opening ceremony was performed by the late Sir Gerald du Maurier. The programme consisted of Clair's *Le Millon* (revived again, as fresh as ever, on our 30th anniversary), a Disney cartoon, a Mack Sennett comedy, and a newsreel. Our policy then, as now, was to conduct the Everyman on film society lines, reviving and presenting the best films, long and short, available from international sources; but with this difference, that the Everyman programmes would be available to the public at large rather than to a limited audience of subscribers.

On the day we opened, Cinema House, (now Studio One), was showing the original German version of *Emil and The Detectives*, the Academy (then under the direction of Elsie Cohen) was showing *La Maternelle*, and the Rialto, which occasionally came up with a foreign film, was showing Marcel L'Herbiers *L'ordonnance*. The Curzon was not in being, the Polytechnic was dedicated to a policy of showing geographical documentaries, the British Film Institute had not been founded, the National Film Theatre was nearly twenty-one years away, and the only cinema in London devoted to revivals, as I recall, was the late Forum Cinema in Villiers Street, which then had Pabst's unfortunate version of *Don Quixote* featuring Chaliapin and George Robey.

To begin with our venture met with very little success. We soon realised that the audience for repertory programmes was extremely small, and because of the comparatively recent change from silence to sound the repertoire was more limited than we had supposed. Many silent films had been scrapped and many of the early sound films did not bear revival. Even so, we were able in 1934 to show a series of programmes which seems awe-inspiring today. Here is a list of *some* (only *some*) of the films we showed. during that year:

A Hitchcock Season
A Clair Season
TABU (Flaherty)
KAMERADSCHAFT (Pabst)
MADCHEN IN UNIFORM (Sagan)
THE ROAD TO LIFE (Ekk)
THUNDER OVER MEXICO (Eisenstein)
THE BLUE ANGEL (von Sternberg)
M. (Lang)
TURSKIB (Turin)
POIL DE CAROTTE (Duvivier)
THE BLUE LIGHT (Reifenstahl)
DER TRAUMENDE MUND (Czinner)
THE GUARDSMAN (Franklin)
LIEBELEI (Ophuls)
LA MATERNELLE (Benoit-Levy & Epstein)
EN NATT (Molander)
CHARLEMAGNE (Colombier)
CONGRESS DANCES (Charell)
SUNSHINE SUSIE (Saville)
ROME EXPRESS (Forde)
LE ROSIER DE MADAME HUSSON (Deschamps)

In 1936 we gave no fewer than six seasons of films. These were:

A Marx Brothers Season
A Clair Season
A Lang Season
A Lubitsch Season
An Astaire–Rogers Season
A Capra Season

Despite these mouth-watering, programmes, the early years were years of anxiety and crisis. The success of certain films, *The Guardsman, The Blue Light, Madchen in Uniform, Der Traumende Mund, The Road To Life*, and our Hitchcock and Clair seasons, were encouraging, but for quite a long time the continued existence of The Everyman could be attributed only to the refusal of the managing-director to accept the plainest evidence of defeat. Looking back at those days the first indications of better things to come might perhaps be seen in the result of our showing of a quite unpretentious little French film directed by Siodmak, prophetically entitled *The Slump is Over*. It attracted exceptionally large crowds and thereafter our audiences gradually grew, continued to grow and eventually reached a level which dispelled most financial worries and encouraged the expansion of ideas. In 1936 we gave in addition to the six seasons of films already mentioned a long survey of the first forty years of film-making entitled *A History of The Film*. In 1937 we gave the world premiere of Jean Vigo's *Zero De Conduite* in a full programme of surrealist films.

For three of the war years The Everyman passed into other hands but early in 1946 we resumed occupation. At that time the problem of film supply was difficult. New films were coming in very slowly from the Continent. Prints of many famous films had been mislaid or destroyed during the war. We therefore decided to revive some of the most interesting wartime and contemporary films such as *Citizen Kane, The Magnificent Ambersons, Double Indemnity*, and *The Southerner*, together with some older films of which we managed to discover prints, such as *Madchen in Uniform, Quai Des Brumes*, and *Les Bas-Fonds*. These films attracted large audiences and helped to establish us again, and when a little later on we were able to achieve one of our earliest ambitions and show such masterpieces of the silent screen as the *Birth of a Nation, Intolerance, The Cabinet of Dr. Caligari, The Last Laugh, Metropolis*, and *An Italian Straw Hat*, we attracted a new generation of cinemagoers who, with those who had followed us from the beginning, combined to form a wider and larger audience than before.

Today the audience for what used to be called the "unusual" film has seeped into the circuit cinemas and, in the London area at any rate, you will rarely experience much difficulty in finding a French, Japanese, Swedish or Russian film almost on your doorstep. Only a few weeks ago, the Everyman was, ironically, the only one of the four cinemas in Hampstead *not* showing a foreign film! Still, we keep our policy unchanged, and are happy to do so. Dilys Powell wrote of us not so long ago: "The Everyman has been run by people who like the cinema instead of regarding it as purely a business or a duty." 'Twas ever thus, and so remains.

THE DIRECTOR SPEAKS

Bryan Forbes

I think that on the subject of their own films, directors should be seen and not heard. With more and more conviction I am led to the belief that we should "never complain, never explain".
Just as the mystique of the theatre has been eroded by the gossip columnists – who have done their level worst to reduce Sir Laurence Olivier to the status of the Boy Next Door, while at the same time elevating every pathetic little scrubber whose chest measurements are in reverse ratio to their talents to the pedestal of fame, so that now the mystery of the theatre and the romance of actors is as tatty as Berwick Market at closing time – so have the inner workings of the cinema been too inexpertly examined by a new breed of lamentably ill-informed journalists posing as film critics. They have been much aided and abetted by me and my kind, for we have all been too easily seduced. Those transient pleasures, the television interviews we all give on the eve of our premières; those wistful "at home" articles we are foolish enough to give to the women's magazines; those acid drops in the oceans of print that in our conceits and ambitions we donate – what have they to do with the making of films? Nothing.
The making of a film, like the writing of a novel, is a lonely pursuit, complicated by the fact that the role of the creator is superimposed upon an industrial pattern. Great acting has to be forged in the glare of arc-lamps, and in the shadows of union rules and regulations. To commit a performance to celluloid is not a matter of chance inspiration, but the coming together of perhaps a hundred people with little or nothing in common except to earn a wage, who work under factory conditions not so far removed from Detroit and Coventry. Films are big business where the return of capital investment is at all times as important as the creative urge, and for the most part more important. Instead of the films themselves being the realm of make-believe, the mechanics of the financiers are the true fantasies. The film-maker today is hedged around with wanton idiocies, conditioned to accept as inevitable foolish answers to straight questions, beaten to the ground with regulations that a child of five would reject out of hand. The wonder of it all is not that films are still made, but that good films are still made. What should be a world of shadows has become a shadowed world.
But, to return: "Never complain, never explain". The public are never interested in our troubles – and why indeed should they be? Do we judge a Van Gogh by the state of his ears or the brilliance of his canvases? The object of all art, it is said, is to conceal art, and we must cover our tracks, not reveal them.
The making of a film is a battlefield and we should tend our own wounded and become blood donors to our own kind. The true function of anybody engaged in a war of creative purpose is to totally ignore the feelings of the enemy. For nobody can or ever will truly define what the enemy wants – all critics are wise after the event, never before, and one invariably has to aim at their arses in retreat, not the whites of their eyes. Peaceful art is dull art, and the nature of the beast is always to be in revolt. So, if you'll forgive me, I'll return to the barricades. In silence.

THE STORY OF

The auditorium at the new Odeon, St. Martin's Lane, dominated by the 44 ft. by 20 ft. suspended screen.

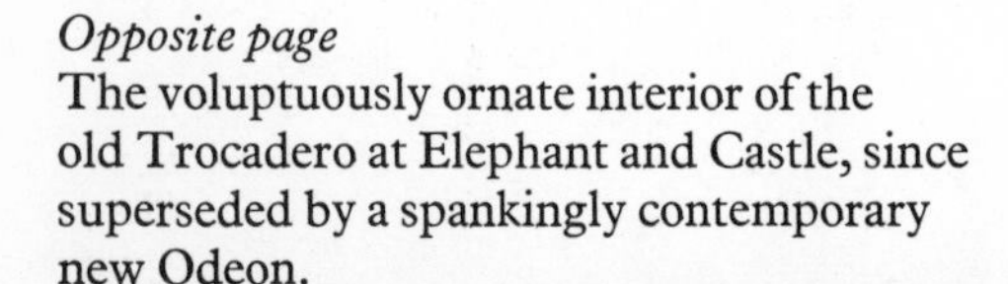

Opposite page
The voluptuously ornate interior of the old Trocadero at Elephant and Castle, since superseded by a spankingly contemporary new Odeon.

THE PICTURE PALACE

Ivan Butler

For many filmgoers, the autumn gloom of 1967 took on a shade darker hue with the closing of the old Plaza, Lower Regent Street, during so many years the "home of Paramount Pictures", and one of the last of the old guard of pre-war Palaces in London. Two smaller cinemas, better adapted to modern techniques, are to take its place, but to the older picturegoer at any rate, it seems like one more link broken with the romantic past history of the British cinema. The first commercial film show was given on February 20, 1896, under the auspices of Quintin Hogg, by Louis Lumière at the Polytechnic Hall in Regent Street, where the Cameo–Poly now stands. Its success was such that it was transferred to the Empire Music Hall in Leicester Square – as a side-show. Simultaneously, Robert W. Paul staged a show at the Finsbury Technical College, and later at Olympia. Other showings at music-halls and variety houses followed – the films being generally used as a "send-'em-home" item at the end of the programme. A few months later enterprising exhibitors started using converted shops, one of the first being in Fife Road, Kingston upon Thames. As a whole, this early experiment failed to interest, however, and the "living pictures" were relegated to fair-ground marquees, where they flourished. The converted shop idea never completely died, and early in the century their popularity began to grow. One of the most famous of all attractions, "Hales Tours" – a sort of film travelogue with the audience seated in a realistically unsteady train coach – opened in a couple of transformed

shops in Oxford Street and Hammersmith Broadway. Later, disused chapels also were converted, some being sold complete with organ, and from this developed the cinema organ – the Mighty Wurlitzer with its multitudinous stops and heaven-scaling platform.

In 1905 the first building to be built specifically as a cinema (by an American named George Washington Grant) opened in Wilton Road, Victoria. It was called the Bioscope, later the Biograph, and was used as a prototype for further houses. The Biograph survived two World Wars (having its doors blown in during the Second) and – seating 680 on a single floor and with a thrice-a-week change of programme – is still flourishing today. Almost as early, and also still very much in existence, was the Cinema House, Oxford Circus. In 1934, under Sir David James, it became the Studio, and later Studio One when Studio Two (one of the very few actual news cinemas remaining) was added underneath it, replacing a Chinese restaurant. Studio One, an independant house, today specialises in "family programmes" (an occasional A – no X), and has become a home for Disney productions.

Many of the small cinemas which sprang up during this period survived years of competition with near-by Palaces, serving a useful complementary purpose in presenting smaller-scale films and revivals. The Royal, in Kensington High Street (affectionately known as the "little cinema under the big clock' – both now gone) was typical of hundreds, entered by a narrow passage leading to the back of the shops. There throughout the afternoon the lady pianist battled bravely with her mood music, joined promptly each evening (regardless of what was going on on the screen) by the trio which struck up and gave life to the whole proceedings.

* * *

The first news-reel cinema opened in 1906 in Bishopsgate, called the Daily Bioscope. Years later numbers of small cinemas would be refurbished and given a new lease of life as news-reelers, until the advent of television caused many to close, or to be taken over again as feature houses. As it became clear that the films were here to stay and mightily grow, the business side rapidly developed. Cinema circuits were soon formed, a notable pioneer being Electric Theatres (1908). The first major circuit was started in 1909 by Ralph Jupp and known as PCT (Provincial Cinematograph Theatres), formed with the intention of providing every town of more than 250,000 inhabitants with a grand-scale picture-palace. By 1920 PCT owned some seventy cinemas; in 1928 it became associated with Gaumont-British but retains its identity. Another important circuit was built up by Montague Pyke in 1910, composed of smaller cinemas, seating about 450 and erected to a standard pattern. They provided a two-hour programme with a top price of a shilling.

By 1914 the development in size and number of cinemas was well established. The Marble Arch Pavilion was opened that year, and the original New Gallery in Regent Street was another early arrival. World War I inevitably held everything up, but the Golden Period followed soon after. The Tivoli opened in 1923 with Rex Ingram's *Where the Pavement Ends*, and reigned over the Strand for thirty-five years until demolished in 1958 to make way for shops and stores. For most of its time it was a member of the PCT circuit. Among its highlights were the silent *Ben-Hur, The Trail of '98*, the All-Star Warner Bros. revue *The Show of Shows* and seasons of Walter Forde's excellent but forgotten English comedies (surely deserving a showing at the National Film Theatre?).

In 1925 the Capitol, Haymarket, opened its doors with Raymond Bernard's spectacular *Miracle of the Wolves*. This tastefully decorated and comfortable cinema, which boasted a notably fine orchestra under Paul Moulder, was one of the pleasantest of all the Palaces. Garbo silent features made their début on its screen. It was later refurbished as the Gaumont, recently demolished, and replaced by the Haymarket Odeon, underground but imposing.

Five months later the rebuilt and greatly enlarged New Gallery reopened with *The Lost World*. Noteworthy presentations included the early Douglas Fairbanks colour film *The Black Pirates* and the famous weepie *Seventh Heaven* – shown alternately with a live orchestra and Movietone accompaniment, the former receiving critical preference. The first full-length Disney cartoon had enraptured children and adults alike, cooing over Snow White and her dwarfs as the war clouds gathered. The cinema was taken over in the fifties by a religious body and is now the New Gallery Evangelistic Centre. The recently defunct Plaza arrived in 1926 (with Dorothy Gish in *Nell Gwyn*); the Astoria in 1927 (*The Triumph of the Rat* –

Ivor Novello); the Regal, Marble Arch in 1928 with the early Jolson sobbie *The Singing Fool.* This cinema is now the magnificent Marble Arch Odeon, with a moving staircase to the *stalls* – the only one in the country. In the same year, on the site of the old music-hall of the same name, rose up the Empire, home of Metro-Goldwyn-Mayer – opening with *Trelawney of the Wells,* later showing the first real musical *The Broadway Melody*, and now completely transformed to accommodate the new style films. It was joined by its little sister, the elegant underground Ritz, in 1934. Once again in 1928 the Carlton, originally a theatre, turned to films with the air epic *Wings*, including Clara Bow and a screen which enlarged at spectacular moments. Innumerable others opened and flourished during this great period in outer London and the provinces. In general they were built on "legitimate" theatre lines, with proscenium, orchestra pit, tabs and stages on which prologues of singers and high-stepping dancers preceded the main feature – often with little enough relevance to its content.

* * *

The mid-twenties also saw the opening of the first "art" – or, preferably, "specialist" – cinema, where foreign and other less-commercially regarded films were to obtain a showing. This was the Avenue Pavilion, which stood near the Palace Theatre in Shaftesbury Avenue. Under the management of Leslie Ogilvie, it built up a fine tradition which (through the Avenue Pavilion itself later became a news-reel house and is now gone) has been carried on elsewhere ever since – most notably at the Academy in Oxford Street. The

The Biograph in Wilton Road, Victoria. Built in 1905 it was the first building built specifically as a cinema, later renamed the Biograph, it still flourishes.

The main entrance to the new Odeon Theatre in St Martin's Lane.

larger houses sometimes ran foreign seasons, in particular the Marble Arch Pavilion with *Metropolis* (1926) and other UFA films. The high reputation of the Academy was pioneered by Elsie Cohen in 1929 and carried on in the present day by George Hoellering. The building now comprises two additional exquisite small cinemas, the tiniest of which started life as a club. The trio form a mecca for the discriminating filmgoer, and whatever reasons some of the huge crowds pouring in to see *Ulysses* may have for their first visit, it is to be hoped that some of them will return for less sensationally publicised films.

On Boxing Day, 1933, the little Everyman Theatre in Hampstead (which had earlier seen the first production of Noël Coward's play *The Vortex*) turned to films and, under J. S. Fairfax-Jones became the first real repertory cinema. Concentrating on revivals and seasons of foreign and other pictures of special interest, it has sustained an unwaveringly high standard ever since. The Everyman opened with René Clair's *Le Million*, which was repeated to celebrate its thirtieth birthday.

The following year the Mayfair Curzon opened with a German romance about Schubert, *The Unfinished Symphony*. The building was famous for its luxurious seating and general comfort. It was to the Curzon that, shortly after the war, the French film on the life of *Monsieur Vincent* (St Vincent de Paul) drew all denominations in astonishing queues. The cinema was recently closed for some time, reopening in 1966, somewhat grimly decorated but more luxurious than ever, with *Viva Maria*.

Another small early cinema now pursuing an interesting policy of first-run specialist films is the Paris–Pullman in South Kensington. Originally, in 1911 known as the Electric Theatre and later as the Boltons, it became a "legitimate" theatre for a short while after the war, then began its new and exciting career under Richard Schulman, a career continued under new management, with club attached, in 1967.

With the coming of the talking picture many of the smaller cinemas faced financial problems of installation, and numbers disappeared altogether. In London and other big towns, on the contrary, erstwhile "live" theatres were converted to show sound films. The Leicester Square Theatre opened as a cinema in 1930 with *Viennese Nights*, its most notable run being, perhaps, *The Best Years of our Lives*. The Dominion, Tottenham Court Road, had only a short life as a home for spectacular musical plays before turning to films. *The Sound of Music* has broken all records here.

The Alhambra Music Hall gave way in 1937 to the Leicester Square Odeon (*The Prisoner of Zenda*). It was redecorated and reconstructed on a magnificent scale in 1967, reopening with *Smashing Time*.

Daly's Theatre, long famed for its Edwardian musical comedies, was taken over by Warner Bros. and rebuilt on a grand scale. It opened in 1938 – entitled, naturally enough, the Warner – with *Robin Hood*. With the advent of wide-screen films it was refitted and reseated, the first film in its new style being *Robin and the Seven Hoods*. The first modern 3–D films were also shown here.

The London Pavilion turned from a long series of revues and musicals to films in 1934. Many of the more adventurous British pictures are launched here, notably *Tom Jones*, *It Happened Here*, *Poor Cow* and the Beatles' films.

The Piccadilly Theatre became a cinema during the early talking period, showing the first full-length (and execrable) talkie, *The Terror*, but after a short period reverted again to plays. More recently the Cambridge Theatre ran a short season of Gala films, opening with *La Religieuse*, but present plans are to use it for revivals of musical comedies. The Stoll Opera House had been showing films for some years before its demise. Nowadays the relatively small but aristocratic Royalty Cinema occupies a part of the new building on the site, and is at present leased by Gala Films.

* * *

No attempt can be made in this short survey to disentangle the multifarious strands of the big present-day circuits, whose beneficent tentacles spread over the whole country. Very much condensed and simplified: the PCT circuit became associated with Gaumont-British in 1928, and ABC (Associated British Cinemas) was created by John Maxwell the same year. The Biggest Brother of all, Rank, came into the picture literally in 1933, and took over the Odeon circuit from Oscar Deutsch in 1939. In the same year Odeon took over Paramount cinemas. In 1941 Rank became chairman also of Gaumont-British. Few urban cinemagoers are not within reasonable travelling distance of an Odeon (Rank), Gaumont (Rank), ABC, Essoldo or other smaller circuit cinemas. Essoldo, running about eighty cinemas throughout England, was founded at Newcastle in the early thirties, the name being formed from a combination of the names of its founder.

The Marble Arch Odeon
above: The auditorium from the screen.
left: The foyer, showing the box-office and the escalators which lead to the lounges and auditorium.

Essoldo cinemas are generally called Essoldo, but a number in the Rank circuit may be by other names than Odeon or Gaumont (e.g. the Metropole and New Victoria in London). Changes can sometimes prove confusing. In one typical medium-sized town a few years ago there were five cinemas: a Regal, a Gaumont, an Odeon, a Carlton, an Empire. The Regal is now the Essoldo, the Odeon is a dance hall and the Gaumont is now the Odeon, the Carlton is still the Carlton but is now a Rank cinema as well as the Odeon which was the Gaumont. Only the little Empire staunchly retains its title as well as its independence.

At the outbreak of war all cinemas were closed by law for a short period. During the Blitz, programmes finished around seven o'clock. Building and development were, of course, at a standstill. About 330 cinemas were bombed, but in central London total casualties were comparatively few. The bomb which caused havoc and tragedy in the Café de Paris went through the roof and floor of the Rialto, Coventry Street, which had started life many years ago as the West End Cinema, and the Cameo–Royal in Charing Cross Road was badly damaged. By the end of the war attendances were soaring, and they continued to do so until about 1949 – the year ironically, when cinemas were once again permitted to light themselves up. The gradual return of counter-attractions such as motoring undoubtedly contributed to the fall – accelerated violently by the spread of television a few years later. To counteract the tiny TV screen, cinema screens started to expand and take on strange shapes in order to accommodate the super-spectacles which were being made in the hope of luring people away from their little sets. In 1953 Twentieth-Century Fox showed the first Cinemascope film, *The Robe,* at the Odeon, Leicester Square. Exhibitors faced more financial headaches over the expense of installing new equipment and screens, as other techniques followed. The Astoria presented *Around the World in Eighty Days* in Todd–AO, and more and more strange "scopes" and "visions" arrived, culminating (so far) in Cinerama. The London Casino in Old Compton Street, which started life in 1930 as the Prince Edward Theatre, was adapted to house this cinematic mammoth, which has now also taken over the Coliseum Theatre – for long the sister variety house to the London Palladium – and provincial houses.

To accommodate the huge curved screens and stereophonic sound, and to avoid engulfing the audience altogether, much interior alteration was necessary. The auditorium began to lose its "live theatre" appearance as proscenia disappeared, front stalls moved back, and large sloping carpeted areas took the place of orchestra pits and organ lifts.

* * *

The news-reel theatres which abounded in London and the larger provincial towns before and after the war began to dwindle as television took over their job with improved immediacy, though their close relations the cartoon-and-comedy-short shows still continue to a smaller extent. Many of the news-reel theatres were comfortable and charmingly decorated little cinemas – a modern version of the Bijou house – and have, fortunately, been taken over as speciality cinemas, often showing a mixed bag ranging from esoteric foreign films to nudies and seXeys. An important post-war concern is Gala Films, founded in 1951 by Kenneth Rive and running, among others, the two long-standing Tottenham Court Road cinemas now known as the Berkeley and the Continentale. They also have a lease on the handsome Royalty, Kingsway, and in 1967 ran a season at the Cambridge Theatre. Gala cinemas generally show first-run foreign films and, in occasional revival double-feature programmes, afford a welcome opportunity of catching up on two missed pictures at once.

Three leading circuits of "mini-cinemas" are the Cameo, Classic and Jacey. The present Cameo–Royal started as a news theatre well before World War II and changed to its present policy soon after it. The Polytechnic (where Lumière held the show referred to above), was taken over in 1941 as a news theatre, and started to build its high reputation as a specialist cinema, the Cameo–Poly, in 1941 with *The Secret of Mayerling*. Unhappily, there is a strong likelihood that this famous little theatre, with its unique link with the past of cinematograph history, may shortly be closed to accommodate the growing number of Polytechnic students. Cameo–Moulin began life as the first modern-style news theatre in 1930, taking its present name and turning to continental pictures of the more racy type when television decreased the public for news films. The latest acquisition, Cameo–Victoria was built by the Claverings in 1936. It opened as a news theatre, then showed classic-type films in 1947 and in November continental.

The circuit is run by Basil Clavering, whose family have been in the business for years, at one time owning the Capitol, Haymarket. Recently Cameo was acquired by Classic Cinemas, but is to retain its identity and policy.
The first Classic opened at Croydon in 1935, and the circuit now owns about ninety theatres throughout the country, running a lively and invaluable policy of revivals and seasons devoted to particular directors, stars or foreign films. This policy remains unchanged though the circuit now runs a number of larger-scale cinemas also. A feature of its administration is a constant redecoration and modernisation.
The Baker Street Classic was opened by the circuit in 1937, the Windmill (once the famous Home of Non-Stop Revue) in 1965, and the Piccadilly, originally a bare underground barn, was first used experimentally for a circular cinema, then entirely rebuilt as a Classic.
Jacey Cinemas (the name evolves from the initials of the founder, Joseph Cohen) was started in 1932 and led in the provinces by opening the Oxford Cinema, Birmingham, as a specialised house for news and interest features. Later the company expanded into news theatres throughout the country.
In 1960 it bought the Monseigneur chain.
A recent development is the opening of Jaceyland, at Baker Street Station, once a news theatre and now modernised and specialising in full-length Disney pictures. The seating includes individual boxes in the back stalls. Jacey also run the two Gala cinemas in association with Kenneth Rive, and the Cinephones in Oxford Street, London, and elsewhere, belong to the circuit.

Of paramount importance was the opening, in October 1957, of the National Film Theatre in its permanent home built under an arch of Waterloo Bridge and cunningly adapted to its constricted space. With its daily change of programme (sometimes three times in one day), its range from the earliest silents to pre-releases during the London Film Festival, its projection equipment enabling the silents to be run as originally intended, and its installation of head-phones so that untitled foreign films can be given an English commentary, it performs a unique service for both students and the general film enthusiast. Its programmes are arranged generally in definite series based on a period, a country or a personality. Two full NFT theatres are being opened, in Manchester and Newcastle, and over twenty part-time theatres are planned for other towns. Arrangements are also well under way for a smaller, specialist theatre (approximately 160 seats) adjoining the present building. Another major event was the opening of the fine *new* Columbia in Shaftesbury Avenue, February 1959 – first film *Gigi*; and the Prince Charles, off Leicester Square, after a brief period as a theatre, turned to films.

* * *

As to the present and future – statistics can provide plenty of gloom for the pessimist. Official figures for 1966 show the drop in both attendances and takings to be continuing. Away from mathematics, however, there is plenty to stimulate. The opening towards the end of 1967 of the austere but impressive *new* Odeon in St Martin's Lane (with a smash-hit in *Thoroughly Modern Millie*), the massive refurbishing of the Leicester Square Odeon, the under-way construction of the new twin Plazas – whatever their future name may be – are significant events in London's West End at any rate, and a new Odeon will be completed in Stockton by the spring. In addition, the total number of "specialised" cinemas command an audience unthought of in past years. Anybody who has seen a cinema film only on the ill-defined, cramped, unsteady, audience-lacking tube of a television set has not really seen it at all: no criticism or judgement based on such a viewing is of much value. In time this realisation will surely spread throughout the country. The modern cinemas may be less lush, less plush, less gold-and-glittery than the old – but they are challenging, vital and often beautiful, more comfortably seated, better designed for seeing the screen wherever you sit, and in general have their attention focused more on the presentation of the film than the incidental luxuries, which can only be to the good. But many of the old friends remain as well, and through all their story runs the inspiring thread of the first cinema ever – still going strong in Wilton Road, Victoria.

* * *

The first new theatre to be built in Britain in 1968 was opened on April 25th at Stockton-on-Tees. It is a Rank Theatre Odeon, of stadium design with a central circle area, 1,225-seat auditorium, and licensed bar. The opening film was *Thoroughly Modern Millie*. The total cost of the building, erected on the site of the old theatre, was £150,000, including full equipment.

RELEASES OF THE YEAR IN PICTURES

(You will find more detailed information about the films illustrated in a later section of this volume—The Year's Releases in detail)

Of all the films in the considerable cycle of religious screen spectacles that received a fresh lease of life with the advent of Cinerama (and *The Robe*), Dino de Laurentis's *The Bible . . . In The Beginning,* for Fox, directed by John Huston, was probably the best, certainly the one made in the best taste (if you exclude Palo Pasolini's *The Gospel According to St Matthew* which was a different kind of film altogether and certainly no spectacle). Based on the first chapters of Genesis, it relates man's tempting by the Devil, his fall and expulsion from the Garden: seen going from Eden in fear and shame, Michael Parks as Adam and Ulla Bergryd as Eve.

It was Burton himself, together with wife Elizabeth Taylor, who made possible the screening of the Oxford University Dramatic Society's production of Christopher Marlowe's *Doctor Faustus*, for it was their company which put up the money to transfer it from stage success to screen. Burton directed himself to considerable effect as the Doctor whose love of learning and fair women make him barter his soul to the Devil – the latter, in monk's cowl, played brilliantly by Andreas Teuber.

Opposite
After nearly a year's premier run in London, Julian Blaustein's vast-scale story of General Gordon, *Khartoum*, was at last generally released. Charlton Heston played the General, the hero of Khartoum, so sadly let down and finally martyred for political reasons. Behind that headdress is Laurence Olivier, playing the General's enemy, the fanatical Mahdi whose followers provided "the enemy" in a number of extremely spectacularly-staged desert battles.

Though not all car racing enthusiasts waxed enthusiastic about M-G-M's spectacular *Grand Prix,* it did more than any previous film to take the audience into the cockpit of a racing car and give them all the thrills of driving around some of the most famous of Europe's race-circuits at more than 100 m.p.h. Tieing these sequences together; a story of the men who drive, with James Garner as a more ruthless type savagely determined to be first past the chequered flag.

Robert Wise's *The Sand Pebbles* for Fox (he directed and produced) was a gargantuan adaptation of the Richard McKenna novel about an American gunboat isolated on the Yangtze river during the Chinese ferment of the 20's and the adventures and misadventures of some of the crew, notably of Steve McQueen as the non-conformist Holman (right) and Richard Attenborough as the unfortunate Frenchie (centre). Left, Charles Robinson, as Ensign Bardelles.

After a fantastic three years at the Dominion cinema in London, during which period it became established as the greatest money-maker of any film ever made, Fox's *The Sound of Music* had a special selective release this year. The wonderfully winning Julie Andrews is seen singing "My Favourite Things" with the seven motherless Von Trapp children – whose governess and step-mother she becomes.

58 Quite obviously Peter Brook's film for U.A. of the Peter Weiss play *The Persecution and Assassination of Jean-Paul Marat as Performed by the Inmates of the Asylum of Charenton under the Direction of the Marquis de Sade* (surely the longest film title ever?) isn't ever likely to get more than a limited floating release, for this straightforward, no concessions, adaptation of the Royal Shakespeare Company's production, with its flesh-creeping, blood-curdling horrors and final murder and riot, isn't ever likely to appeal to more than minority audiences. Shown: Glenda Jackson, Ian Richardson (as Marat) and Susan Williamson.

Another film which, premiered as far back as April 1966, because of its astringency and black comedy now seems unlikely to ever have a general release is Tony Richardson's macabre little piece for M-G-M, *The Loved One,* based on the Evelyn Waugh satire "The American Way of Death". Shown: John Gielgud, Roddy McDowall.

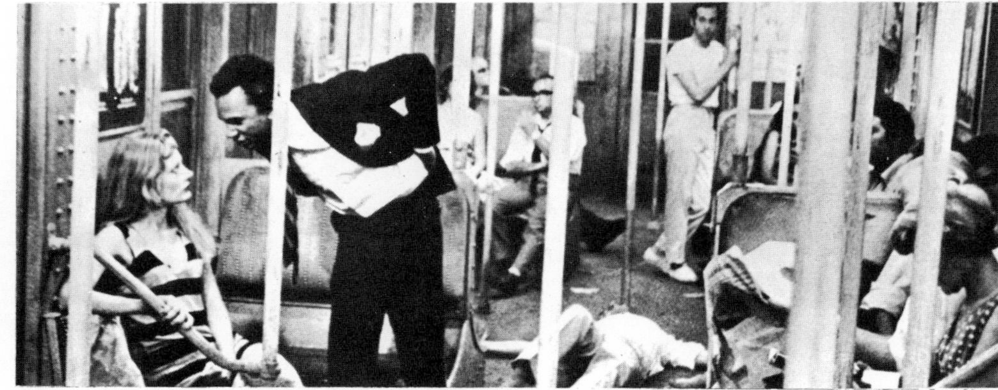

In his last feature cartoon, *The Jungle Book,* based on Kipling's "Mowgli" stories, Walt Disney was back to his highest standard and this delightful story of a little boy's adventures among the animals of the Indian jungle had verbal as well as visual wit, and was easily one of the most entertaining animated feature films in years.

Anthony's Harvey's shoestring film of the Leroi Jones stage play about racial prejudice *Dutchman* was quite an achievement from any angle, helped to success and added significance by the brilliant playing of the only two characters: Shirley Knight as the sexy little white trollop who goads and reviles a fellow New York subway traveller, a peaceable young negro, played by Al Freeman Junior, into an outburst of primitive violence.

60 Warner's *Up the Down Staircase* was notable if only for an outstanding performance by Sandy Dennis, as a young teacher having to face up to her first job, trying to force some sort of basic education and discipline into her class (which, set in a slum district of New York, appears to consist largely of morons, thugs and subnormal teenagers) and eventually winning some sort of small victory in spite of all the routine which sometimes appears to leave no time for actual teaching.

Coincidentally, Columbia's British film *To Sir, With Love* was a slight – more sentimental – variation on the same theme, for here again a new teacher has to fight hard to make good his first job, trying to knock some sort of education and civilised behaviour into a class of insubordinate young thugs, an effort complicated in his case by the fact that he is coloured! Sidney Poitier played the role with authority.

Opposite
The 1966–7 period has been particularly rich – after some lean years – for the Western, several of the new ones being outstanding. One of the best, Columbia's *The Professionals*, was set along the Mexican border and described an expedition of four tough characters (three of them shown, the Negro, Woody Strode, the explosives expert, Burt Lancaster, and Lee Marvin the leader – (the fourth, not shown, was Robert Ryan): financed by a millionaire to recover his wife, Claudia Cardinale, kidnapped by bandits.

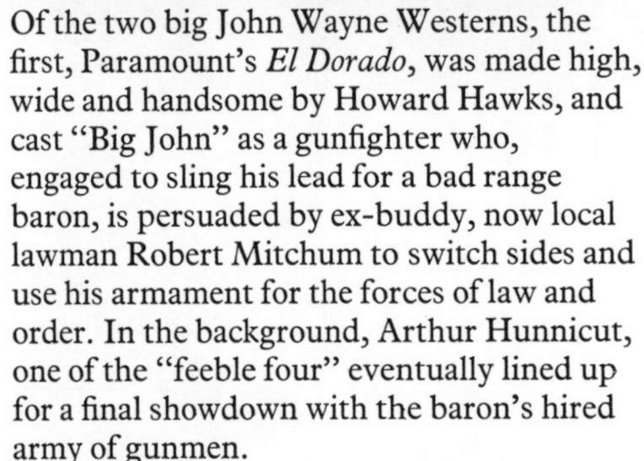

Of the two big John Wayne Westerns, the first, Paramount's *El Dorado*, was made high, wide and handsome by Howard Hawks, and cast "Big John" as a gunfighter who, engaged to sling his lead for a bad range baron, is persuaded by ex-buddy, now local lawman Robert Mitchum to switch sides and use his armament for the forces of law and order. In the background, Arthur Hunnicut, one of the "feeble four" eventually lined up for a final showdown with the baron's hired army of gunmen.

In U.I.'s *The War Wagon* Wayne played a rancher whose land has been stolen and at the same time been framed into a prison sentence by another big land-grabber. When he comes out of jail, paroled, John plans to get even by holding up the villain's iron-clad, gatling-gunned stagecoach carrying the gold dug up from mines on John's own ranch! And helping him, the gunman employed originally to shoot him down, Kirk Douglas!

Robert Mitchum was star (with Richard Widmark – seen in a tight spot – and Kirk Douglas, not shown) in Harold's Hecht's expensive U.A. production *The Way West*, a story about a wagon train struggling along the old Oregon trail in 1843 and finally overcoming all obstacles. A big, incident-filled Western this, but with some of the story angles and some of the characters oddly undeveloped.

Another star with two Westerns to his credit was Dean Martin and the novel angle of one of them, U.I.'s *Rough Night in Jericho*, was that he played the villain (and played him straight, without any comedy touches), an ex-lawmen now turned town terroriser; killer, blackmailer and just about everything else.

The other movie *Texas Across the River* was a very different kind of Western and a very different kind of role for Martin. From the same U.I. studios, this one was a cheerful "send-up" of some of the more familiar sagebrusher situations.

The very busy James Coburn was the anti-hero of Paramount's *Waterhole 3*, playing a character who will do – and does – anything to get his hands on some stolen gold bullion but quite willing to dally a little while along the way in order to carry out an odd rape or so – Margaret Blye, watching Coburn leaving her to ride off with the all-important gold.

James Garner gets his bullet in first – receiver is unfortunate Steve Ihnat. An incident in John Sturges' continuation of his story of Wyatt Earp (first related in his 1957 movie *The Gunfight at the O.K. Corral*): *Hour of The Gun,* in which the revengeful Wyatt uses his sheriff's badge to cover a campaign of personal revenge on the Clanton gang survivors.

Among the year's crop of Westerns were a number of "foreign" productions, usually made in Spain and including the second in the U.A. "Man With No Name Series", *For a Few Dollars More,* starring a taciturn Clint Eastwood as a bounty hunter who will stop at nothing to bring in – preferably dead – any man with a price on his head. Brutal, cliché-ridden like the first film (*A Fistful of Dollars*), it was again wonderfully visual.

Another of these "European Westerns" was *Seven Guns for the MacGregors*, an Italian–Spanish production about the struggle of a family of Scots immigrants trying to establish themselves in a tough Texas at the turn of the century.

Walt Disney contributed *The Adventures of Bullwhip Griffin*, which was set in the Gold Rush days and told a story about the way that a gentleman's gentleman was caught up in the great Klondike treasure hunt – Roddy McDowall, seen with his hands raised, top right.

Not strictly a Western but near enough to be squeezed not too unfairly into the category was Ivan Tors' film for Paramount, *Africa – Texas Style*, in which Hugh O'Brian played the cowboy imported from Texas by a British (John Mills) wild-life rancher who has the bright idea of breeding wild animals as a means both of conservation of the wild life and of providing meat for the hungry natives.

Jack Clayton's *Our Mother's House* for M-G-M was a grim, somewhat macabre (and spasmodically effective) story of a family of children who are so terrified at the thought of possible separation and the orphanage that when their mother dies they bury her in the garden and keep up a pretence that she is ill or away. Eventually their mysterious "father" materialises and with him comes the final tragedy. Dirk Bogarde as the father, Pamela Franklin as the eldest daughter.

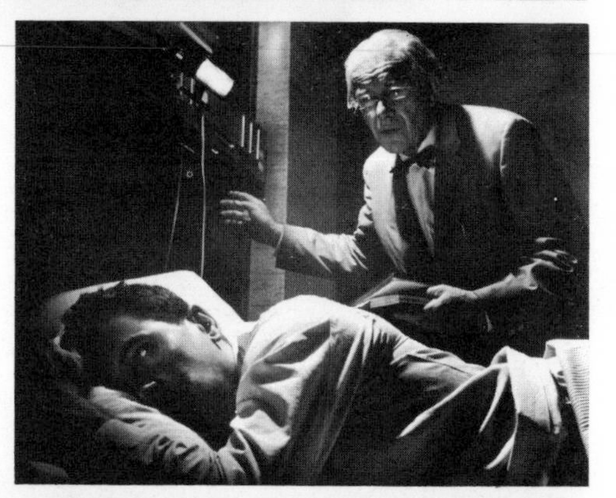

Another unusual thriller and one which didn't seem to gain the critical acclaim and wide showing it deserved was John Frankenheimer's *Seconds* for Paramount, which was based on the macabre David Ely story about a man – Rock Hudson – given a second chance in life but only, as he gradually becomes aware, at horrible cost.

A magnificent performance by James Mason completely dominated *Stranger in the House,* Pierre Rouve's direction, for Dimitri de Grunwald, of a Georges Simenon story. Mason played the central role of a barrister who after his wife had left him has more or less opted out of life but is forced right back into it when he finds a body in the attic and his daughter involved with the group of young people suspected of committing the crime.

Taking years to come to this country, always frowned upon by the censor, *Lady in a Cage* was finally shown this year by Gala. Olivia de Havilland's performance was the dominating factor in this slice of cinematic Grand Guignol about a semi-invalid woman who, trapped in the lift in her own house, is forced down to the level of an animal by a group of morons who break in, pillage, murder and torture before being defeated by their own weapons.

Controversial Eddie Chapman, as played by Christopher Plummer, faces up to the suspicions of German Gert Frobe, while an already convinced Yul Brynner watches in this scene from Warner-Pathe's *Triple Cross*, based on the book "The Eddie Chapman Story", the story of a real-life safe-cracker and double agent, who managed to fool a lot of people on both sides during the war.

Robbery was Stanley Baker's film from start to finish. He thought of it, set it up, fought for it through a maze of legal jungle, produced and was himself star of this meticulously observed and minutely recorded story of a Great Train Robbery!

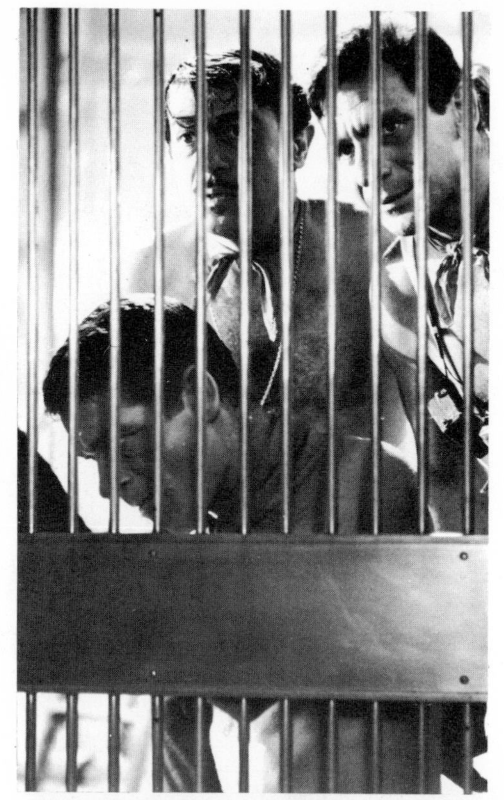

More crime in Joseph E. Levine's Paramount film *Carnival of Thieves* (shown in America with the jollier title of *The Caper of the Golden Bulls*) in which Stephen Boyd (lock-picking in centre) played a former bank robber unwillingly dragged back to the game and forced by blackmail to blast open, for a gang, the vaults of the Bank of Spain under cover of the annual carnival at Pampalona.

Warners' *The Naked Runner* was a spy story in the new, cynical tradition, with Frank Sinatra the unhappy victim of an intricate and confusing British Secret Service plot to erase a man who has defected to the other side of the curtain.

Warners' *The Shuttered Room* was a highly unlikely but coldly chilling thriller about a mad old Aunt shut up in the attic who occasionally emerges for a little red-blooded mayhem and murder. Gig Young and Oliver Reed (victim) were among those involved.

Craig Stevens played the trouble-maker of the title in Paramount's *Gunn,* taking on the pretty tough job of bringing to book the murderer of the gangster boss who once saved his life. Highly complicated, and often confusing, it was at the same time gripping in its expert thick-ear detection way.

Pretty wild, and certainly again highly complicated in plot, *Fathom* was another thriller which achieved its object of light-heartedly entertaining. Everything – and everybody – centred around Raquel Welch – shown being "frisked" by Tony Franciosa after being caught bending over a dead body.

Shirley Eaton somewhat unexpectedly played the leader of a global organisation planning to take over the world and run it in the female way in Anglo's *Sumuru,* based on the Sax Rohmer thriller.

Steve Plytas, Miki Iveria and Julian Glover have a grim little discussion in London Independent's *Theatre of Death*, a thriller about a series of vampire murders which take place against the foreboding backgrounds of Paris's centre of macabre entertainment, the so-called Theatre of Death.

An unpleasant moment for Diane Clare in the Rank British thriller *The Trygon Factor*, in which Stewart Granger played the superior sleuth trying to get at the truth behind the gold-melting nuns living in one of Britain's stately homes – a house in which masked men and murders are everyday events!

Burgess Meredith as the mysterious *Doctor Diablo* – who shows five visitors to his booth at the fair what their horrifying futures are going to be. The "goddess of destiny" is shown with her skein of life and shears of fate, ready to use the one on the other . . .

The Deadly Bees start the attack . . . in the Paramount thriller whodunnit of that title about a man who trains a lethal brood of the insects to carry out his orders and murderously remove from his path the people he decides must die.

U.A.'s *Danger Route* was another of these highly involved espionage thrillers in which Richard Johnson (seen with one of his more interesting "leads" – Diana Dors) is the ex-Commando British agent more or less blackmailed by his bosses at M.I.5 into yet one more murderous adventure.

Confrontation between Margaret Lee, Maurice Kaufmann and Anthony Newlands in Anglo's thriller *Circus of Fear*, a murder story set against a circus background.

72 And the circus was again the background for Columbia's thriller *Berserk*, in which Joan Crawford (centre: Michael Gough is to her left) played the owner of a travelling Big Tent set-up which is beset by a series of violent deaths and mysterious accidents.

Patrick Allen and Sarah Lawson face up to the unpleasant facts of *The Night of the Big Heat*, a science-fiction piece from Planet Films, which told a story about some mysterious beings from Outer Space who land on a small British island and for their own nasty reasons start to heat the place up!

Another and excellent Science Fiction thriller was Hammer's well-produced *Quatermass and the Pit*, the story of an antedeluvian spacecraft – formerly employed on the Mars–Earth shuttle service! – dug up with occupants intact during tube excavations. Examining the fast decomposing creatures, James Donald and Andrew Keir.

Violence has been one of the most prevalent features of the movies recently: sometimes meaningless, less often an integral part of the story. It was a large part of the motivation of Warners' chain-gang drama *Cool Hand Luke*, in which Paul Newman most ably played an individualist always in rebellion and never finally subdued in spite of plenty of sadistic treatment from wardens and fellow chainees.

Violence, too, was one of the main ingredients in M-G-M's painfully gripping *The Dirty Dozen*, about the training of a group of civilian killers given a chance to escape the noose if they will volunteer to be trained for a desperate commando-like expedition into occupied France during the last war. Brutal but effective trainer was Lee Marvin, shown carrying out a little work-out!

Violence, again, in Sam Spiegel's *The Happening* for Columbia, the story of a kidnapping entered into light-heartedly by a gang of moronic young layabouts, which suddenly turns sour on them as their victim finds out the disillusioning truth about his own position. Anthony Quinn as the kidnapped: Faye Dunaway and Michael Parks as the kidnappers.

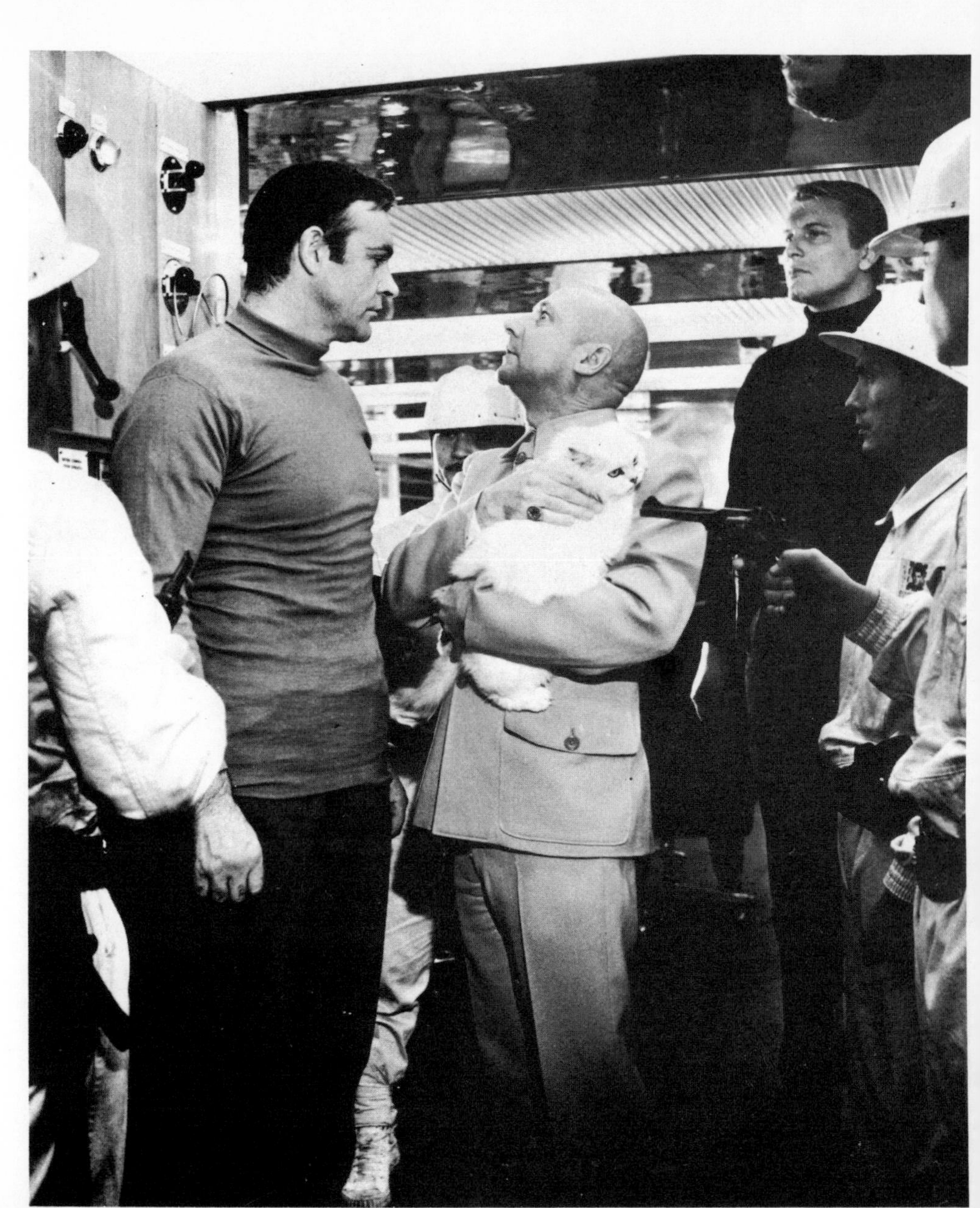

Plenty of violent happenings also in one of the best of the Bond films, *You Only Live Twice,* one of which was a superbly organised air battle between Bond in his mini-copter and four larger battle-copters belonging to the nasty Spectre organisation whose plans for atomic war M.I.5 ask Bond to put a stop to. Sean Connery was again Bond (the last time I'll play the role, he threatened). Seen facing up to the villain, Donald Pleasance.

One can always depend on finding plenty of strong-arm stuff in the "Uncle" series of thrillers and Robert Vaughn and David McCallum in M-G-M's *The Karate Killers* used something stronger than their wits to prevent those horrid THRUSH boys from getting the professor's secret recipe for turning seawater into gold!

Though this scene looks charming enough, there was plenty of rough and tumble in Fox's addition to the Flint series, *In Like Flint*. This act by the versatile Flint, played as usual by James Coburn, takes place in Moscow, where he dances with ballerina girl-friend Yvonne Craig in order to find out more about a feminine plot to "take over" the world, and a plot by less feminine plotters to take over the world from them when they've taken it over!

The busy Coburn also starred in Columbia's interesting movie from director-writer Bernard Gerard, whose individuality was stamped firmly on his *Dead Heat on a Merry-Go-Round,* in which Coburn played the crook who in the end is a little too ruthlessly clever so that in stealing one fortune (from a bank) he unknowingly passes up an even larger, legal one.

But easily one of the most bloodily violent, yet at the same time, paradoxically enough, beautiful and exciting films of the year – also one of the most commercially successful – was Warner–Seven Arts' *Bonnie and Clyde,* which recreated the true and terrible story of bankrobbers Clyde Barrow and Bonnie Parker, who in the 1930's joined forces to head a gang which spread death and terror through the American South-West until they were betrayed and ended their lives in a carefully planned police massacre. An outstanding performance was contributed by Faye Dunaway as Bonnie.

Opposite
A bloody mass execution was the climax of another excellent gangster film, Fox's *The St Valentine's Day Massacre,* the story – based on fact – of the gang war in Chicago in the twenties between the Al Capone and Bugs Moran mobs which ended in a wholesale slaughter which stirred the horrified city into belated action.

SCHNEIDER
TAILOR SHOP
APARTMENTS FOR RENT
DRESSMAKING SEWING · LACE BUTTONS
TAILOR
POLICE

Stewart Granger as the great white hunter who hates the changes that are coming to his beloved wild Africa and undertakes a last expedition, with client Kaz Garas, primarily with the big intention of settling scores with the dangerous rogue elephant who has killed his pal. Paramount's *The Last Safari*.

Far more light-hearted if equally lethal violence was in Hammer's new film based on the old legends of Sherwood Forest, *A Challenge for Robin Hood,* in which the new, athletic Robin hero was Barrie Ingham, here teaching a mail-man his place!

Rank's *The Long Duel* was one of those large, basically simple adventure stories which don't ask you to take them too seriously: although it was claimed to be based on fact. Yul Brynner played the Dacoit outlaw leader whose forces are defeated by the British, who lure him and his men into a bloodily hopeless attack on a train bristling with arms and armour.

The Slender Thread (to life) of the title of the Paramount picture is that which holds a would-be suicide, the thread which those in charge of Seattle's Crisis Clinic cling to while they set in motion the machine which will, they hope, be able to avert another suicide. Telly Savalas played the professional; Sidney Poitier the volunteer amateur; both trying to find the woman who has threatened on the phone to end her life.

One of the greatest difficulties these days is deciding which film comes from where; what the actual origin of a movie is. For instance, many of the year's releases with English sound-tracks, titles and even players, were made abroad and dubbed later. Typical example, Jules Dassin's *10.30 p.m. Summer*, with Greek Melina Mercouri and Spanish newcomer Julian Mateos as stars (others: Britain's Peter Finch, Germany's Romy Schneider), screen-played by France's Marguerite Duras (with director Dassin) and released by America's U.A.

Tony Richardson's *The Sailor from Gibraltar* was made in France with an international cast that included Jeanne Moreau and our own Ian Bannen as co-stars. It concerned Miss Moreau's search for her mysterious sailor lover, almost as unreal as the story, an ambitious one from Marguerite Duras.

Also made in France was Fox's *Rapture*, about a retired Judge and his simple-minded young daughter (Melvyn Douglas and Patricia Gozzi) who live in a house over-shadowed by a sense of doom and who are brought to tragedy by the arrival of a young escaped prisoner.

80 One of the first examples of real Franco-British cinematic co-operation was Rank's Francos–Kenwood production *Two Weeks in September*, in which the star was Brigitte Bardot, who had difficulty in making up her mind which of her two boy friends she'll finally settle for: this one is Laurent Terzieff.

Opposite
Fox's *Road to Saint Tropez* was a real one-man-band effort, a so-called "anti-travelogue" made in French with an English commentary (spoken by Fenella Fielding) and written, directed and produced by ex-pop singer Michael Sarne. The woman was Melissa Stribling, the boy Udo Kier, and the girl Gabriella Licudi.

Another, less ambitious, pop singer was Paul Jones, who appeared as the star in *Privilege,* an odd sort of film made by Peter Watkins about a future British government using a glum, masochistic pop star as a means of controlling and bringing the teenagers to heel.

Easily one of the greatest performances in one of the most memorable (and, incidentally conventionally treated) films of the year was that of Dame Edith Evans in Bryan Forbes' *The Whisperers*, a deeply intuitive and moving study of old age which Forbes both wrote and directed. The clerk with a warm feeling for the old woman: Gerald Sim, a nicely thought out performance.

America's pre-occupation with marriage and divorce laid the foundations for several of her best comedies. Columbia's *Divorce, American Style*, was a highly cynical, richly satirical examination of wedded bliss and, more especially, ex-marital poverty, when after the split-up the husband is reduced to penury by the alimony and his only hope for financial re-balance is to marry his ex-wife off to somebody else! Jean Simmons and Jason Robards (ex-partners) discuss the happy possibility (for Robards) of her marrying newly divorced Dick Van Dyke.

In the same wittily sophisticated vein was Fox's *A Guide for the Married Man*, in which Richard Morse teaches willing pupil Walter Matthau how, when and where to deceive (how *not* to do it illustrated by this moment of truth for horrified wife Ann Guilbert, finding hubbie Joey Bishop cosily entertaining his friend Sharyn Hillyer) but is himself hoisted on his own petard.

84 One of the best and wittiest Hollywood films, *Barefoot in the Park,* from Hal Wallis for Paramount, was also on the same theme – and concerned the troubles in the marriage of a young couple – Robert Redford and Jane Fonda, two beautiful comedy performances – in their tiny, hopelessly inconvenient flat high under the roofs of Manhattan. It's interesting to note, by the way, that beneath all the fun of this trio of brilliant comedy movies there were very serious human problems.

Seven Arts–Warners' *You're a Big Boy Now* was a very different sort of comedy, though still concerned with love. It had a very slim story, musical numbers, extremely modern direction and a couple of nice young stars in Peter Kastner and Elizabeth Hartman.

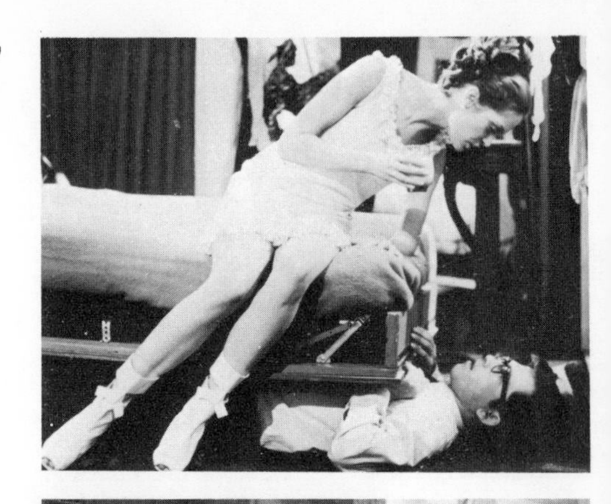

Rank's Michael Winner film *The Jokers* was a mixture of thrills and smiles, with its story about two brothers (Michael Crawford and Oliver Reed) and the wild, but successful, plot they dream up (for the sake of the notoriety they crave) to lift the Crown Jewels from the Tower of London, a jape that goes sour when one double-crosses the other and sends him to jail for the crime!

Fox's *One Born Every Minute* (released in America as *The Flim-Flam Man*) gave plenty of – fully accepted – comedy chances to George C. Scott, as the wily old "con" man making his crooked way across the South American States but finally caught up with by the law – in the person of hayseed sheriff Slade (Harry Morgan).

Richard Lester's *How I Won the War* was a comedy of sorts, a satire about war in general and war films in particular which turned out to be an odd mixture of laugh and shudder, slapstick and bloody tragedy, decorated with all sorts of gimmicky touches. It starred, among others, Roy Kinnear and "Beatle" John Lennon, who, however, contributed only a brief role.

Though not all the critics agreed, the third Eric Morecambe and Ernie Wise film, from the Rank stable, *The Magnificent Two,* with its stronger than usual story about a couple of travelling salesmen-innocents caught up in a South American revolution, was probably their best large-screen work to date.

86

One of her more appealing performances made Stanley Donen's Fox comedy *Two for the Road* a triumph for Audrey Hepburn, who more or less stole the film from her co-star Albert Finney, with the less rewarding role of the boorish young architect who beds and weds her and then finds there's friction as well as fun in the married state.

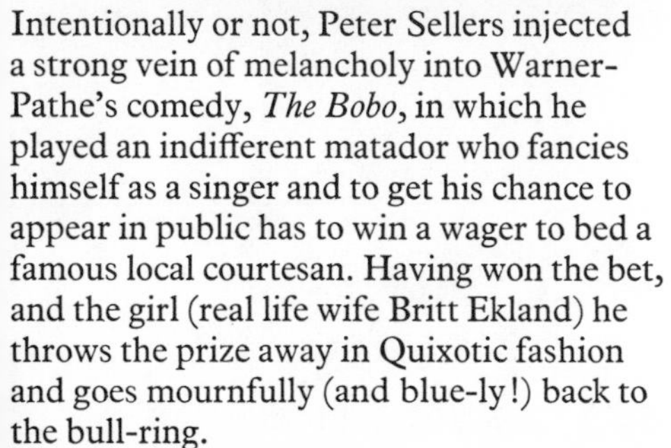

Intentionally or not, Peter Sellers injected a strong vein of melancholy into Warner-Pathe's comedy, *The Bobo*, in which he played an indifferent matador who fancies himself as a singer and to get his chance to appear in public has to win a wager to bed a famous local courtesan. Having won the bet, and the girl (real life wife Britt Ekland) he throws the prize away in Quixotic fashion and goes mournfully (and blue-ly!) back to the bull-ring.

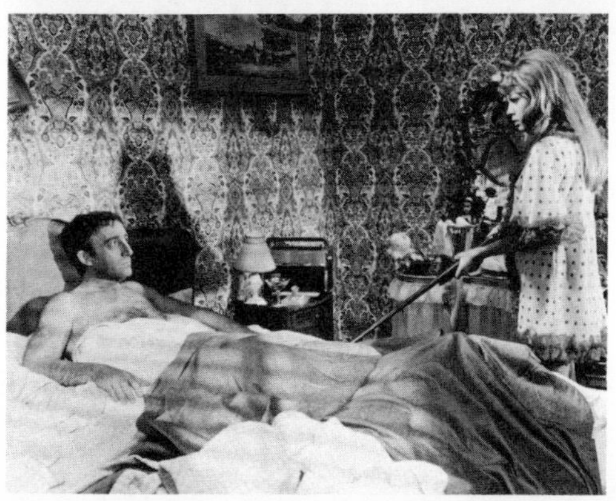

Loosely constructed, not always smooth in its story line, Alexander MacKendrick's crazy comedy for M-G-M, *Don't Make Waves,* with its story of marital meanderings in (sometimes!) sunny California, had some very funny moments and some highly effective sequences. Star was Tony Curtis – shown chatting up one of the bathing belle beauties.

The oddly-titled Disney comedy *The Gnome Mobile* was all about the adventures of tycoon grandpop Walter Brennan and his grandchildren ("Mary Poppins" youngsters Matthew Garber – behind the bars – and Karen Dotrice) and their search through the giant Redwoods forest for a suitable female companion for their new friend, the two-foot-tall gnome they find so sadly lonely.

Lionel Jeffries comes to grief and his odd machine gets an unintended ducking in Anglo-Amalgamated's *Jules Verne's Rocket to the Moon*, a Victorian science-fiction chapter about an 1875 spacecraft built for a voyage to the moon and based on some of Verne's fascinatingly imaginative writing.

U.I.'s *The Perils of Pauline* was a modernised version, in colour, of the sort of thing, which, in her cliff-hanging silent serials, made Pearl White a great star of her day. This time it was Pamela Austin – shown comforted by Pat Boone after her car has been smashed by a train! – who had to stand up to all the perils that the screen writers could dream up for her.

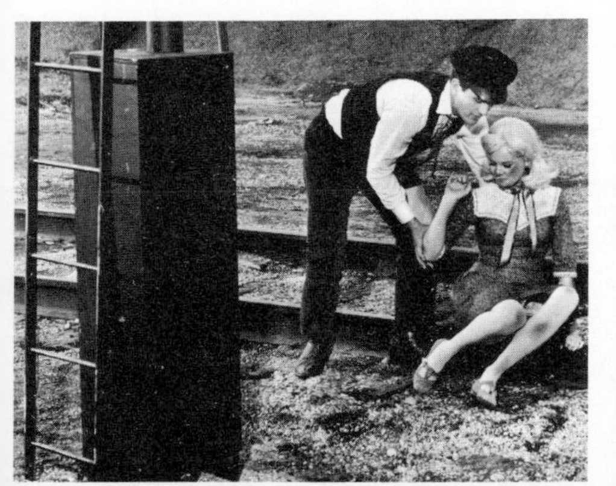

Jerry Lewis continued to turn out his comedies, written, directed, produced and starring himself. Typical was the Columbia-released *The Big Mouth*, in which he was involved with stolen diamonds, dead frogmen and his own villainous double.

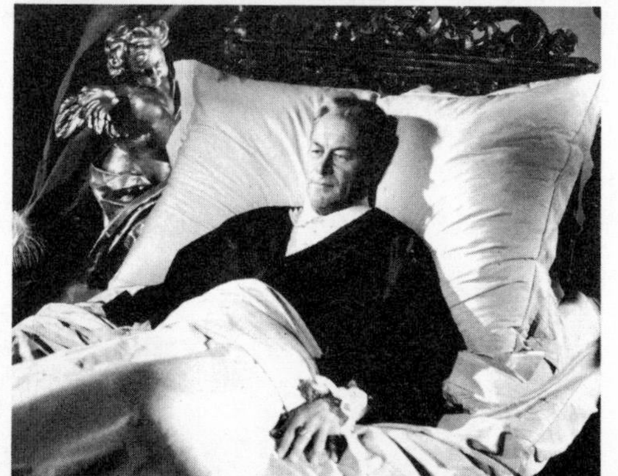

One of Hollywood's most literate creators, Joseph L. Mankiewicz, wrote, directed and produced the Charles Feldman–U.A. film *The Honey Pot*, a polished variation on the "Volpone" plot, a stage performance of which, indeed, gives wealthy, urbane Englishman Rex Harrison (left) the idea of inviting three of his ex-mistresses to see how they will react to the news that he is dying: discussing the possibilities, Adolfo Celi, Maggie Smith and Capucine.

Neat idea behind Paramount's *The Swinger* was the difficulties of a nice young girl – Ann-Margret, with Tony Franciosa – who is forced into the position of having to prove that she really knows the naughty life she writes about in her very successful stories.

Pop fashions come and pop fashions go and Elvis Presley, one of the pioneers of much that is now almost old-fashioned in this with-it world, goes on successfully making musical films. He sang nine numbers in M-G-M's *Double Trouble*, in which the slim connecting story was about the way he finds the unpleasant things that happen to him are really intended to happen to the young English girl whose adoration for him leads her to follow him around the world.

Hayley Mills, as a sort of Cinderella who, in U.I.'s *Pretty Polly* during the few days she stays on in Singapore after her guardian dies after too much food and a quick bath, takes her first lover (a not very pleasant character, played by Shashi Kapoor, seated) and grows up to complete womanhood.

Brilliant in every department and one of the best films of the year as a result, U.A.'s *In the Heat of the Night* was a whodunnit with racial undertones: the story of a strange, at first antagonistic but increasingly mutually respectful alliance between a coloured detective from out of town and the less bright local sheriff, getting together in order to find out the murderer of a respected local citizen. The team: Sidney Poitier and Rod Steiger.

Also set in the deep American South and equally concerned with the problems of colour prejudice was the 1967 Otto Preminger film released by Paramount, *Hurry Sundown*. Michael Caine was oddly cast as the Southern bounder (married to Jane Fonda) whose greedy and ruthless scheme for making money out of her lands turn on and ruin him.

Opposite
Though it may have had a rough censorship journey in various parts of the British Isles, Joseph Strick's remarkably ambitious and in part highly successful attempt to adapt to the screen the vastness and the richness of James Joyce's *Ulysses* was a big hit in London, where it opened at the Academy in the June of 1967 and is still running at presstime, in mid-'68. Barbara Jefford was wonderful as Molly and Milo O'Shea equally successful in cinematically re-creating the gentle Irish-Jew Bloom.

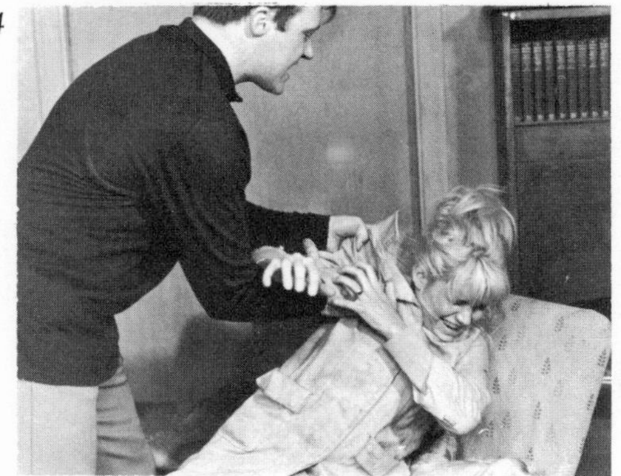

Roughest and rawest of the wave of British kitchen-sink dramas spawned by the TV tide was Joseph Janni's production of *Poor Cow*, in which Carol White made a great personal hit (following her TV success in the same subject) as the girl of the title, a young lady whose marital and extra-marital adventures with burglar husband and his burglar friend, and other equally unpleasant characters, are sordid and sad and keep her finally in the gutter she makes no real effort to get out of.

Rita Tushingham, the little 'un, and Lynn Redgrave, the big 'un; the two friends who come from Ooop North to London to taste its swinging life in Paramount's *Smashing Time*, and having tasted its snob boutiques, false pop world, wild Carnaby Street and other with-it wiles, go back home not particularly sadder but certainly wiser girls.

Paramount's *Up the Junction* continued the cycle of films about the seamier side of – London – life with an amusingly incredible story about a little Chelsea Rolls-Royce-type dolly (pretty Suzy Kendall and banana – in reflective mood) who throws up the good life for a rough – and apparently ready! – sort of existence in the slums of Battersea because she finds there some sort of fulfilment, especially with a cockney lad who dreams of better things and goes to jail when he makes them come illegally true.

Wendy Craig and Orson Welles share a spotlight in Michael Winner's determinedly with-it comedy for Rank, *I'll Never Forget What's 'Isname*, which was all about an advertising executive who decides to opt for the simple life but, having opted, finds it all too complicated.

Also very, very determinedly with-it and swinging was Clive Donner's U.A. comedy *Here We Go Round The Mulberry Bush*, which was full of pretty little dollies, lots of bad language and young sexual hungers in its story about a lad who searches for sex, doesn't quite know what to make of it when he gets it, but then decides to go on seeking it, anyway! One of the prettiest little dollies, Judy Geeson, seen with co-star Barry Evans in his first film role. But the film was actually stolen by older-timers Denholm Elliott and Maxine Audley, as a snobby, hard-drinking suburban couple, in a short satirical sequence which was for some the high-spot of the movie.

Peter Rogers continued to regularly carry on with his cinematic Carry Ons, even if he did temporarily get away from the series' normal title with his *Follow That Camel*, which might, anyway, have as well been called "Carry On Legionaires!". This offered considerable fun at the expense of the old Foreign Legion – officered by Commandant Kenneth Williams and Sergeant Phil Silvers.

96

The Plank, written and directed by Eric Sykes, with himself in the leading role, was an exhaustive examination of the amount of humour which can be obtained with, by and around the piece of wood of the title as it is carried through London. Carrying it, Tommy Cooper.

Footnote – and a golden footnote, too – to a golden age of cinema: Spencer Tracy and favourite co-star Katharine Hepburn in Columbia's *Guess Who's Coming To Dinner*, which was completed only three weeks before Tracy's death. Tracy in his last role played a liberally-minded, crusading newspaper owner suddenly faced by his daughter with the negro she wants to marry!

James Earl Jones, Richard Burton, Alec Guinness, Elizabeth Taylor and Peter Ustinov – the starry line-up in Peter Glenville's M-G-M production of Graham Greene's novel *The Comedians*, with its strong indictment of a dictatorial regime in Haiti behind its story of a rather sad, illicit love affair.

A bitter moment of truth as young and ruthless star Patty Duke tears off the gorgeous auburn wig of stage veteran rival Susan Hayward to reveal that her real hair beneath is thin and white: a melodramatic moment from Fox's adaptation of Jacqueline Susann's 'sensational' best-seller *Valley of the Dolls*.

In mingled feelings of hate, fear and anticipation, the family await the regal entrance down the stairs, on the occasion of *The Anniversary*, of the three men's man-eating momma Bette Davis (right), who rules them all with scathing contempt and ruthless brutality. The sons: Jack Hedley, James Cossins and Christian Roberts. The wife (of the first): Sheila Hancock. The girl-friend (of the second): Elaine Taylor.

Frank Sinatra as *Tony Rome*, a cynical private eye, quizzes lovely stripper Deanna Lund at her caravan home she shares with her plump lesbian friend in Fox's tough detective thriller, made along the lines of the classic Bogart movies of the 30's.

Peter Falk, attorney turned detective, and Britt Ekland are both involved in the complicated crookery of the theft of the priceless Macedonian piece of shrine jewellery in M-G-M's *Too Many Thieves*.

One woman – but what a woman, Rosana Podesta! – is among the *Seven Golden Men* in the Warner film about their neat plot to break into one of Switzerland's best banks and steal the contents under cover of taking the road up! And it succeeds; it is only with the aftermath, when thieves begin to live up to their reputation and fall out, that everything starts to go wrong.

Lee Marvin, (with Angie Dickinson as his wife's sister) framed by his wife and her crooked friends, goes to jail in M-G-M's *Point Blank* because he's too beaten up to resist, takes his jail medicine and comes out coldly determined to kill every one of those who sold him down the river.

Norman Rodway, Suzy Kendall (one of the year's busiest as well as prettiest new stars) and Tony Beckley as a rather nasty trio in Paramount's gripping, quite brilliantly made but always creepingly unpleasant *The Penthouse*, about two young men who break into a flat and torture the owner and bait and then rape his young mistress.

That intrepid "UNCLE" team of Robert – Solo – Vaughn and sidekick David – Illya – McCallum returned to the large screen in M-G-M's *The Helicopter Spies*, in which they are assigned the task of finding and obtaining a terrible new thermal heatray weapon which in the wrong hands could bring about a new world dictatorship. All very slick, and amusing – and ludicrous!

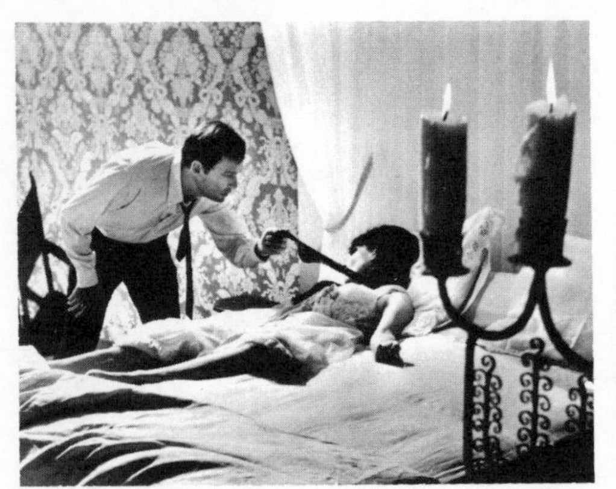

The most involved and confusing Harry – Cockney – Palmer adventure yet, Harry Saltzman's *Billion Dollar Brain*, was all about his somewhat puzzling adventures as he tries to foil a mad Texas oil millionaire's plan to smash the Soviet Union by organising a revolution in Latvia! Shown, Karl Malden as the millionaire's crooked aide, Michael Caine as Harry and, in the background playing the 'cello, the late Francoise Dorleac.

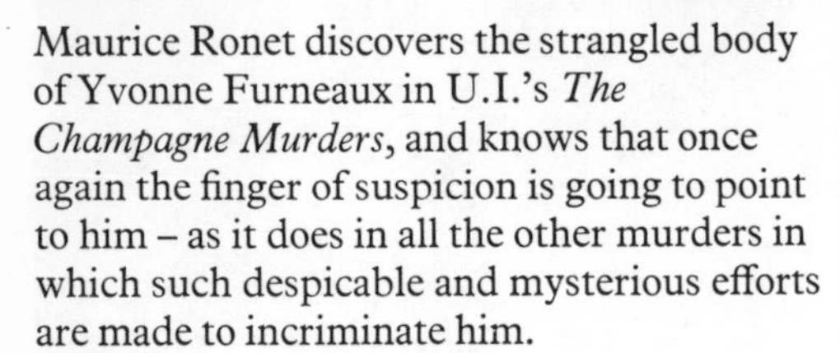

Maurice Ronet discovers the strangled body of Yvonne Furneaux in U.I.'s *The Champagne Murders*, and knows that once again the finger of suspicion is going to point to him – as it does in all the other murders in which such despicable and mysterious efforts are made to incriminate him.

The siege of the killer is finally on in U.I.'s *Madigan*, the story of the "normal" sort of thing that goes on behind the façade of a typical American city police force as they grapple with the many problems posed hourly. James Whitemore, left, as Chief Inspector; Henry Fonda, centre, as the worried Commissioner, and Frank Marth, right, as detective lieutenant.

Lovely Camilla Sparv as the bone of contention between villain Jeremy Kemp and hero Stephen Boyd in Columbia's *Assignment K*, which was all about a British toy manufacturer who uses his frequent business trips to Germany as a cover for his own small spy ring established there, and who suddenly finds that, dangerously for himself, his secret is a secret no longer.

Janice Rule in provocative pose in Columbia's *The Ambushers*, third (and possibly the liveliest) of the Matt Helm series of comedy spy adventures. Matt's task (played as usual by Dean Martin) is to recapture the stolen flying saucer and to rid the world of yet another would-be take-over by an unpleasant would-be dictator.

Apparently on leave from "UNCLE", David – Illya – McCallum turned up as the American Narcotics Bureau's best under cover agent in M-G-M's *The Heroin Gang*, in which he is set the tough – as you can see – task of smashing a Mafia-inspired, multi-million-dollar drug-theft plan.

Golden Era brought Sherlock Holmes back to the screen, in the person of Christopher Lee, with Thorley Walters as Dr Watson: they're seen sharing a fire as Holmes ruminates in *Sherlock Holmes and the Deadly Necklace*.

In masks, Katharine Ross, James Caan and Simone Signoret act out a weird cultist play in U.I.'s odd little thriller *Games*, which was about a series of practical jokes which turn sour when they lead to murder.

Odder still was M-G-M's gloomy little thriller *Eye of the Devil*, with its entirely unlikely story about a remote and primitive little French community who demand that their Marquis be sacrificed with black magic rites if their vineyards fail three times in a row – as they have done this time. David Niven played the strangely willing victim – shown with judge and jury and pretty little witch, Sharon Tate.

Tarzan and friend Leo: the new large-muscled ape man, first conceived by Edgar Rice Burroughs, is Mike Henry, who in Paramount's *Tarzan and the Great River* goes to the help of his Professor friend when the latter fights the depredations of the local Leopard Men.

The strip-teaser dopes the drink as the unsuspecting victim carries on pouring out the champagne in Golden Era's London thriller *The Phantom of Soho*, with its sorting out the murder suspects against a strip-teasing background.

It was the performance of Paul Newman which made Rank's *The Secret War of Harry Frigg* a great deal more entertaining than it might otherwise have been. He played the ace U.S. escapee sent to Italy in order to be deliberately captured and so help from the inside a bevy of P.O.W. Allied Generals escape to the outside! The German Commandant on the receiving end is Warner Peters; Vito Scotti is the player on the left.

Among the year's best Westerns, Paramount's *Will Penny*, in which Charlton Heston brought a hard breath of reality to the character of the title, a fifty-year-old illiterate range-rider who sees the cold touch of age on his shoulder and unselfishly shrugs off the love of a good woman because of it, finally riding on and off in the true Bill Hart manner.

108 Another grand Western portrait was supplied by Burt Lancaster in U.A.'s *The Scalphunters*, in which he played a trapper trapped (by Redskins) into parting with his season's harvest of pelts in exchange for an escaped negro slave – Ossie Davis – whom he then recruits to follow his furs until they can be stolen back.

And a Western with a difference was M-G-M's cheery little opus called *The Fastest Guitar Alive*, with musical numbers supplied by the star, Roy Orbison, whose guitar has the slightly unconventional gimmick illustrated – in a tight spot it can be made to spit, accurate, lead!

One of the calmer moments in M-G-M's *The Mercenaries*, with drink-ruined doctor Kenneth More taking the decision to stay and help with the native woman's childbirth although the rebels are nearing the small religious community, and he knows their arrival will inevitably lead to his death. Concerned onlooker in plaid shirt is Yvette Mimieux.

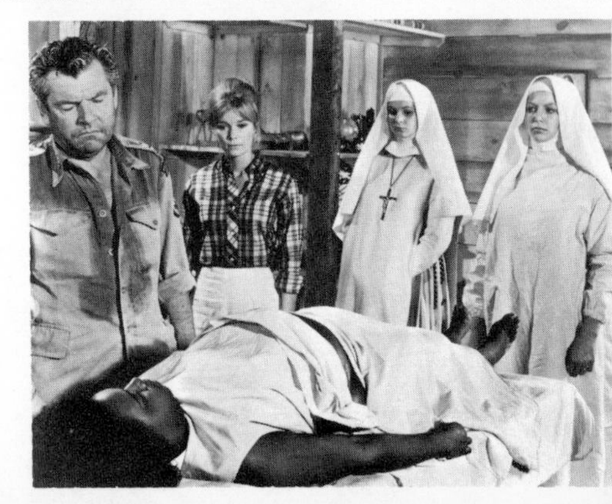

A rather strange little effort was Seven Arts' *Once Before I Die*, which John Derek both directed and produced and in which he played a major role. It was all about the efforts of a company of mixed American-Phillipino Cavalry to get to Manilla, with pretty passenger Ursula Andress, after the Japanese surprise attack on the island. As it turns out, Miss Andress is the only survivor of the long trek.

Jack Palance and Fernando Lamas, friendly enemies and rival Hong Kong junk owners, settle an argument with a little game of Russian roulette in U.A.'s old-style adventure melodrama *Kill A Dragon*.

A game of chess in Golden Era's spectacular reconstruction of really ancient history, *The Fabulous Adventures of Marco Polo*, the thirteenth-century traveller who journeyed from his Venice home to present himself at the Court of the great Kublai Khan.

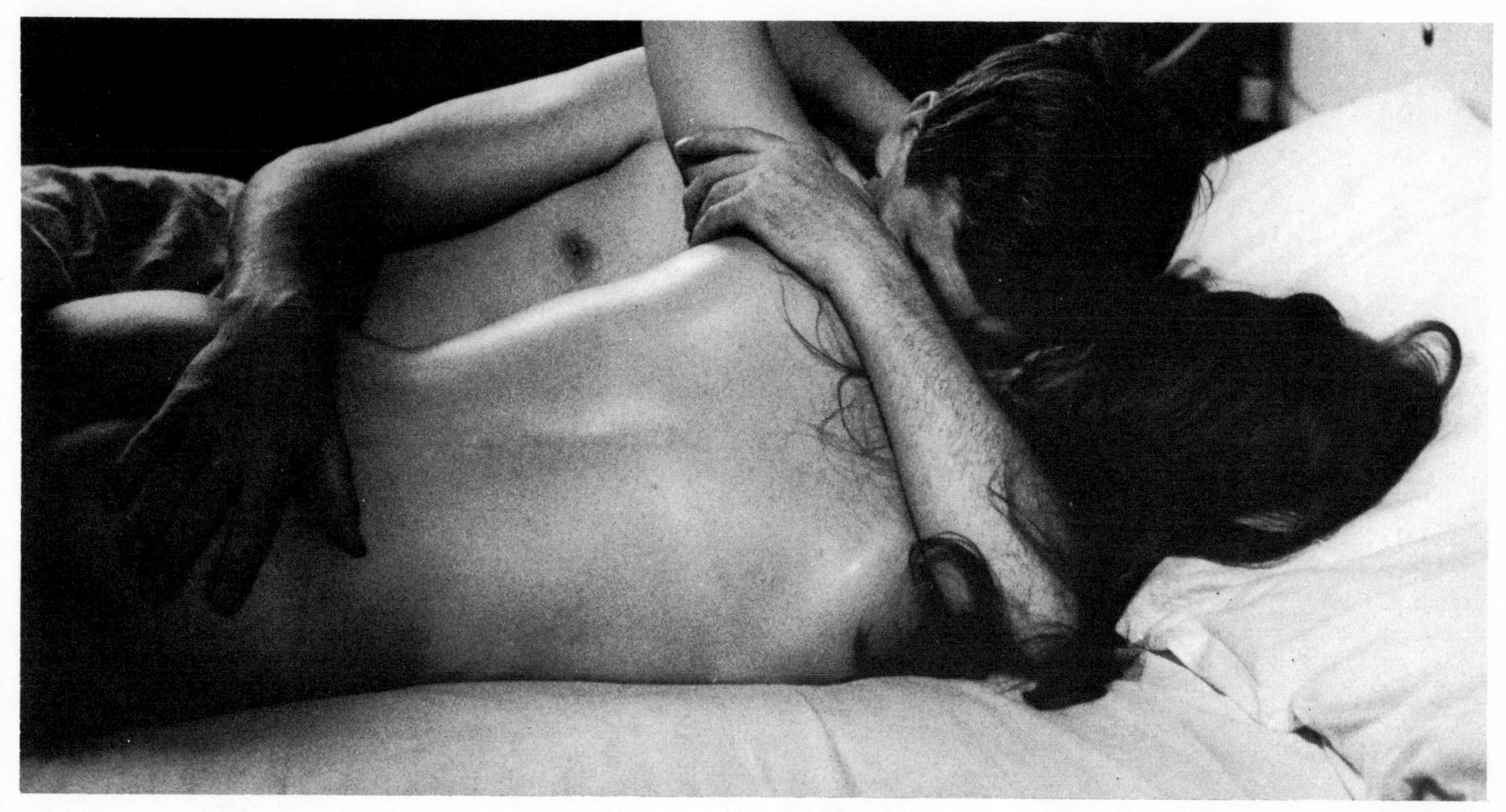

Opposite
Adventure of a completely different kind in *The Endless Summer*, an hour-and-a-half feature documentary about two expert surf-riders as they ride the waves in all sorts of places across the world.

Pretty newcomer Lucio Mondunio played the leading role in the Richard Schulman–Bachoo Sen British production *Her Private Hell*, taking the role of the out-of-town innocent who comes to the big city hoping to become a fashion model, but is seduced and used by her seducer for pornographic pictures.

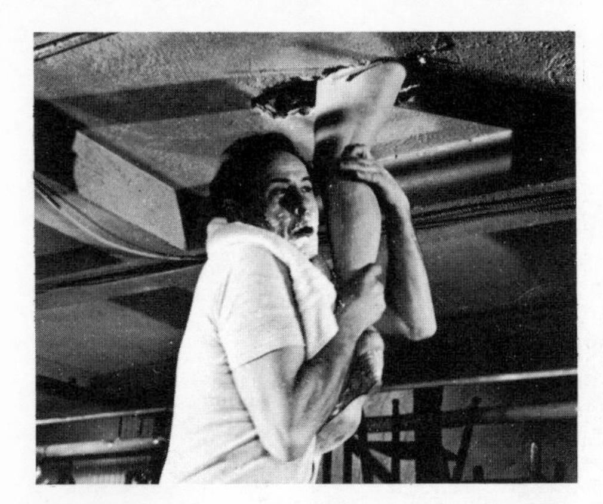

The real-life husband-and-wife team of Eli Wallach and Anne Jackson co-starred for the first time on the screen in Murray Schisgal's own adaptation of his stage success *The Tiger Makes Out*, in which the leading character is a woman-chasing postman who learns his lesson dearly when he picks up a culture-vulture who considers she's far too intelligent to stay a housewife all her life.

One of the more way-out films of the year, American William Klein's made-in-France *Who Are You, Polly Magoo?*, an odd mixture of dreams and reality telling the story of the rise and fall of a fashion model – delightfully played, incidentally, by Dorothy McGowan.

Continuing his series of well-made, always obviously sincere films, producer–director–star Cornel Wilde, came up with *Beach Red* for U.A., a story of an American Army group's assault on a Japanese-held island in 1943, a bloody business which leads to pain, death, degradation – and nothing else! With leader Wilde in this attack scene, Burr de Benning.

Knowing that his physically neglected wife (Elizabeth Taylor) is having an affair with his superior officer (Brian Keith), the homosexually inclined major (Marlon Brando) sits stiffly in the background as the game – of cards – proceeds. From the Warner–Seven Arts film *Reflections in a Golden Eye*, a story of a collection of – very – unpleasant sexually disturbed characters living on an Army station in Georgia. John Huston directed and made them interesting – though certainly not likeable!

A, rather understandably, *Bedazzled* Dudley Moore, cosily comforted by curvaceous Raquel Welch in the first (Fox) film to be made by Moore and his TV comedy team-mate Peter Cook. It was an uneven skit on the Faust theme.

Having already had some fortune-making medical fun in their *Carry On Nurse* (1959), those inveterate and prolific cinematic "Carry Oners" Peter Rogers and Gerald Thomas (producer and director) returned to the hospital ward to repeat the dose in this year's *Carry on Doctor*, in which Kenneth Williams played the slightly *outré* doctor! Patient, Charles Hawtrey; matron, Hattie Jacques.

Lurking in the shadows of his very funny, rumbustious portrait of the Pirate Captain in Walt Disney's comedy *Blackbeard's Ghost* were memories of both Charles Laughton and Robert Newton! The young athletic coach who brings Blackbeard back from limbo was played by Dean Jones, the pretty little professor who "falls" for him by Suzanne Pleshette.

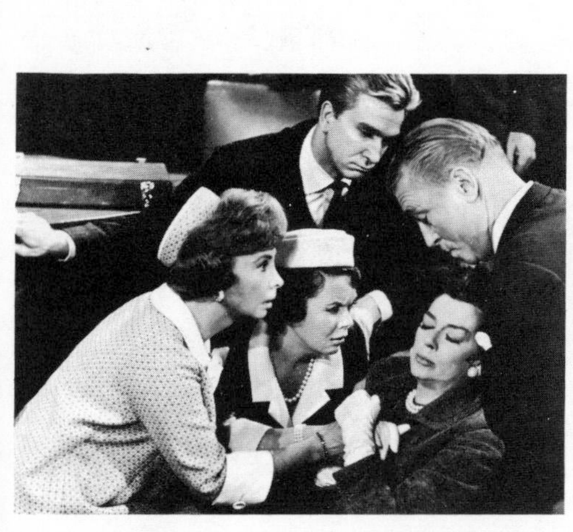

Rosalind Russell, fighting to legally prove her sanity in U.I.'s Ross Hunter production of *Rosie*, passes out in court during the hearing. Solicitously surrounding her: Audrey Meadows, Vanessa Brown, Leslie Mielsen and Brian Aherne, the last as the legal gentleman whose interest in this very wealthy widow are not wholly legal.

Slim gimmick in U.A.'s aptly named spy thriller *Operation Kid Brother* was that the star was Sean's younger brother Neil Connery (right) and the film made plenty of tongue-in-cheek allusion to the fact as it told its highly unlikely story about a group of crooks trying to blackmail the world into parting with half its total gold! Bernard Lee, left, played one-of-ours!

116 Reminiscent at times of the tough thrillers of the 30's, U.I.'s *New Face in Hell* was all about a thick-ear, always hard-up but doggedly persistent private eye (George Peppard, shown getting a roughing-up) who is hired by a nasty tycoon as a bodyguard for the man's mistress – but intended, it is eventually revealed, to be the sitting-duck victim in a pretty sordid murder plot.

Confused, cornered double-spy Laurence Harvey in Columbia's *A Dandy in Aspic* begins to realise that his Russian masters have no intention of letting him go back home after his British masters have given him the impossible assignment of "removing" his other, Soviet self! It was all rather incredible and also a little glum.

Don't sleep with your staff, even when they're as pert and pretty as Susannah York, is the lesson which should have been learnt by British brain Dirk Bogarde in Paramount–British's *Sebastian*, a stylish but strictly unromantic and certainly unlikely story of Britain's brilliant, mini-skirted, Bogarde-led Office of Decoding! On the other hand, as it is the girl's (and his!) baby daughter's rattle which leads him to solve the latest and most difficult Soviet satellite code, maybe one should ignore lessons!

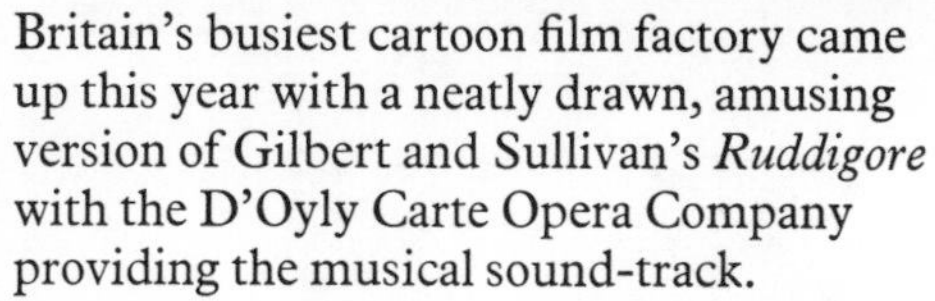

Britain's busiest cartoon film factory came up this year with a neatly drawn, amusing version of Gilbert and Sullivan's *Ruddigore* with the D'Oyly Carte Opera Company providing the musical sound-track.

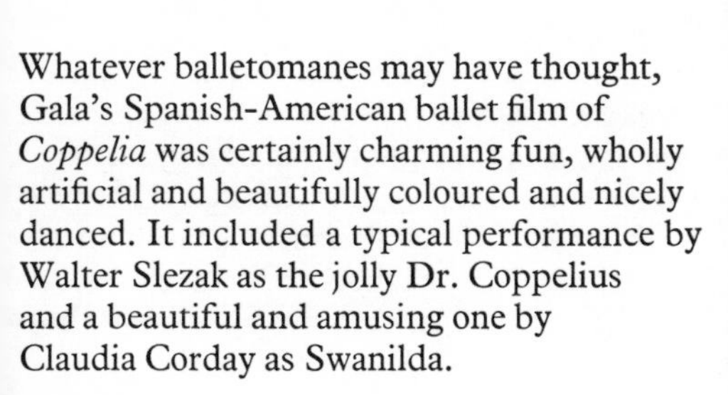

Whatever balletomanes may have thought, Gala's Spanish-American ballet film of *Coppelia* was certainly charming fun, wholly artificial and beautifully coloured and nicely danced. It included a typical performance by Walter Slezak as the jolly Dr. Coppelius and a beautiful and amusing one by Claudia Corday as Swanilda.

The French comedy (with English dialogue – and a wide general release) *Don't Look Now . . . We're Being Shot At* combined the gallic talents of Louis de Funes and Bourvil with the typical English contribution of Terry-Thomas. The young man completing the quartet is Mike Marshall.

When it was first brought here a dozen years ago Columbia's *The Wild One* was refused a certificate by the censor and only received one or two limited showings. Now generally released in a more permissive climate it confirmed the idea that those twelve years have seen a very great change in censorable attitudes: but it is still a powerful, disturbing film, about a gang of motor-cycle thugs led by an almost inarticulate braggart (Marlon Brando – seen with Mary Murphy) who descend on a small American town and proceed to take over and terrorize it.

The Vengeance of She was a typical Hammer thriller, based vaguely on the Rider Haggard character, about a girl mysteriously "drawn" from Europe to an Eastern city hidden in the desert and there hailed as the returned, immortal Queen. Chosen for the part, mid-European beauty Olinka Berova: with her, John Richardson as the country's ruler.

It is said that Pierre Boule, author of "Bridge Over the River Kwai", wrote *Planet of the Apes* for fun, though the underlying theme, that of a place and time when the apes have transferred places with man (the latter now the despised animal, hunted for sport) was serious enough. Anyway the Fox film of the story was certainly fun, with Charlton Heston the captain of a spaceship which lands four thousand years into the future – and comes into conflict with the ape men and their culture.

Ajanette Comer defends Anthony Quinn, the fugitive mistaken for a priest and forced by circumstances to keep up the pretence in M-G-M's *Guns for San Sebastian*, a story set in South America in the 18th century and allowing Quinn plenty of opportunity to suffer and struggle and emerge bruised but triumphant.

One of the Big Westerns of the year, in size, scope and screen-dimension (originally shown in Cinerama) was Cinerama's *Custer of the West* with Robert Shaw (left) as the General whose hunger for glory eventually took him to disaster and death at Little Big Horn, where he and his men (some of them shown in relaxed mood; Jeffrey Hunter and Ty Hardin) made their historical "Last Stand".

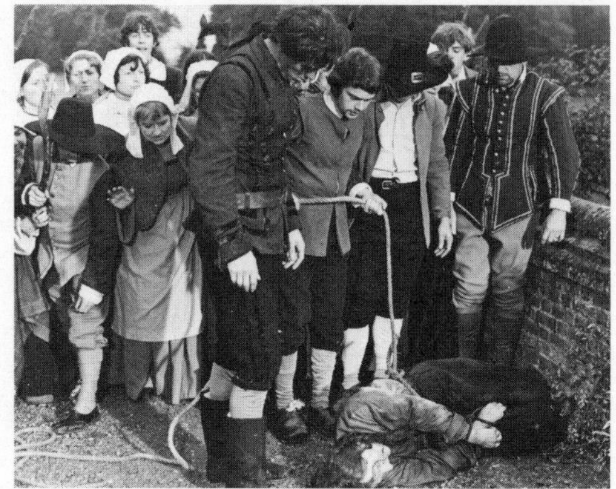

Tigon's *Witchfinder General* was about an opportunist magistrate who during the British Civil War rode the villages of England seeking out, trying, condemning and carrying out ritual murder of anyone accused of witchery – and doing it at three pounds a – burnt – head!

Two old hands at playing in Westerns were co-starred in Warners' *Firecreek*. Henry Fonda was the bad man leader whose gang take over a small town in which James Stewart (foreground) is the part-time, peaceful sheriff forced eventually into deadly confrontation with the force of evil they represent.

Arthur Kennedy and Glenn Ford, unwilling partners in M.G.M.'s *Day of the Evil Gun* brought together by the need to rescue the former's future and latter's ex-wife from the hands of the Redskins who have captured and sold her to a neighbouring tribe.

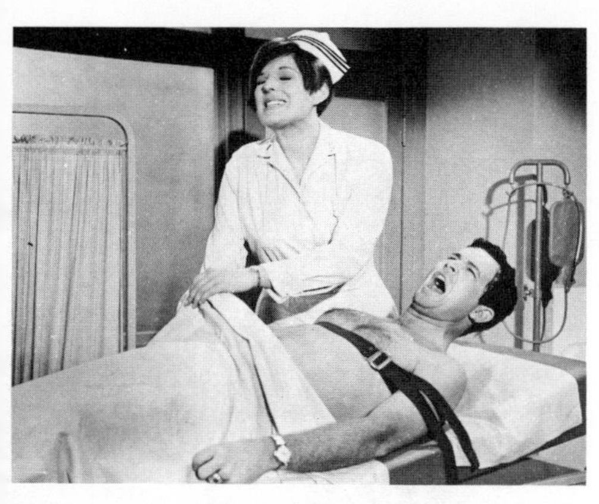

You might well fill in for yourself the greater part of this caption for a scene from U.I.'s comedy about the American Navy (in peacetime): *Nobody's Perfect*. Agonised patient is Gary Vinson.

Dean Martin up to his neck in trouble – pretty trouble, in the person of Stella Stevens – in Columbia's lengthily-titled marital (and extra-marital) comedy *How to Save a Marriage and Ruin Your Life*.

Doris Day, a belligerent would-be sheep rancher in – infuriated – cattleman's country, is prepared to back her argument by gunplay in her altercation with Peter Graves in U.I.'s comedy Western, *The Ballad of Josie*.

Van Heflin as *The Man Outside*, an American agent who gets the sack for not telling his bosses about his suspicions about one of his men and then becomes involved in a complicated series of plots and counter-plots, crosses and double-crosses against authentic London backgrounds in this London Independent Producer's release.

Gordon Scott as the son who rebels against his ruthless cattle baron father (Joseph Cotten) in Planet's Western *The Tramplers*, leaves home and so starts the inter-family struggle which stops the power- and land-hungry dictator spreading his domain further across Texas.

Pushing or pulling? In any case magician Vincent Price needs a little of his magic to get him out of this tight corner in Planet's *House of a Thousand Dolls*, in which his magicianship is really just a polished front for his real money-making business of white slaving.

Portrait of a father and daughter – and you'll find this strange family in Tigon's *The Blood Beast Terror* with Robert Flemyng as the nasty scientist who uses daughter Wanda Ventham in some spine-chilling experiments which lead to his own death at her hands.

Peter Sellers consoles sorrowful widow Shirley MacLaine so well at the funeral of her husband that by the time it is over she is ready and willing to go off with him . . . one of the seven diverse and separate episodes in the de Sica-directed Fox comedy *Woman Times Seven* – Miss MacLaine demonstrating her ability by playing all seven women.

Double-decker swinging entertainment provided by a zinging Elvis Presley and lots of glamorous support in U.A.'s *Clambake*, yet another in the several money-making films that Presley continues to turn out annually some twelve years after creating a new "Pelvis" pop trend with his first movie, *Love Me Tender*, in 1956.

Dame Edith Evans and the new secretary – Barbara Feldon – who at first seems likely to spoil butler Dick Van Dyck's (left) long-term plan in U.I.'s *Fitzwilly Strikes Back* to give his penniless old lady boss the money she needs for her charitable works by setting up a number of highly nefarious plots which include stealing the entire Christmas Eve takings of a famous New York store.

That old gag? Yes, Bobe Hope and a banana peel in *Eight on the Run*, Hope's own U.I. production of a story about a bank clerk who, suspected of embezzlement after finding a fortune (thanks to that banana), doesn't wait to reason why but flees with his family – including the oversize dog – stoutly pursued by the law.

The *Yours, Mine and Ours* in the U.A. comedy of that title are the nineteen children (ten his, eight hers, the additional one theirs!) which is the combined total of their families from their respective former marriages. He is played by Henry Fonda. She by Lucille Ball and the fun is based on a factual case in the marital records of North California.

The Rev. Smiling Gentleman is really a psychopathic killer whose pride in his work is such that he always chats to his legal pursuers about the crimes he commits – until he oversteps the mark and talks once too often and too long. A showy part for Rod Steiger and the film is Paramount's *No Way to Treat a Lady*.

Edward G. Robinson as the old professor who after thirty years of watching a diamond merchant from his classroom window decides upon retirement to gather a few crooked friends and rob the place of ten million dollars-worth of goods! With him, pretty secretary Janet Leigh: in Paramount's *Grand Slam*.

Warner-Pathé's thriller *Assignment to Kill* was about an investigation of the mysterious sinking of two ships belonging to a crooked financier (investigator-in-chief was Patrick O'Neal, seen doing his not always essentially unpleasant job).

Raymond Stross's Warner-Pathé film *The Fox* was an adaptation of the D. H. Lawrence novel about a delicate relationship between two girls living on a remote farm in Canada (girls: Sandy Dennis and Anne Heywood) which is strained and broken when a young man arrives on the scene and one of the women finds herself falling in love with him.

THE NEGLECTED ONES

Footnote to the Releases of the Year in Pictures

As you look through the detailed list of the releases of the year you'll probably be a little surprised at a few of the inclusions and feel certain they *must* have been released before this! The films in question are:

The Best Man, premiered in September 1964.
A Child is Waiting, premiered in July 1966.
The Greatest Story Ever Told, premiered in April 1965.
Lilith, premiered in November 1966.
The Reward, premiered in November 1965.
The Visit, premiered in August 1965.

The films have **not** been included in any previous FILM REVIEW for the simple reason that, *very* undeservedly, they have never received a general release; in fact in nearly every case – *The Greatest Story Ever Told* is the exception, it did get a very limited release – the film in question has never been shown since its premier season except at one or two cinemas more recently, when it has been shown as a "revival"! When one considers the rubbish that does sometimes get a countrywide release the neglect of these films is puzzling, for they are all in their way of special and in some cases of outstanding entertainment interest.

Take U.A.'s *The Best Man*, which was Gore Vidal's own adaptation of his stage play about dirty American politics, telling a story about the ruthless struggle, in which accusations of mental instability and homosexuality are used as exchange weapons, for nomination of U.S. President. Absorbing, convincing, bitingly amusing and finely played by a cast including Henry Fonda, Cliff Robertson, Edie Adams, Margaret Leighton and old-timers Lee Tracy, Gene Raymond and Ann Sothern, it was such a good movie that one wonders why it was never more widely shown? One shies away, of course, from any thought that it might have been because of its unpleasant picture of American politics?

Above
Henry Fonda – *The Best Man.*

Less outstanding, but certainly brave and interesting, was Stanley Kramer's *A Child is Waiting* which tackled, long before *Warrendale* the question of the mentally defective. In this Burt Lancaster gave a first-rate performance as the new head of a national institution for backward children who is anxious to try out new methods, and Judy Garland played a do-gooder who becomes too involved with one of the children. Kramer used some actual mental defectives in the film. *A Child is Waiting* had its faults, it was admittedly a little sentimental, but it was thoughtful and sincere.

Burt Lancaster – *A Child is Waiting.*

The Greatest Story Ever Told because of its size and its specialised subject is the one in this set which one can understand not being widely released. And, too, it came at the tail-end of a cycle of religious films. But it was one of the best; austere and completely anti-De Mille. Typical of the seriousness of the production was the selection of the actor to play the Christ, Max von Sydow.

Max von Sydow – *The Greatest Story Ever Told.*

Lilith was one of the last films to be made by the late Robert Rossen and in spite of an occasional hint of pretentiousness it clearly showed his considerable talent as a movie-maker. Warren Beatty played the occupational therapist who becomes emotionally entangled with one of his prettiest patients, Jean Seberg, who gradually and tragically disillusions him. Though not a great film, *Lilith* deserved a far wider showing than it had.

Warren Beatty and Jean Seberg – *Lilith.*

It is easier to show equanimity about the lack of attention that *The Reward* got from the men who book the movies. Always magnificently photographed, it opened wonderfully but later disintegrated as it told its story of the chase in Mexico of a man with $50,000 on his head, a chase that leads to death or disaster for nearly all concerned. With a cast including Max von Sydow, Yvette Mimieux, Efrem Zimbalist, Jun., and Gilbert Roland it was, again with all its flaws, still a great deal better than many a film – and many a Western – which won a wide general release during the period.

The Visit marked one of Ingrid Bergman's now rare screen performances, playing a – very – wealthy widow who triumphantly returns to her home-town in mid-Europe and then, after the civic welcome, publicly announces the reason for her return: she will offer the town a million dollars if they will kill the man – still a citizen, and a respected one – who with forged evidence drove her out when she was a girl! And after the offer she sits back and watches the place fester and corrupt as the townsmen discuss the fantastic bribe! A strange film, an unlikely one (though based on a Lunts' Broadway stage success) but well enough acted to make it worth, one would have thought, a wide showing.

Gilbert Roland, Efrem Zimbalist, Jun. and Yvette Mimieux – *The Reward.*

Ingrid Bergman and Anthony Quinn – *The Visit.*

THE CONTINENTAL FILM

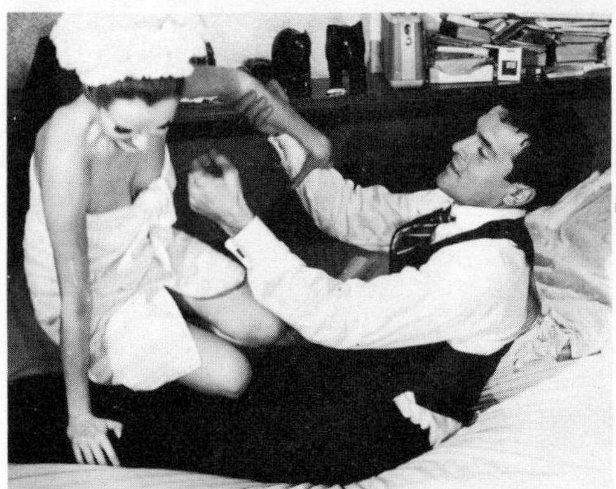

From France

Alain Jessau, who made *Life Upside Down,* was still concerned with dreams and reality in *Jeu de Massacre – Comic Strip Hero,* a strange but fascinating comedy about a fiction writer suddenly faced by a man who claims to be the "hero" character he has created! Eventually the writer (Jean-Pierre Cassel), his pretty wife (Claudine Auger), the "hero" (Michael Duchaussy) and his mother (Eleonore Hirt) settle down to a strange, complementary team to produce a highly successful comic strip series.

An odd contribution from France was *Massacre for an Orgy*, a satire on sex and sadist films which went so far in both directions that by the time the censors had finished with it little but shredded cinema remained! And the director's name was listed as Jean-Loup Grosdard!

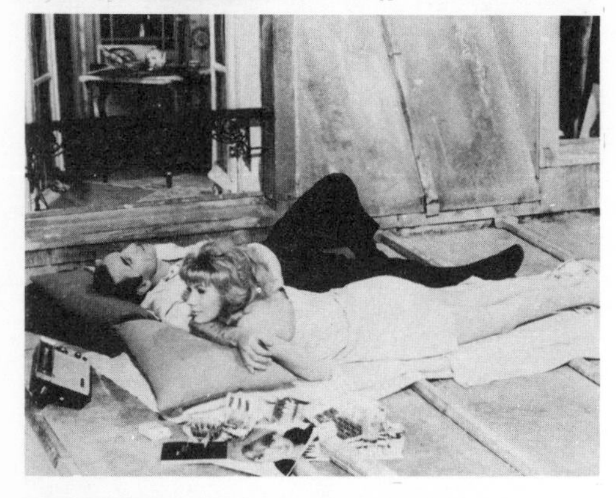

Contemporary's importation, *Paris in August*, was a romantic comedy about an English girl in Paris (Susan Hampshire) who meets and falls in love with a Paris shop assistant (Charles Aznavour) whose wife is away with their children on their summer holidays. It had charm, and it was coy!

Already several "Angelique" films, adaptations of Sergeanne Golon's popular stories, have been made and enjoyed a considerable success in France and elsewhere. But only now has the first of these been seen in Britain, *Angelique – Marquise des Anges* – with gorgeous Michele Mercier playing the title role in the action-filled, eye-filling melodrama.

Shown this year, the more or less completely reconstructed (by Renoir himself) Jean Renoir film of 1937, *La Marseilles*, a fine, patriotic pageant of French history only previously seen in cut, even butchered versions! The great surprise was to see how modern and up-to-date it looked, with many of it's technical qualities far ahead of their time.

Jacques Rivette's *La Religieuse*, based on the 18th-century Diderot story about the misadventures of an innocent young girl pushed unwillingly into a nunnery, had long been banned both in France and elsewhere. Now that it was seen here it proved surprisingly harmless, not at all shocking. Anna Karina played the girl.

136 Vintage performances from Bourvil – all the more impressive by being so restrained and non-comic – and Michele Morgan helped to make *Fortunat* one of the memorable movies of the period. He played a bibulous poacher and Resistance worker assigned during the war the task of getting the lady and her children through to Toulouse.

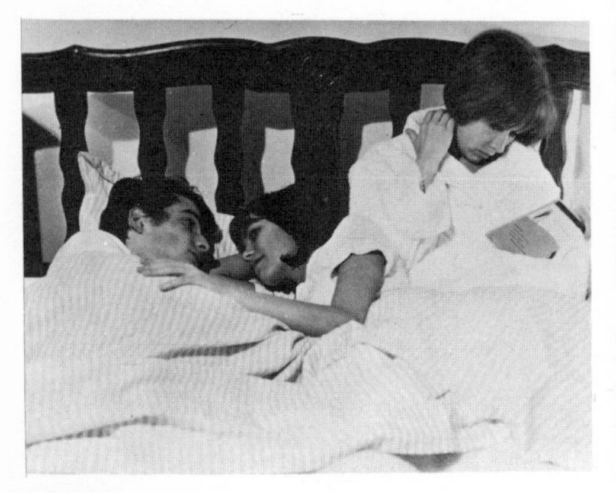

Masculin-Feminin was a typical Jean-Luc Godard effort, in which with his usual bag of tricks he set out to present a picture of Paris youth. The intimate trio: Jean-Pierre Leaud, Chantal Goya and Marlene Jobert.

The two young players, amateurs both, whose sincere performances helped to make Edouard Luntz's *Naked Hearts – Les Coeurs Verts*, a documentary-style story of young layabouts in Paris, far superior to the usual kind of film of this nature.

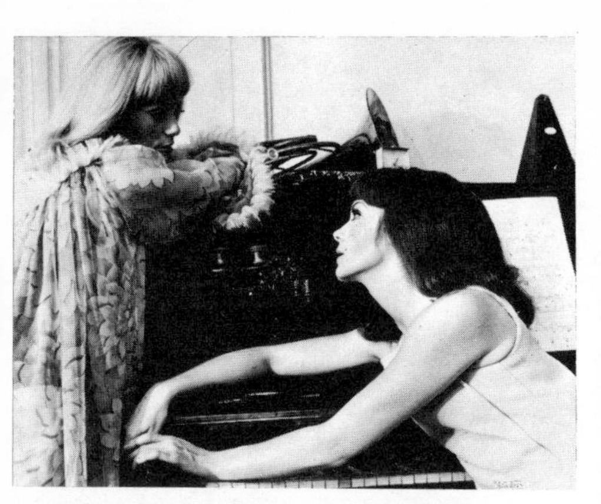

Jacques Demy's *The Young Girls of Rochefort* was another charming musical from the man who made *Les Parapluies de Cherbourg*. It was shown both in sub-titled (best) and "dubbed" versions. Included in the cast were real-life sisters Francoise Dorleac (shortly after killed in a car accident) and Catherine Deneuve.

Claude Pierson's *Ils Sont Nus – Days of Desire* was a shock sex film about a strange family living in poverty along the lonely, sand-dune girt sea-shore. Rita Maiden is the young woman finding resistance difficult.

Roger Vadim's adaptation of Zola's *La Curee – The Game is Over* cast Peter McEnery as the young man who falls in love with his beautiful young stepmother (Jane Fonda) and so sets off the chain of events which brings unhappiness to both, and ruin to her.

Catherine Deneuve as the cold wife fascinated by whoredom; the Japanese visitor client; and Jean Sorel as the Madame in Luis Bunuel's *Belle de Jour – Day Girl.*

The sextet of short episodes, *The Oldest Profession,* was actually a Franco-German co-production, though French-speaking and, largely, French-cast. The first episode showed the start of it all, right back in caveman times, with woman learning how to put a price on herself!

Joel Barbouth, Dominique Erlanger and Pascale Cori-Deville in the mud in J. L. Bastid's odd mixture of sex and kinky adventures, *The Pussycats.*

The Two of Us – Le Vieil Homme et L'Enfant, with its humanity, its charm and its unashamed warmth of sentiment, took the moviegoer back automatically to the vintage, pre-war years when the French cinema was pre-eminent. Even more so in that one of that era's more considerable players, Michel Simon, played the lead, as the old Jew-hating reactionary who, during the war, unaware of the child's racial origin, grows to love the small Jewish boy that has been sent to him and his wife for safe keeping. The boy was played by Alain Cohen.

Like Ingmar Bergman in Sweden, Robert Bresson in France works cinematically towards ever greater simplification and divorce from all sentiment and his *Mouchette*, based on the great French Catholic writer Georges Bernanos's book, was a completely uninvolved, anti-sentimental relation of the grim story of a teenage girl brought up in direst poverty in a remote provincial village who, when she is raped by the local epileptic drunkard and her mother dies, decides death cannot be so painful as life and rolls her way to suicide in the local lake!

Though so deliberately played down, the final effect of Bresson's telling of this depressing tale was almost stunning in its impact. Nadine Nortier gave a beautiful performance as the girl.

Another French film with a pre-war, vintage flavour was the, this time, unashamedly sentimental film *An Idiot in Paris*, with Jean Lefebvre as the provincial village idiot who has his dreams of Paris but finds them far, far from reality when a friend eventually takes him there. But if simple he's not *too* idiotic, so he takes a pretty little prostitute (Dany Carrel) back with him when he goes, planning to buy a farm with her nest egg!

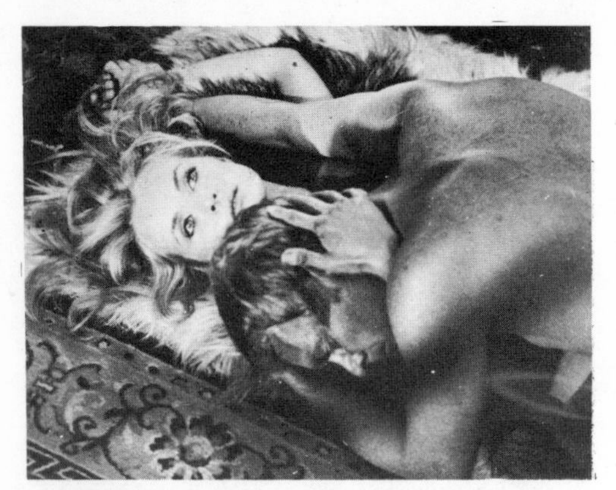

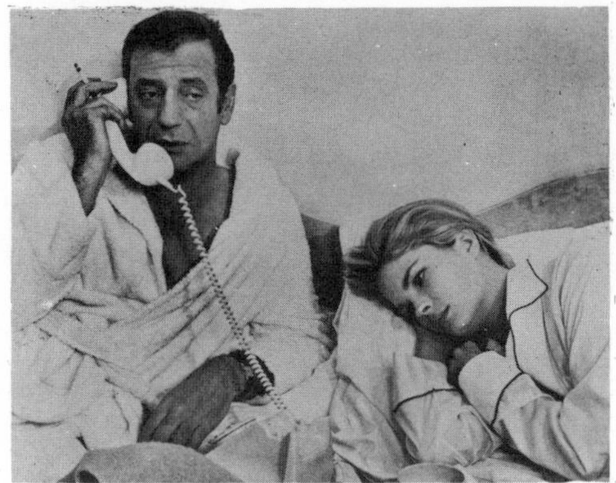

Claude Lelouch's *Vivre pour Vivre – Live for Life* showed deep insight into married life with its story of a faithless TV news reporter (Yves Montand) who eventually realises the worth of his marriage. The girl who nearly succeeds in breaking down the marital habit: Candice Bergen.

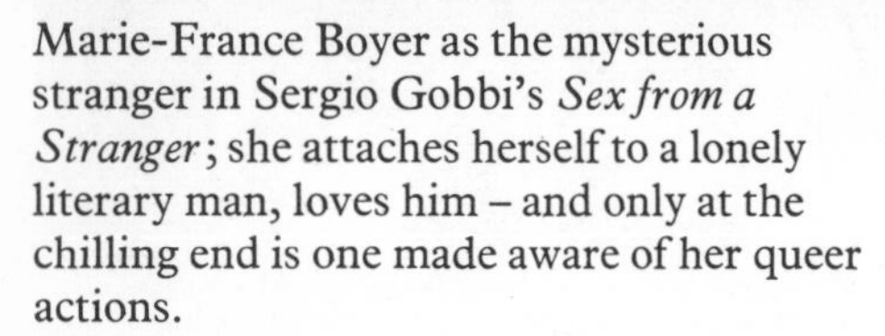

Marie-France Boyer as the mysterious stranger in Sergio Gobbi's *Sex from a Stranger*; she attaches herself to a lonely literary man, loves him – and only at the chilling end is one made aware of her queer actions.

Christiane Minazzoli wanders along the beach dreaming of the days and nights of passion in Antoine d'Ormesson's *La Nuit Infidel – Unfaithful Night*, a poetic story of a man and a woman and one night in the Camargue.

From Italy

"The most impressive of the religious films ever made" was the verdict of many who saw Pier Paolo Pasolini's *The Gospel According to St Matthew*, which in a documentary manner, and very convincingly, told the bible story of the life and death of Jesus, played by Enrique Irazoqui.

Marcello Mastroianni bares his breast to the bullets and Ursula Andress, unbared, sends a few back in return in Elio Petri's science-fiction thriller *The 10th Victim*, which was about a macabre and deathly game played as a substitute for war at some time in the future.

The Italians do portmanteau pictures better than anyone, and go on doing them, too, as was nicely illustrated by the amusing *Sex Quartet*, which consisted of four short films directed by four directors and with four highly glamorous stars, Claudia Cardinale, Raquel Welch, Monica Vitti and Capucine (the latter seen with Alberto Sordi), involved in sexy situations

Luciano Salce's *How I Learned to Love Women* was a typical, happy, chuckly Italian sex comedy, the story of a young man whose sex education is provided by a string of diverse – and all-star! – beauties such as Nadja Tiller, Michele Mercier, Anita Ekberg and Elsa Martinelli in a series of amusingly amorous episodes. But the girl who gets student Robert Hoffman in the end is the patient, prudent but determined young woman Romina Power – shown providing her part in the curriculum.

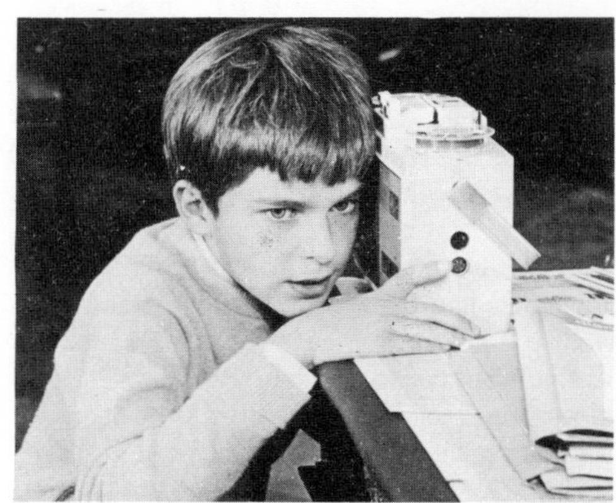

Wholly Italian, though wonderfully well dubbed into English, was Luigi Comencini's *Misunderstood*, an adaptation of a rather sentimental story by Florence Montgomery about two small motherless boys in Florence, sons of the British Consul there, and the tragedy which results from the widower's inability to communicate with the elder lad – Stefano Colorgrande. The film turned out to be surprisingly amusing, with a great insight into the child's world.

From Sweden

Ingmar Bergman's latest film *Persona* was his most fined-down picture yet: an economically related story about an actress who has a breakdown and the nurse who takes her away to a lonely sea-shore cottage for convalescence, and the way in which their personalities waver and merge and finally appear to switch! Deeply personal, difficult but fascinating and capable of almost endless meanings. Bibi Andersson played the nurse; Liv Ullman the unspeaking patient.

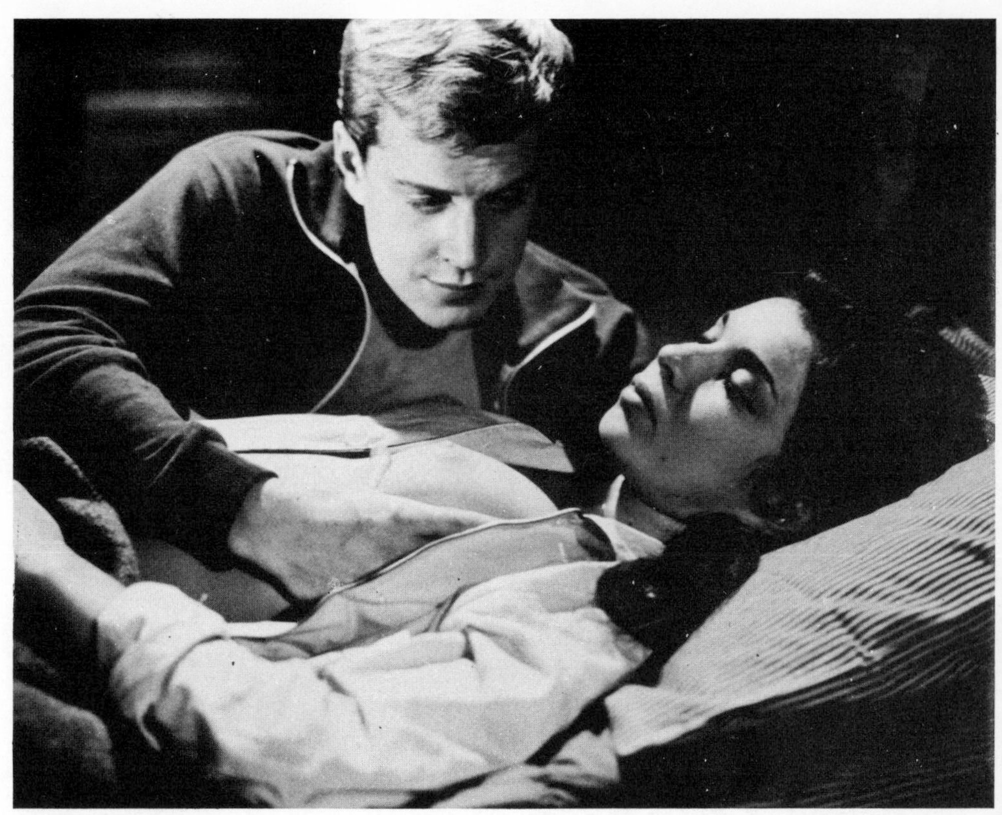

A new Swedish director, Gunnar Hoglund, was responsible for *My Love and I – The Royal Track*, an ambiguous but always interesting film about a man who after ten years again takes Sweden's "Royal Track" walk across the mountains in order to see if the girl he loved and lost will be there to meet him. But whether he does meet her, or dreams he meets her, what is reality and what imagination remains undefined. But it was a film which, once seen, could never be completely forgotten. Maude Adelson played the Jewish girl; Mathias Henrikson her lover.

The 17-year-old guest Jacob (Ole Soltoft) looks across at the girl he may one day marry (Ghita Norby): her parents, Ole Monty and Bodil Steen. In Anneliese Meineche's *Seventeen*, a story of an adolescent youth's initiation into the joys of sex during his hectic summer holidays.

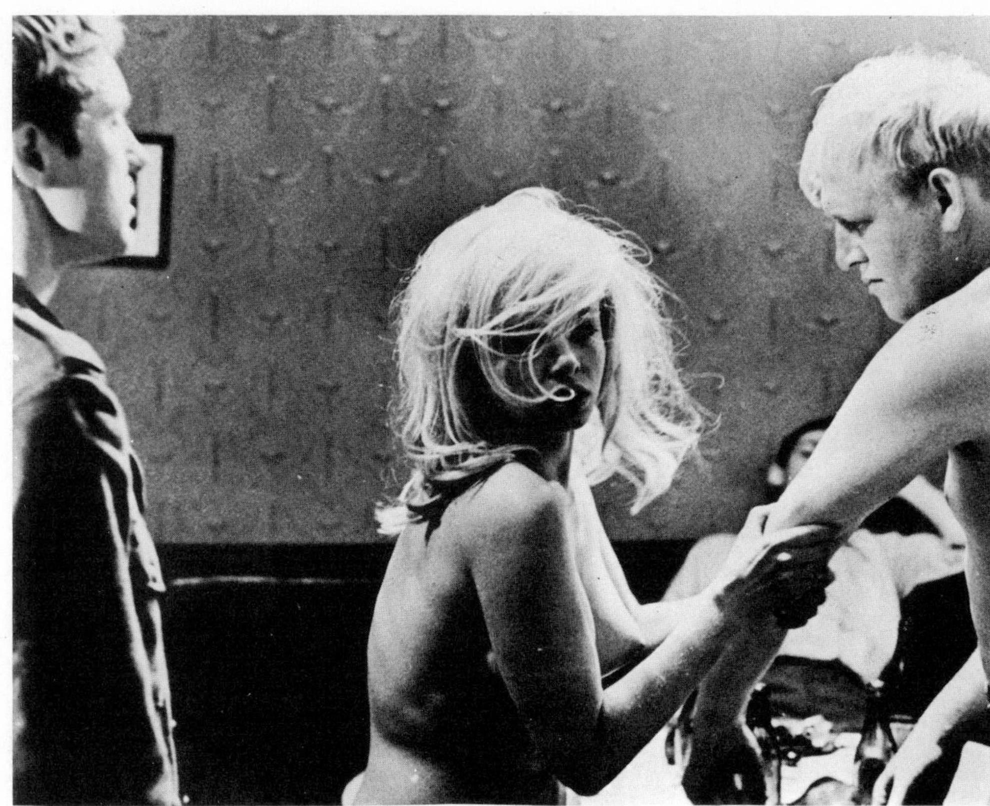

The girl, Signe Stude, the boy, Hans Ernbach (right), in the wild party scene which is so important to the story of Han Abranson's fascinatingly evil *The Serpent*.

148 Hailed by all the critics as one of the most completely lovely films of the year was Bo Widerberg's *Elvira Madigan*, the story – based on a true incident which has almost become legend – of the ecstatic but always hopeless, and inevitably tragic, summer romance in Denmark of an Army officer deserter and a tight-rope walker, the couple played beautifully by Thommy Berggren and Pia Dagermark.

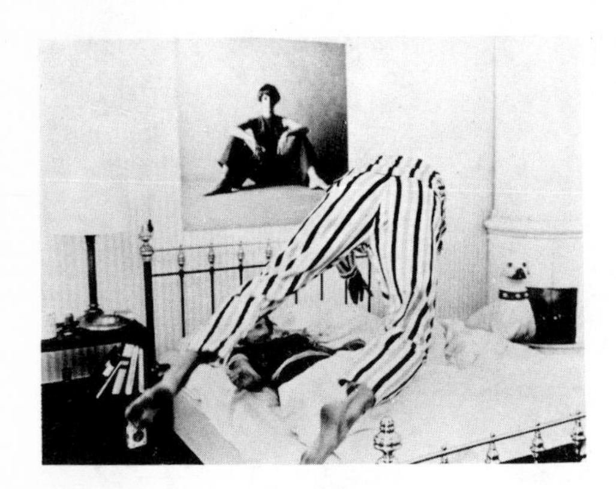

Jonas Cornell showed himself to be a young director of great promise with his *Hugs and Kisses* (he also wrote the script) which, taking the old, old farce situation of a husband–wife–lodger triangle, smoothly and effortlessly obtained a great deal of fresh and delightful fun out of it.

Nils R. Muller's *The Other Sex* was all about a group of young people who go on a camping weekend but find things work out very differently from what they had – at least sexually – expected!

From Poland

Barrier was a fascinatingly obtuse film about a girl tram-driver and a restless young medical student and their romance seen against a background of modern Poland. It was full of allusions which must have meant more to its people than to anyone outside the country.

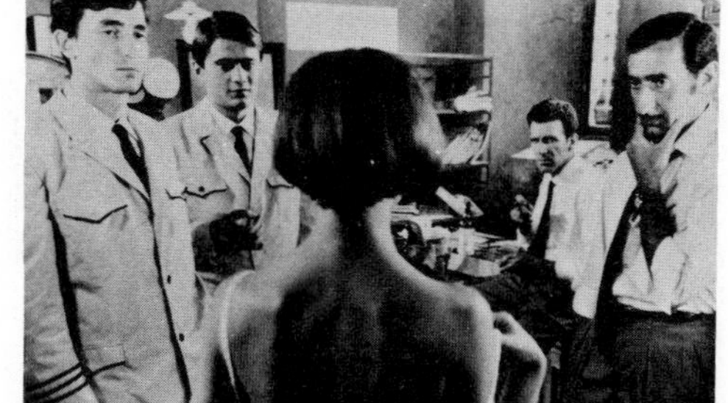

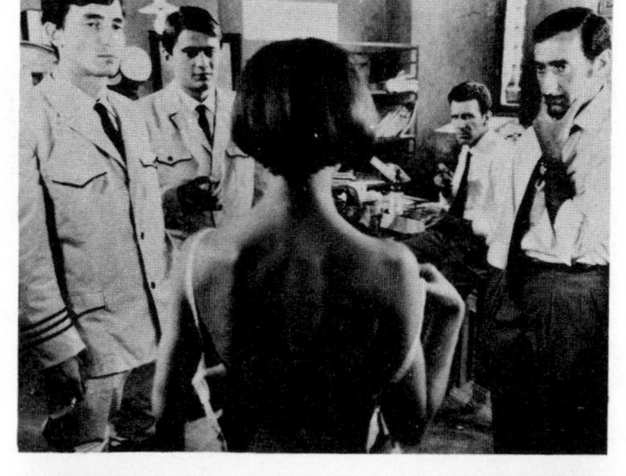

Emmanuele Riva, apprehended suspect revolutionary, prepares to strip in front of her police interrogators in the French–Italian–Yugoslav production set in Latin America, *Bitter Fruits – Soledad*.

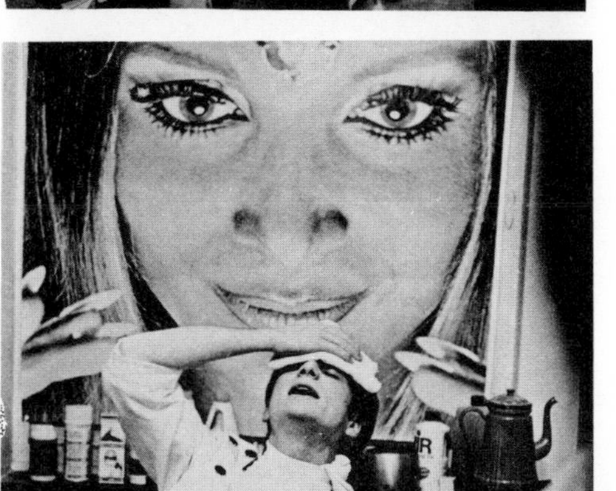

Though French-titled and with a largely French cast, and made in Belgium, *Le Depart* was a Polish film made by a promising new young director, Jerzy Skolimowski. It starred Jean-Pierre Leaud, whose crazy love for cars hides his blossoming love for women.

From Hungary

Suitable scene for the title, *Cold Days*, Andras Kovacs' compassionate film about four men accused of taking part in a 1942 massacre, in prison in 1946 awaiting their trial and thinking back to the horrible circumstances of the occasion when everyone on sight was rounded up and shot down into holes in the Danube ice.

Miklos Jansco's *My Way Home* was a strange, gripping film about the tragic-ending friendship between a young Soviet soldier and a Hungarian student prisoner (Andras Kozak and Sergey Nikonenko) set against a wonderfully drawn and atmospheric picture of the confused and turbulent period at the end of the war.

From Czechoslovakia

The three jolly men in "Orphan Rudolph's Adventures", the third and most hauntingly memorable of the three stories in Jan Nemec's highly individual *Martyrs of Love*, which beautifully captured the strange, paradoxical world of dreams.

Vaclav Neckar as the young train trainee Miloš who, apprenticed during the war at a little wayside railway station where the *Closely Observed Trains* (Nazi troop trains) go speeding past unstopping, learns within a few hectic hours the facts of love and of life and grows to manhood and a patriot's death in a touching climax.

From Greece

Dimitri Papamichael as the building operative who becomes a famous cabaret singer in a charming little musical from Greece, *Dancing the Sirtaki*. The girl is Aliki Vouyouklaki.

Made wholly on location in the small Grecian island of Skyros, *Cry in the Wind* was a story about two young rebels struggling towards love in an incredibly primitive, closed community.

From Holland

From Yugoslavia

The Human Dutch was another of Bert Haanstra's wonderful documentaries, a warm and sympathetic look in depth at his own country and its people: and winner of a whole string of international prizes, quite deservedly so.

Winner of a number of prizes, Alexander Patrovic's *Happy Gipsies* had one of the misleading titles of the year, for a less happy lot than these unfortunate people, living in mud and poverty, would be hard to imagine. They buy and sell goose feathers, live a primitive life in which a duel to the death over a girl doesn't appear all that unusual – it was all a fascinating, and in one sense colourful insight into how the other half lives!

From Israel

One of the rare examples of a film from that country, a warm, noisy comedy built around the talents of ace comedian Topol, as *Sallah,* the Oriental Jew who arrives in Israel with his large family and is forced to come to terms with the new life there.

From Japan

No, this isn't a railway signal cabin – it's the armoury of Lord Matsudaira's Armoury and the "levers" are the long Samurai swords. A scene from Masaki Kobayashi's *Rebellion*, a dramatic story of a family driven to revolt by the inhumanity of their lord in the federal Japan of some 240 years ago.

The boy Mathieu Carriere begins to learn about physical love from Barbara Steele in the prize-winning German film *Young Torless*, which was presented by Amanda Films. It was about the boy's refusal to interfere – until too late – with the systematic degradation and torture over a period of one of the pupils by two others.

Helga Ander and Jurhen Jurge enjoy a little amorous romping in Robert Fritz's basically tragic *Madchen, Madchen – Girls, Girls,* in which the drama springs from the fact that a girl falls in love with the son of the man whose mistress she has become.

156 **From India**

Mahanagar – Big City was another small screen masterpiece from Satyajit Ray, who produced, directed, wrote and even composed the background music for this facinating picture of Contemporary Calcutta, where the emancipation of women leads to disquiet among the younger generation of men and open hostility among the older. Beautiful Madhabi Mukherjee played the wife who goes out to work and for a time becomes the main provider for the home, to the disquiet of her husband, played by Anil Chatterjee.

THE FILM ON TV

Alan Eyles

Such is the wealth of films offered on British television that it's hard to recall the time when a real film fan turned up his nose at the box and clung to his notion of seeing films "properly" in the atmosphere of a cinema. He had a point, of course. It is disheartening to see the rich details of the image lost on that small screen, a film perhaps stripped also of colour and cinemascope proportions, clumsily abridged, and interrupted by commercials.

For most people the local cinemagoing choice breaks down into the ABC or Rank release programme of the week; at home, TV offers a choice of about ten films a week (more at holidays). Some admittedly clash; some have been seen on TV before (or perhaps in the cinema originally); only the occasional foreign film is **new**. But the range is still greater than that offered by the cinema outside of the largest cities.

It's ironic that the country as a whole pays more attention to old films on TV than it does to new ones. The audience for a film put out nationally by the BBC at a peak viewing time will usually total between 7 and 15 million – which is frequently double the entire *weekly* cinema attendance (close to 6 million on average). Of course, the home viewers are far less appreciative and less discriminating than those who make the effort to go out and pay to see a film and TV is regrettably too often viewed as a complete alternative to the ordinary cinema attraction. But certain films not given their due by the cash customers, or only sketchily released to cinemas, may eventually be appreciated by a mass audience on TV where prejudice against a theme or lack of stars is not so important when the habit of tuning in is so strong and straightforward.

Cinema owners have never been happy about the free competition of TV. For many years they successfully kept most post-war films out of its reach. Even now they have been able to keep TV waiting a minimum of five years (from the date of cinema release, foreign-language films being excepted). By contrast, in the United States it is possible to see features – particularly the box-office failures – at home in less than two years.

The immediate limit now on the number of American films seen on ITV is the 15 per cent maximum of foreign material permitted by ITA regulations (this covers new American TV series too), while the same approximate limit is adhered to on a voluntary basis by the BBC. That this frequently imposes a strain on the independent companies' programmers is well known; and old British features often have to be hurriedly substituted for American ones to keep to the quota. Still, it is obviously right that TV should largely concentrate on originating its own material; and we shall have to wait for an extension of viewing hours to expect an increased number of films on TV.

Due to this limited intake, TV has been a buyer's market. The companies still wait to be offered batches of films, knowing that to display any interest in particular titles merely ups the price. The procedure is to select pictures from a list of about twice the number agreed on, and the price currently averages out at £5,000 or more a film (compared with half that figure for much older films a few years back). Rights usually run for five years; some films are restricted to two or three showings, others have no limitations imposed. As the backlog of popular ones dries up, the present meagre price is bound to rise sharply. The more recent films are the most prized and independent companies have the edge here, being prepared to go a little higher in price. (The various stations group together to buy prints or buy national rights and circulate their prints to other regions.)

ITV generally has scant regard for the artistic qualities of the films it shows and they are often ruthlessly cut to fit the rigid length of programme slots. British producers and directors have protested about this mutilation of their work, but to no lasting effect; and famous scenes have been eliminated from such well known American films as *Key Largo*, *The Bad and the Beautiful*, and *The Wrong Man* without even the courtesy of a preliminary announcement (although this of course would draw viewers' attention to ITV's contemptuous assessment of how much they will tolerate).

The different companies vary in the degree to which they give offence. It's a little sad from this point of view that TWW, which was mild in its mistreatment of features, should have been the one TV company to disappear in the recent shake-up. But Granada TV is alone in warranting positive praise from film enthusiasts: it has been able to attract good audiences with a number of excellent older Warner Bros. and Universal pictures specially selected and purchased for the area by its knowledgeable film chief, Leslie Halliwell. Happily, the new company London Weekend Television seems likely to follow similar lines in its programming. However, for a really enlightened policy one has to turn to the BBC where feature films are treated with respect and invariably shown in full, despite the continual planning headaches of fitting in pictures of varying lengths. (Even with commercials and rigid timings, it is not impossible for a TV company to do the same, as Telefis Eireann demonstrates in Ireland; not surprisingly, its standards of film selection are also high.) The BBC's film selectors will even pursue more complete prints than the ones immediately available, as has happened in the case of *All Quiet on the Western Front*, *Anatomy of a Murder*, and *Lola Montes*. While considerations of audience appeal mean that the BBC frequently put on films as bad as those seen on ITV (and the dregs of a package deal have to be aired sometime!), it is evident that a concern for the films themselves also exists. An additional service of the BBC (though it may well occur as an economy measure) is that most films are seen at least twice, thereby helping to overcome the frequent irritation of missing a TV screening. (ITV stations do repeat some films, but not on a regular basis.)

The BBC also does more planning with its films, grouping them under themes. The Western, The Thriller and British Comedy have been some of the highly successful series mounted on particular evenings. More ambitious has been the line of musicals, spotlighting a genre that ITV noticeably avoids (so that even as famous a musical as *On The Town* has had difficulty being seen in ITV areas; and musical comedies are apt to lose some of their musical content when cut for length).

Many of the BBC musicals have been quite old – dating from the late thirties and early forties – and they can be taken with the lengthy "Vintage Years of Hollywood" series as a really noteworthy achievement of the BBC's second channel. What is interesting is that the age and period appeal of these films has been exploited as an asset and not hushed up. But it is regrettable that comparatively little space has been found for early sound films (and the silent cinema has never been touched on). The introduction of colour has hastened BBC 2's progress towards larger audiences led to much "safer" programming. American films are associated with large viewing figures, and a great deal of artistically rich material with low audience potential is likely to remain untouched. A new film from the thirties has become something of a rarity (in which connection it is worthy observing that ITV will now and then come up with a surprise "oldie" and that even BBC 1's key Sunday evening time is occasionally given over to a classic of the middle or late thirties).

Curiously, the pre-war British cinema is very little seen on any channel. Even the Hitchcock films and Will Hay comedies of the thirties haven't been taken up in any detail. However, the foreign film has been accorded a fine welcome by the BBC whose series "International Film Theatre" and now "World Cinema" have over the last few years brought films of art-house standard into the remotest homes. These attract an average of 4 per cent of those who could tune in, but this is still an audience to be numbered in a great many thousands and some of the choices do much better than average.

Interestingly, it is not the work of well known names that does best. Both Bergman and Godard have come off very badly (though it's difficult to imagine that very many viewers had seen *Sawdust and Tinsel* or *A Bout de Souffle* before, and those might have been expected to tune in for a second look). Still there must be considerable satisfaction for David Francis, who selects the series, in the excellent ratings of many lesser known productions (like *The Bandits of Orgosolo*) and of numerous films that are being given a British premiere (excepting, in some cases, for an earlier festival or National Film Theatre showing). Out of 92 films shown in a little over three years, 25 were making their public début. Some of them have been major omissions on the part of the cinema distributors; most have lacked the angles that would have guaranteed success in the present state of the foreign film market (where many of the more enterprising films that do appear have been bought with an eye for eventual sale to television for "World Cinema").

Among the great many, one might mention such pictures as the stark Brazilian feature *Barren Lives*; the outstanding Italian productions *La Sfida* and *Time Stood Still*; the missing films of Andrzej Munk (including *Man on the Tracks*) as part of a complete tribute; the Czech musical *The Hop Pickers*; and among more recent acquisitions Karel Zeman's *The Stolen Airship* (a Jules Verne fantasy) and the prize-winning Bulgarian feature *Sidetrack*.

Unfortunately few of these newcomers have been given the critical attention they deserve. It has not been BBC policy to press show them and TV critics have not felt called on to give them reviews. But the "World Cinema" series has created the breakthrough for subtitled films that British cinema owners never attempted.

As far as other films on BBC are concerned, it is difficult to generalise about what goes down best with audiences. But broad British comedies (like the Ronald Shiner *Up to his Neck*) and films with pronounced women's

The landless peasant of the stark Brazilian drama *Barren Lives* (1963) filmed by Nelson Periera Dos Santos and set in the interior of Brazil. Shown first on BBC 2's "World Cinema" late 1967.

Rosanna Schiaffino in Francesco Rossi's 1958 drama *La Sfida*, shown under the title *Challenge* in the "World Cinema" series – a striking early work by the director of *Salvatori Giulano* and *Hands Over the City*.

A recent "World Cinema" presentation has been *The Stolen Airship*, an engaging fantasy derived from the work of Jules Verne by the distinguished Czech director Karel Zerman, whose *The Jester's Tale* has been premiered in this series.

appeal (like *Random Harvest*) are apt to show up particularly well in the ratings. All kinds of factors have to be considered: the weather, the competition on other channels, and changes of fashion (the renewed interest in *The Desert Song* after its West End stage presentation boosted the appeal of a very poor film version).

Whatever the film fan's attitude to TV, he owes it a debt of gratitude on two counts. Firstly, its insatiable appetite for films to screen in the U.S. has meant that hundreds of negatives have been rescued from decay in the vaults; even the earliest sound films and most humble "B" features have been given a new lease of life. Many old British productions have been more in demand for American TV than in their country of origin. At a recent count well over 13,000 films had been put on the market and at least 11,325 were still available. These lists provide the source of supply from which British companies gain their American features; it also provides the basis on which film fans and scholars will in future years be able to investigate the past. Even if British TV is unlikely to explore the remoter reaches of this vast treasure house, it has already made life much easier for the planners of National Film Theatre seasons and given audiences there the chance to see much that might have remained inaccessible.

Secondly, TV has been entirely responsible for the great boom in film production, which for many years seemed to be slowly dying. The vast new revenues from TV screenings (now so quickly forthcoming that deals can be made for films before they've even been shot) makes film production a much safer proposition. TV itself has been rushing into production to make features, initially for cinema release, then for its own use. The two industries have dropped their ancient attitude of implacable hostility and entered into a merger that promises well – for the greater the financial security of the medium, the more chances for it to be used with imagination and taste.

TO DUB OR NOT TO DUB

W. A. De Lane Lea

Mr De Lane Lea at work in the studio.

The mere mention of the word "dubbing" is anathema, not merely to the critics, but to a host of other people as well. Jean Renoir, one of France's most illustrious directors, who has worked in many countries outside France, including America, said of dubbing: "I hate it. I even believe that in a period of high civilisation like the twelfth century, if people had done dubbing in films they would have been burned in the public square for pretending that man may have one body and two souls."

Be that as it may, until such time as the world decides on one universal language, the dubbing of motion pictures must be regarded as necessary. What is in dispute is whether it is necessary for dubbing to be evil.

Many people, of course, seldom see a picture which is not dubbed. Filmgoers in a whole range of countries see virtually all American and British films – often the bulk of the product shown – in dubbed versions. They have never heard the original voices of Cary Grant or Audrey Hepburn, though they have seen many of their films.

Obviously, producers are not going to limit themselves to having the films they make shown only in their countries of origin or in those in which the same language is spoken. It seems to me, therefore, that the question of whether films should be dubbed is an abstract one. What really matters is *how well* the films are dubbed.

What is a good dubbing job? Is it simply lip movements that fit? No. Good dubbing is this: it is creating an illusion whereby one is led to believe that if the actor – whether he be Russian, French or Chinese – had been asked to speak his lines in any other language, he would have spoken them in the way the audience expects to hear them.

Good dubbing is not just a technical process, but also an artistic one. Each film must be looked at individually. For example: an Italian film showing typical Italian life should not be dubbed with American voices. On the other hand, a Western shot in Italy by Italians and/or Spanish actors can and should be dubbed into the kind of American accent that you would expect to hear in Texas or Arizona.

Classics – Stendhal, Victor Hugo, Shakespeare – can be dubbed with strict national accents. If the Russians make *Othello* you can dub it using English Shakespearean voices.

If, on the other hand, the Russians make a film containing elements of contemporary history, as in *The Ballad of a Soldier*, you should try, in the English version, to give every voice, every character a Russian flavour, not only in the dialogue but in the accents that are used.

Bad dubbing has come about because too many people think that if the lip movements fit, then that is all that is required. This, in actual fact, is the least important part of it. Every film should be examined carefully. The dialogue should be carefully written to preserve the original thought, meaning and flavour and each part, including the very small ones, should be carefully selected.

At De Lane Lea, for example, we do not depend on the technical process, but on casting correctly and then, by our technique, eliminating the nerve-wracking need for the actors to watch for the lip movements of the characters on the screen, thus giving them time to concentrate on their acting performances. When we provided an English version of *Casque d'Or* (*Golden Marie*)

some years ago, we brought over Serge Reggiani, Claude Dauphin and Simone Signoret to speak their own original roles. This was a difficult experience for them but we were able to get them to speak the lines in a French-accented manner which was wholly acceptable. Often we will test some fifty actors for one part, since the criterion is not merely whether the performer can speak the lines well but whether his or her voice seems to be the correct one to come from the face on the screen. For example, we tested twenty-five actors to speak Jean Gabin's lines in *Pig Across Paris* and eventually chose Rupert Davies, not because of his *Maigret* performances but because he sounded just like Gabin.
Similarly, in Jacques Tati's *Playtime*, which we have recently rendered into English, Tati came to London personally and selected every one of the players for the forty-odd speaking roles.
The internationalisation of the film industry has increased the importance of dubbing, because more and more pictures are being made with one or two British or American stars in a cast mainly Italian, or Spanish or German. Perhaps a particular example of this type of film is *Misunderstood*, starring Anthony Quayle, for which we made an English version which had the honour of a Royal Premiere, with Prince Philip in attendance. Not a single National newspaper critic commented adversely on the dubbing. Most of them paid us the compliment of not mentioning it, thereby showing that they had accepted the film as a whole without a jarring note. The others paid us the compliment of praising our work.
Oddly enough, those responsible for dubbing pictures, must be most satisfied when their work passes unnoticed, for the whole aim of good dubbing is to ensure that the audience is not even aware that the picture is dubbed. If we consistently achieve this result we shall remain contentedly back-room boys responsible for one of the important facets of the international motion picture world.

AN ACTOR SPEAKS

by Robert Ryan

I suppose I'm something of an anachronism in these days of "packaging", "cross-collateralising" and setting up big deals in a haze of cigar smoke. I'm not an actor–writer, or an actor–writer–director, or even an actor–writer–director–producer.

I'm just an *actor* . . . and I must tell you that this apparently simple and straight-forward role in life suits me very well.

It has always seemed to me that a man does best what he knows best and over a period now of darn near thirty years I have been trying to fit myself for the profession which I have chosen. Acting is a serious and responsible business and I have no desire to make myself into a walkin', talkin' one-man corporation in which the acting side plays a more and more minor role.

To be a good actor, I believe one must be as far as is possible a whole person. The actor who cuts himself off from life as it is lived by his fellow men must become more and more artificial in his performances. Because surely it is of the essence of this way of living that the performer must be able to create genuine emotions and to do this he must not only observe those around him but

also share their feelings and ambitions.
I am a political animal. I believe that people who live in a society have their rights and obligations to that society and the duty to play their part in its life and in shaping its direction. So in the United States 1968 election I have found it important that I should lend what support I can to the candidate of my choice.
Years ago, when my children were young and we were living in the San Fernando Valley in California, my wife and I came to the conclusion that the schools in the area could not provide the approach to education which we felt was important. Accordingly, in association with some like-minded parents in the area, we founded our own school – Oakwood – to try and give our children the principles in life which we believed to be important. That school, I am proud to say, is still operating successfully.
I make these points merely to emphasise that, right or wrong, I have always tried to play my part in the community and I am convinced that I am the better actor for it.
These days, of course, I am often faced with the dilemma that worries many of my fellow actors, too: the difficulty of finding the acting parts which provide a stimulating and creative challenge. I turn down role after role, but a man must eat and I am not always satisfied with the motion pictures in which I find myself.
Unfortunately, too, in America we do not have the acting opportunities you in Great Britain have with your comparative wealth of provincial theatres, each seeking to present a range of work including classical and experimental productions. It was for this reason that in 1967 I jumped at an opportunity which presented itself to come for three months to Nottingham's Playhouse and to appear in two plays under John Neville's banner. This was a wholly satisfying experience and one which much more than compensated me for the thousands of dollars it cost me. Nottingham's star pay offer of £50 a week did not, I am afraid, really meet my expenses!
Not that I would want you to think that I have not found many of my film roles rewarding. Twenty years or so ago I had an exciting period in my life when I played a vicious racist in *Crossfire* and followed this up with a role as an ageing prizefighter in *The Set-Up*. Over the years since then a good number of challenging parts have come my way, one of them being in *Billy Budd*, which was the film which first brought me into touch with John Neville.
More recently still, a picture like *The Professionals* was a happy acting experience and I look forward to more parts which I can really get my teeth into. Because, you see, I don't think that an actor who really has acting in his blood can ever get blasé about his work: there is always a fresh challenge, some new facet of life to explore.
I am grateful for the opportunities I have had but even happier in the thought that life has new experiences to offer. The day that outlook fades I shall give up!

THE CINEMA LOOKS AT GOD

John Mountjoy

God gives a boost to the box-office! And looking at the wide and extensive panorama of the cinema from its late nineteenth-century birth right to today I can reverently write: As it was in the beginning, is now, and ever shall be. And amen because it is potentially one of his best media.

It is ironic and a little sad that so many of us meet him and religion in the cinema rather than his immediate (but not exclusive) habitat – the church, where his decline and fall – Roman Catholic churches are factual exceptions to this overall opinion – make it all the more important that the camera at least glimpses him as he truly is in his creation, which is you and me.

Some of the first film-makers were priests working with men like Lumière, Gaumont, Pathe; producing simple versions of religious subjects made famous in painting. Walking on the Waters, The Passion, and so on. These were at the beginning.

But whether people go to church or not doesn't alter the proven fact that in varying degrees all of us are interested in right and wrong and the source of their standards. The variations of conventional morality provide plots for the pictures which really means – and shows how untrue thinking can be if carried to its logical conclusion – that every picture is a religious picture. Which, if you care to consider, may not be basically incorrect after all.

In general, religious dramas are clear cut and we aren't likely to find that we are in God's movie country without fair warning. Professional religionists have had good cause to be concerned because no matter what brave phrases might end the film the in-between bits have from time to time run haywire with God's image. But as I advised one protesting parson: Hold it, reverend. You'd never get that audience in your church if you gave them a slap-up London Hilton dinner for free in return. God looked rosier on reflection.

The great – in expenditure and spectacle rather than spirituality – religious films have been *The Ten Commandments, The Sign of the Cross, King of Kings* – and at this point I am writing of the Cinema's comparatively early days. Producers did succumb to arbitrary modifications of Biblical stories and from time to time commerce got the better of the cross.

St Peter wasn't spared in *The Robe,* of itself an exciting story but an unhappily twisted characterisation of the Apostle to fit the fable around which the film story was told. Popular pictures like *The Song of Bernadette, Boy's Town* and *Bells of St Mary's* were successful tries at selling, one might say *soft* selling, religion through romance in the broadest sense. The sensitive Christian might well have deplored their concentration upon externals and heartiness, but then again, Salvation Army singing could grate the Grail.

A legitimate criticism of American treatment could be that it is self-conscious salesmanship, a sort of spelling God in simple terms, a standard one definition of trinity, eternity and infinity with a Roman Catholic nun to say it. But then again, how does a mass-medium tell such a story – in depth?

Perhaps Carl Foreman will get off his war-horse long enough to cope with the enormous demand such a God-story would make upon his brilliant versatility. It is easier demanded than written.

The routine religious exercise seems happier

in the hands of continentals. Perhaps it is because the greatness of God is simplified. Perhaps the audience is put at its ease. No one straightens his tie. No one brushes his hair.

The Gospel According to St Matthew is such a rhythmic, relaxing report that one becomes unaware of its duration. Sub-titles don't affect its flow. It is an Italian film directed by Pier Paolo Pasoline.

Considerable insight, denied for some reason to American producers, by Robert Bresson resulted in *Diary of a Country Priest,* the Bernanos record of his spiritual growth, and likewise Carl Dreyer's *Passion of Joan of Arc* and Delannoy's *Man's Need for God* – all classics in thinking and interpretation on cinema film.

Continental producers put their audiences at ease because they themselves are at ease. Whatever respect they might have for God and religion is subjective not objective. They feel no obligation to touch their hat as they look at something sacred. British and Americans pretend most of the time. And there is something to be said for this, of course. The country is a place of many cinemas – like the mansions in heaven.

On the Waterfront is at one. Aldo Fabrizi's *Rome, Open City* is at another. Gary Cooper as John Doe in *Meet John Doe* rather puzzled the public because it didn't quite conform and at the end lost confidence in its own capability to explain credibly the spiritual and mental catastrophe of this self-discredited evangelist. But it is memorable despite and because of this failure.

Just as everyone can organise the B.B.C. better than the B.B.C., so, too, can critics produce pictures far better than the Carol Reeds, David Leans and Fred Zinnemanns. Perhaps the basic problem is that there is only Zinnemann and not Zinnemanns.

But passing from that piece of pedantry there have been some brave – financial – attempts to grapple with God one way or another in the nearly immediate years.

The outstanding one is Robert Bolt's version of his own play *A Man for All Seasons,* with Paul Schofield as Sir Thomas More; Wendy Hiller, his wife; Leo McKern, Cromwell; Robert Shaw, Henry VIII; Orson Welles, Cardinal Wolsey.

Producers cram their Biblical and religious stories with star names and it is interesting to note the number of "names" attracted by the gold and silver of the cinema screen.

Take the Dino de Laurentis production of *The Bible* which went to the beginning of man – Richard Harris, Stephen Boyd, Ava Gardner, Peter O'Toole, John Huston.

The shrewd, discriminating Stanley Baker allied his talents to Stewart Granger, Anouk Aimee, Pier Angeli for *Sodom and Gomorrah.* Howard Keel's fine singing voice seems gone for ever in screen time and we saw him as *The Big Fisherman,* best forgotten but for the pictorial sequences.

Lavish spectacularism with magnificent costumes were primary credits of *The Ten Commandments,* another Cecil B. de Mille shop-window for God. His sales staff included Charlton Heston as Moses, Anne Baxter, Yvonne de Carlo, Nina Fock, Cedric Hardwicke and H. B. Warner.

A puzzling choice was Jeffrey Hunter as *King of Kings* which, at least, suggested some unusual twists to the Christ story. Harry Guardino was Barrabas – a Jewish resistance leader. Rip Torn played Judas, someone who played his card badly. Siobhan McKenna's beautiful talents were wasted as Mary.

The Story of David, with Jeff Chandler and lesser star-lights like Basil Sydney, Barbara Shelly, Zena Marshall and the exceptionally clever Donald Pleasence, was a sort of Biblical Western notable in that it almost forgot sex and sadism.

Tom Tryon as *The Cardinal,* a piece of ecclesiastical reporting, colourful and interesting became an artisan for the *Story of Ruth,* a hard hitting, devotional, romantic tale with Elana Eden and Viveca Lindfors.

Yul Brynner teamed with Gina Lollobrigida for *Solomon and Sheba,* which was grand, exciting and painstaking.

The Nun's Story, The Singer Not the Song and *The Sound of Music* – if that isn't stretching it too much, slot into religious pictures. It is easy on paper to call for artistic bravery yet now, more than ever, is religious bravery a viable proposition?

Producers may well be fearful that there would be more agony than ecstasy – with apologies to the Heston–Harrison Irving Stone story – in this enterprise, but audiences overpowered by spectacle, sensualised to the nth degree by sex cinema, and blinded by the cleverness of the arty could respond to the refreshment of clear thinking and clear teaching.

The Cinema cannot afford to shirk the supernatural. God's message through his many teachers is a challenge to unbelief. And that challenge can come very alive through this tremendous and dynamic art form used thoughtfully, intelligently and knowledgeably.

Audiences have reached upper school by now.

Jeffrey Hunter as Jesus in
King of Kings.

Percy Smith in his garden.

Opposite page
"Secrets of Nature" series,
Life of a Plant

TRIBUTE TO MR SMITH

Oswell Blakeston

British film-making in the late twenties and early thirties was often devil-may-care farce. A famous director of the time called a great crowd of extras and took a long-shot of a herald reading a proclamation on a balcony. When it was pointed out to the director that one hardly noticed the herald in all the seething activity, he recalled the crowd and – took a close-up of the herald. Then a bright producer engaged a large and highly-paid jazz orchestra to star in – a silent movie.

But while the studios were a shambles, some of the best films ever made in England were taken in a suburban villa by Percy Smith with lights run off 2-volt accumulators!

But let us go back to the beginning. When he was a child, Percy Smith would wait for his mother to kiss him goodnight, and then steal from the house to study the habits of spiders in the marshes. Morning after morning he found himself literally frozen to the ground.

Then, after a very sketchy spell of schooling, his family forced him to take a job in a government office. Tired of copying out a certain form, he smeared paste round a cocoa tin, snatched a roll of a particular kind of thin paper and reproduced hundreds of forms in a flash by dropping the roll down a lift shaft. So somehow, for fifteen years and for twenty-five shillings a week, Percy, out of loyalty to his parents, survived the routine. Then he rebelled and captured a bluebottle and – tied it up.

From that moment, the most riveting films, in the history of British cinema were born. Percy fed his bluebottle with drops of milk on the tip of a needle, and he took a photograph of the bluebottle's protruding

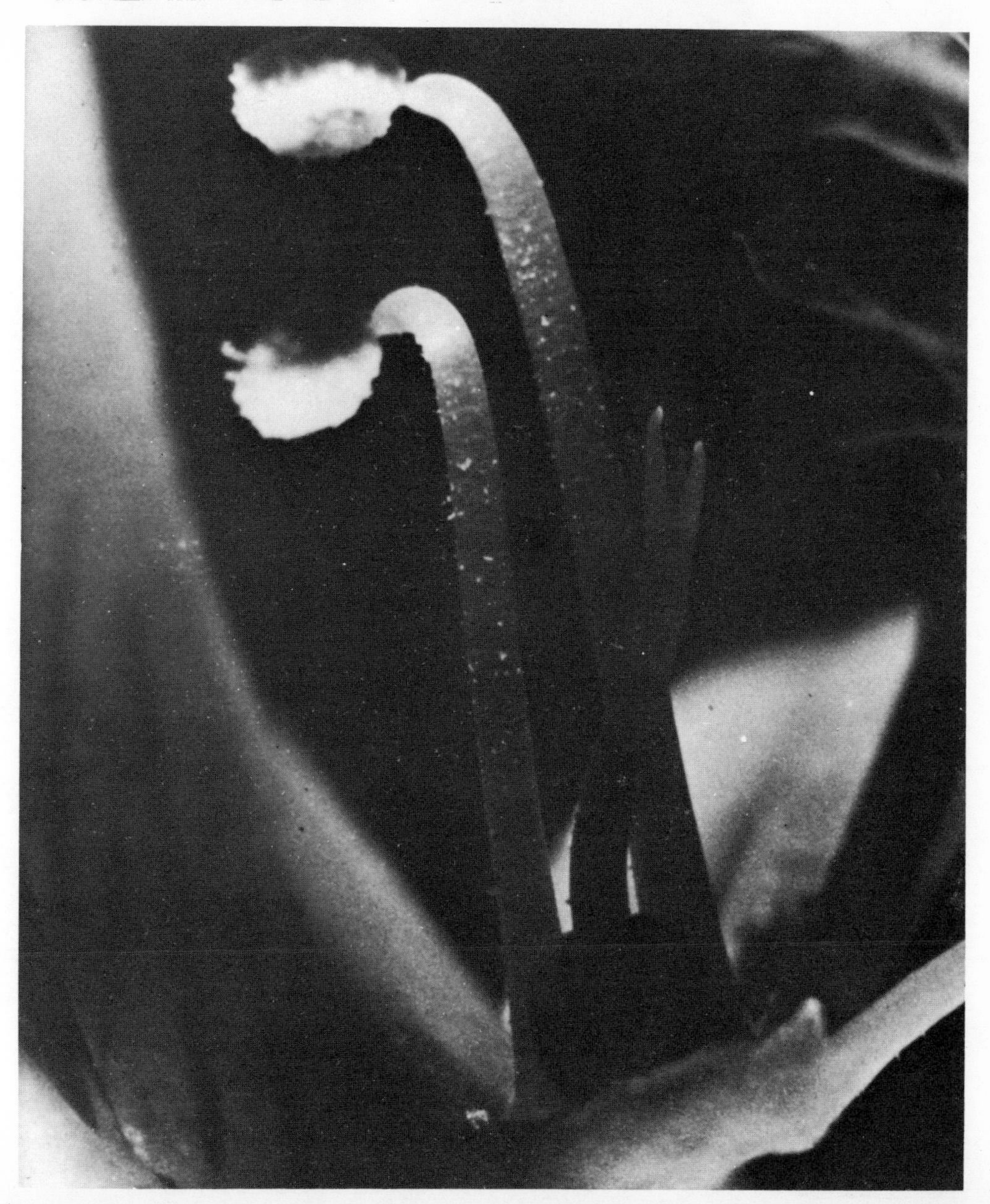

tongue. A friend showed this photograph to a gentleman in Wardour Street who was so delighted with its novelty appeal that he gave Percy a ciné camera, some stock and told him to "do his best".

Percy went into the woods. But it was an old-fashioned camera with a tripod with rigid legs, and Percy had to dig holes in the ground for the legs to get a close-up of a snake on the ground. Sometimes he would ring up the gentleman in Wardour Street to announce that he had got a good shot after the forty-second attempt.

A great career had been launched, although Percy Smith was still a long way from his important *Secrets of Nature* series which showed rival cheese moulds fighting or tiny bean shoots performing sinuous ballets in their struggle to reach the light.

Then World War I intervened, and Percy was drafted as an official ciné operator. On one occasion an early aeroplane charged right into the lens of his camera; and the red hats wanted to know why his photographic document did not show what happened *afterwards*!

The war over, Percy began to build his own studio in a small house at Southgate. He was going to concentrate on taking single frames of film at longish intervals so that when the film was run continuously all movement would be speeded up. He adapted any old camera which could be acquired cheaply, and one was a topical-news camera which had been used in the Russo-Japanese War and was pock-marked with bullet-holes, and another was based on a toy. Gramophone needles were adjusted to touch metal on slowly rotating discs; and when they touched, an electric contact was made, a meccano arm dusted the lens of the camera, a light lit, and the Heath Robinson camera exposed a single frame of film.

There was nothing that these robot cameras could not do – lift a protecting jar off a fragile fungus for the "take", or spin a bit of celluloid to keep cool some delicate organism while the light burnt for the exposure. Percy lived in this home-made shoestring robot world, and he had to be awake day and night!

He might have to check, for instance, that a plant had not grown out of the picture at three o'clock in the morning. So his house and his garden were dotted with alarms ready to summon him or his asistant at any hour to supervise an intermittent camera.

The dedicated Percy never really made much money from his twenty-four-hours-a-day labours of love. Even when his films were making international headlines, Percy remained an "innocent" and the Wardour Street man realised that this born naturalist was not really interested in money and they never bothered him with large cheques. "Oh", he said to me once, "if I had a lot of money, it would do me no good. I'd go too often to the movies, and I'd neglect my work." The "work" of making films as spectacular as epics of life on another planet, of making films which made scientific discoveries.

When Percy was shooting *The Frog*, he wrote to the greatest authority on the subject in England to ask why tadpoles pause before leaving the jelly-like substance which holds them as black specks. Back came the answer: "*Tadpoles do not pause.*" With a faint smile, Mr Smith invited the expert to witness his film sequence of tadpoles pausing.

People simply could not believe that Percy was not a learned scholar ensconced in a sort of Frankenstein laboratory. When a foreign diplomatic deputation arrived in England, the diplomats expressed the desire to meet the maker of such magic films as *Plants of The Underworld* and *Mighty Atoms*. In a panic, high executives shifted Percy from his villa to the Welwyn Studios and surrounded him with "property" apparatus. It was felt that the deputation would never have confidence in the meccano-made cameras and that England, sir, would lose prestige. The diplomats reverently inspected all the bogus scene and almost wept with joy.

But right up to the end, Percy went on making films at Southgate with the same old cameras; and he never lost any of his inspired enthusiasm. When a film magnate consulted him about the best way to rid a loft of a certain pest, Percy replied coldly: "If I think anything is a pest, I make a film about it – and then it is beautiful."

He died in 1945; but many of his films could be reissued. We'd find them more breathtaking than the hordes of extras who charge across the screen in million-dollar Technicolor cavalcades – and more instructive!

MOVIE LANGUAGE

Ralph Stephenson

In his monumental work on *The American Language*, W. H. Mencken makes many references to movie idioms and to the influence of movies on the language.

As well he might – for it is America among English-speaking countries, which has most developed and practised the art of the film. On the film-making side, the United States, between 1920 and 1960 produced six or seven times more films than Britain, her nearest English-speaking rival. This is the picture on the film-making side and, so far as film-*going* is concerned, there is not (despite the British climate) all that difference between the two countries. Nowadays as a minority art, on esoteric as well as popular levels, underground as well as on the surface, film-makers and film-fans are still more numerous in New York than in London. In this country film language and technical terms are current only among a minority, and explained sparingly in the glossaries of books about film technique. The Oxford and Chambers dictionaries show lukewarm interest in *inkies, fishing poles, mixes, dissolves, tear-buckets, breakaways,* or even *horse-operas* and *flesh-peddlers.* Nevertheless, here in England, interest in cinema is more widespread in recent years than ever before, and there are hundreds of intelligent filmgoers who would be delighted to clarify the vague ideas they have about the meaning of *Cinerama, widescreen, Three-D, colour by Technicolor,* and would conceivably be interested also, in knowing more about *lens-hogs, non-actors, double-exposure, first-treatment* and *sneak-preview.*

The first film terms were borrowed from the cinema's parents: the theatre and photography – adding in course of time many terms peculiar to movie techniques and ways of working. The word *movie* itself appeared in 1913 in an *O.E.D.* supplement; and although it was so unpopular with film magnates that the Essanay Company offered a prize of twenty-five dollars for an alternative, they were unable to change the popular usage – the winning word, *photoplay*, got no further than the title of a movie magazine. Early cinemas were called *parlours,* then *theatres,* and the more splendiferous became *cathedrals, mosques, synagogues,* and even *filling-stations. Flea-pit* is an English variant, and in no way synonymous with the American *bug-house,* an adjective meaning "barmy".

From the theatre, for example, came terms connected with lighting: *spots, ash-cans, inkies, cracker-boxes, friers* and *dish-pans* for kinds of lights; the *gaffer* or *juicer* with his *carbon-monkeys* and *grunts* (assistants) – for the staff. Terms for actors were common to stage and screen: *zombie* for a coloured performer, *cobra* for a sexy actress, *finger-wringer* for a tragedienne, *walrus* for an actor with a moustache. A *tear-bucket* (an elderly actress playing mother parts) could *emote* in front of a live audience as well as before the camera; an agent was a *flesh-peddler* whether he handled stage or film starlets; the *casting-couch* might form part of a stage as well as the film impresario's stock-in-trade; and a *death-knell* (or cancellation of a call for extras) might be sounded on the stage of a musical as well as on a studio lot. The same applies to the traditional *breakaway,* any weapon so lightly made it could be used without harm in a knock-about farce scene – a sugar bottle, a paper club, a cardboard chair – *breakaways* are as common and as useful still on the stage as on the screen. And the gag that brings a roar of laughter is a *belly-punch,* a *buffaroo* or a *hup-cha-da-bub-cha* whichever the medium.

On the other hand, terms relating to camera work or photography belong to the cinema: *lens-hog* (no explanation needed), *bulber* (photographer), *jockey* (assistant cameraman), *bungalow* (the housing of a soundproof camera), *stockade* (protection for the camera when animals are being filmed or there are other dangers), *spaghetti* (for film itself). Another field belonging to the movie is sound recording: a *mike monkey* is the one who manipulates a *fishing pole* or *mike-boom,* and there is a whole series of words to describe *gremlins* or *termites* on the sound-track – *bloops, gargles, canaries* and *wow-wows.* Other words which belong more especially to the world of celluloid are *sheepherder* (assistant director in charge of extras), *first-broom* for the head of properties, *beard, muff* or *feather-merchant* for an extra with his own natural whiskers, *beef* for a labourer, *bump-man* for the expert who does the stunts. The cinema has originated the *sobbie* or *weepie,* the *cliff-hanger* (melodramatic serial) and *horse-opera* (the familiar Western).

Much of this is simply frivolous slang, and, however apt or amusing, cautiously avoided as far as possible by the serious lexicographer, who is hard enough put to it to struggle with the scientific jaw-breakers, words like *panoramograms, anaglyphs, vectographs, lenticular screens* or *xerographic animation.** We can safely leave many of these to the lexicographer,

---

* All these are systems of 3-D, except the last, a dry-photo method of making cartoons.

just as he can leave us with our *tear-buckets, belly-punches, and cliff-hangers.* But there is a whole middle range of serious terms in common use, which need clear, compendious definition for the benefit of the average, intelligent filmgoer. *Cinemascope* for instance, what is it exactly? There are other allied terms like *wide-screen and Cinerama* as little understood, and to explain them it is necessary to discuss generally, cinema screens and their development.

Cinema Screens

Screens today come in different sizes and (although their shape is always rectangular) different dimensions. The difference lies in the relation of horizontal width to height, known as the *aspect ratio*. Early in the cinema's history this ratio was standardised to correspond with the proportions of the picture in a movie camera taken on 35 mm. film, and for years (from the twenties to the fifties) this stayed the same. The picture was 1 to 1.33 (100 feet high, say, to 133 feet wide) and it is known as *normal* or *academy* ratio. It is still the natural size of picture to take on 35 mm. film.

Then, early in the fifties, with a flourish of trumpets and a roll of drums, *Cinemascope* was introduced. This was a short, wide rectangle like the opening of a letter-box. Cinemascope ratio is taken to be 1 to 2.50 but it can vary from 1 to 2.65 in the camera and be cut to 1 to 2.25 in the projector to allow for an optical instead of a magnetic track alongside the picture. It needed different screens, different projectors, different cameras, different films, in some cases different cinemas. Cinemascope cost a packet, and most small cinemas couldn't afford it. It was fine for the sweep of a river, or of a mountain range, but not so good for the heroine's shy smile (50 feet across) or young love's first tremulous embrace. Nevertheless, it caught on and it was clear audiences liked (or could be persuaded to like) the new shape.

A compromise to solve the problem of average cinemas was reached with the introduction of *wide-screen*. This was wider than the old academy ratio, but nowhere as wide as Cinemascope. Average *wide-screen* ratio is 1 to 1.75 but it varies from cinema to cinema, 1 to 1.68 in many Odeons, 1 to 1.85 in many ABC cinemas. For the cost of a set of lens, a masking plate and a new screen it could be installed in any cinema and pictures could be made on 35 mm. film, with or without masking in the camera. The only trouble is that for movies made on the normal or academy ratio (and remember this is still the natural ratio for 35 mm. film) wide screen cuts off a strip at the top and the bottom of the picture. In many cinemas today at least some films are shown so that the composition intended by the film-maker is lost.

Another wide-screen system but one that never caught on, was Paramount's *Vista-Vision* introduced in the early fifties. This used a 35 mm. print but fed it through the camera and the projector, horizontally. Technically this was the logical way to use 35 mm. film to take wider pictures: the gauge of the film corresponded to the height of the screen and any width of picture could be obtained by feeding more or less length of film through the camera at each exposure. But somehow *Vista-Vision* never became popular.

Cinerama went one better than Cinemascope, the picture on the screen was immense, the biggest that had ever been seen – it was in fact three academy-ratio pictures shown side by side with a ratio of nearly 1 to 4, the movie taken and shown by a special camera and projector with three lenses, three turrets and three strips of 35 mm. film feeding through simultaneously.

But alas – the shooting equipment was so unwieldy, that filming a full-length dramatic feature was almost prohibitive in cost, and most Cinerama programmes were consequently travelogues or simple sequences – rides in trains, sledges, switchback railways. Furthermore the projection was unsatisfactory – there is almost inevitably some vibration in projection equipment, and the joins between the three pictures showed – disastrously enough whether they went down the middle of the third chorus girl or the thirty-third column of the Greek temple.

Then came *Todd–AO* (AO stands for American Optical Company) developed and used by Mike Todd in the film *Around the World in Eighty Days*, (director Michael Anderson) made in 1956. The movie was universally popular, made a fortune at the box-office and established the new system. This simply used an enormous strip of film 70 mm. wide which was projected on a huge screen almost as big as the threefold screen of Cinerama, and which gave a picture as spectacular and as all-enveloping, and without the complications in filming, or the drawbacks in projection, of Cinerama. In course of time Cinerama acquired the Todd–AO process and nowadays what audiences in London see at the *Casino* and the *Coliseum* is 70 mm. film projected on a huge screen. The original three-turret process with joins, is dead as a stuffed duck. It is interesting to note that Mike Todd was not the first to try and introduce wider film. The first attempt was in 1896 and, I am told, can still be seen on Brighton pier (the film was 65 mm. wide) under the title "What The Butler Saw".

The inventor was Fred Baker of Butchers Film Service, a dentist turned film-maker, and experimental showings were given at the Palace Theatre, Cambridge Circus, the camera being called a Mutograph and the projector a Mutoscope. Later there were at least two other systems, Fox's *Grandeur* and a system developed by R.C.A. The difficulty of the early systems was getting enough light to provide adequate illumination for the double-width film. By the time Todd came along improved arc-lamps had solved the problem. Which goes to show, that it is not enough for an inventor to originate something new and good – he has to choose his time and place.

Panavision is a term sometimes seen. It is a form of control during shooting, by means of a screen or frame attached to the camera which shows the area covered by the various ratios. This enables the director to frame his shots so the resulting film will be suitable for projection on virtually any aspect ratio. Films made in panavision can be distributed more widely, and there is less likelihood that they will be mangled in projection.

Colour Systems

Colour systems are another little-understood feature of the cinema. We see *Filmed in Eastmancolour* or *Colour by Technicolor*. What do they mean? Again a brief look at history is useful. Colour was first applied to film in 1906 by G. A. Smith of the famous Brighton School, and the system called Kinemacolor. Some of these early prints obtained delightful pictures, but the processes were not practicable on a large scale. Not until the thirties when Technicolor brought out a three-colour subtractive system – first used in Disney's *Flowers and Trees* (1932), & *La Cucuracha* (1934) did colour become a commercial proposition.

Colour systems in the cinema are either subtractive or additive. A subtractive system stains the projection print in layers with colours complementary to that desired on the screen. When the white light of the projector shines through, all colour except one shade, is "extracted" by the complementaries and the desired shade shines through to show on the screen. All early systems and all present-day systems are subtractive. The only additive system was Dufaycolour, developed in 1933, in which the film was criss-crossed with a shadow-mask, a "reseau" of colours, which built up a picture by adding coloured lights.

Technicolor was the first company to evolve a practical 3-colour subtractive system. But the Technicolor system was dependent on the use of dyes and it has been superseded by Eastmancolour, a true photographic system. Nowadays the different trade-names Technicolor, Agfacolor, Ferrannicolor, Sovcolor and Fujicolor all conceal a basic similarity of process – all are in effect, variations of Eastmancolour. The quantity and kind of chemicals in the emulsions and the order of colour layers, may differ, but the principles are the same. Three layers in the camera sensitive to the three primary colours, producing in the final print, three layers which between them will filter out all but the shade desired on the screen.

Modern colour systems are versatile, rich and sensitive. The director can exercise control over a colour film at three stages of the production: *first* in drafting a colour script for the film, and co-ordinating the preliminary work of set-designer, property-man and dresser; *second* in using lights, gelatines and paint sprays during the actual shooting; *third* in the laboratory where variation in printing can make all the difference to the final result. In ordering prints from the laboratory use is made of a "cinex" strip which gives twelve choices of printing from the faintest to the strongest colour. One depth of colour may be chosen for the whole film, or different choices made for different scenes. The possibilities are endless, see the films *The Red Desert*, *Juliet of the Spirits* (*Giulietta Degli Spiriti*), *Le Bonheur*, *Un Homme et une Femme*, *Belle de Jour*, *Far from the Madding Crowd*.

Speed

A third matter which sometimes causes confusion among audiences, is the speed of films. In the early days with hand-cranked cameras speeds were variable and projectors could also be run at different speeds. Nevertheless, during the silent era and until the introduction of sound films in the late twenties the speed of films was very much slower than at present, and the figure of 16-frames-a-second (or 16 pictures a second) was generally not far out. With the introduction of sound films with the necessity of running the sound-track at an absolutely regular speed, cameras and projectors were

standardised at 24-frames-a-second, the minimum speed which would give good sound reproduction.
Silent films should clearly be shown at silent speed but certain problems arise. Many modern projectors can only go at sound speed. If a silent film has a sound-track added, it is impossible to run at the right speed for the picture (16 frames) and the sound (24 frames) and a compromise – generally to repeat every second frame – has to be reached.
Films on television present another problem. In this country television is broadcast at the rate of 50 cycles (or 50 pictures) a second. For sound films, each frame is simply broadcast for two cycles which gives a speed of 25 pictures a second – near enough to the right speed (24-frames-a-second) to be acceptable. A voice may occasionally seem high-pitched or the music a little sharp – but most human ears are not sensitive enough to detect the difference. In America TV is broadcast at 60-cycles-a-second – sound films are broadcast two frames for two cycles then half-a-frame for two cycles joining to the next half-frame of the following group of $2\frac{1}{2}$. This, by a more complicated process, again gives a speed of 25 frames, the same as on English TV. So far as silent films are concerned, these are sometimes simply shown at sound speed with all the action speeded up. However, for better results the film can be "stretched" by printing every second frame twice, although this does cause slight distortion in the action.

Random Definitions

What about other terms? There are dozens of them and the choice has to be a personal one. Here are a few (in alphabetical order) which seem (to me) most likely to be useful:
ACTION: What the director (or his assistant) calls out when he means business. It puts everybody (actors, camera crew, sound engineers, electricians and the rest) on their toes ready for the click of the *clapper-board*. When the action is finished the director calls *cut*.
BACK PROJECTION: In unusual situations or buildings adapted from other purposes, there is sometimes no room for the normal projection box at the rear of the auditorium, but room for it behind the screen. In this case the image can be thrown on the back of the screen (possibly using mirrors) and will show through it, and be seen by the audience. *Back Projection* on to a screen may also be used in film-making. In this case the picture thrown on the screen is usually large-scale, outdoor scenery which blends with the rest of the props to form a seemingly natural setting for the action.
BLOW-UP: A photographic enlargement usually to considerable size. Also the making of a larger gauge print or negative, from a smaller guage, e.g. 35 mm. from 16 mm.
CAMERA ANGLE: The direction – from below, above, at a horizontal angle, etc.–from which an actor or scene is photographed.
CLOSE-UP: A very close view of any object, often an actor's face or part of the face.
CROSS CUTTING or *PARALLEL ACTION:* The dramatic construction which cuts backwards and forwards between the heroine facing a fate worse than death at the hands of the villains, and the hero rushing on horseback to save her. One of the cinema's earliest contributions to the art of suspense, and still going strong.
DEPTH OF FIELD: The distance from foreground to background which will appear in sharp focus when a scene is photographed.
DOLLY: A platform on wheels, sometimes also on rails, to carry the camera (and cameraman) during moving camera shots.
DOUBLE-EXPOSURE: One image superimposed on another. Used for memory, ghosts, etc. Obtained by exposing the same film twice, under carefully controlled conditions.
DUPE or *DUPLICATE:* A duplicate negative, made from the original negative by means of a *fine-grain print, duping print* or *lavender*.
ESTABLISHING SHOT: A shot to let the spectator know where he is. Traditionally an establishing shot comes at the beginning of a scene, the camera then moving in to close-ups of expression, significant detail, etc. However, nowadays, an establishing shot frequently comes in the middle or at the end of a scene, and the camera pulls back from a mass of close detail to surprise the spectator with an unexpected location.
FLASH-BACK: The cinema's equivalent of past tense. Starting from the present, the film goes back into the past to trace a thread of the story, follow a memory, explain a background, reveal a guilty secret. Music, distortion, a line of dialogue – many different means, depending on the skill and style of the director, are used to introduce a flash-back, and tell the audience the film is going into the past.
LOCATION: Location shooting is filming outside the studio using real rather than artificial settings.
MIX or *DISSOLVE:* A translation between one sequence and another in which

the second picture appears on the screen before the first has disappeared. A particular case of *double-exposure*. A *SOUND MIX* is the process of combining the various sound elements in making the final sound-track for a film.
MONTAGE: The French word for assembling the various single shots to make the final film. The English equivalent is *CUTTING* or *EDITING*.
NON-ACTORS: Short for "non-professional actors". Films are unique in their ability to use the naturalness of the non-professional to advantage, as for instance in *The 400 Blows*, *Bicycle Thieves*, *The Gospel According to St Matthew*.
PAN: Movement of the camera on a fixed base to sweep the scene, either to give a general picture, or move from one point of interest to another.
RUSHES: All the shots (often many *takes* of the same scene) filmed in the studio or on location, and projected the same day or as soon as possible after, to give the film-makers an immediate opportunity to view, select the best shots, or repeat scenes if necessary. The editor will then go on to make a *rough-cut* of the film.
SCENARIO (*FILM SCRIPT*, *TREATMENT*): *Film script* is generally preferred nowadays to *scenario*. Writing for a film may go through many stages. First will come a *treatment* or general description of the film. In some cases a *STORY-BOARD* may be prepared, a series of sketches to help visualise the action. The final *SHOOTING-SCRIPT* will list the individual shots (with type of shot and possibly length and camera angle) give full dialogue, setting, other sounds, music.
SLOW MOTION and FAST or *ACCELERATED MOTION!* If the camera is deliberately run faster than normal, and the film then projected at normal speed, the movement shown on the screen will be slowed down. If the camera is run slower than normal, then movement on the screen will be speeded up. Fast and slow motion can be used for scientific purposes and, dramatically, for comic or tragic effects.
SNEAK-PREVIEW: Showing a film to a random audience to test their reactions before it is released.
TELEPHOTO LENS: The development of telephoto shots has changed film style a good deal and is capable of brilliant effects. It also facilitates candid-camera work, since the subject is unconscious of being filmed.
THREE-D: There are many possible systems, some listed earlier in this article. The system used in the early fifties was stereoscopic, and necessitated the audience wearing special glasses.
TRACKING: A camera movement contrasted with *Panning* (QV) in which the camera is moved bodily, often on a *dolly* (QV).
ZOOM: Another modern development in camera lenses. By simply turning one component of the lens, the focus changes and in a moment, the camera can, in effect, be brought near (as with a telephoto lens) for a close-up, or taken away for a long shot.

A Well of English Undefiled

There is one final way in which the movies have affected the English language: As Mencken points out, the American film was the most potent influence in bringing the racy idiom of North America to this country. In 1920 the following appeared in an Associated Press report: "England is apprehensive lest the vocabularies of her youth become corrupted through incursions of American slang. . . . it is the subtitle of the American moving picture film which, it is feared, constitutes the most menacing threat to the vaunted English purity of speech." When the American talkie began to replace the silent movie, there was a fresh outburst of indignation. "The talkies have presented the American language in one giant meal, and we are revolted", said *The Daily Express*.
But before World War II began *The Times* gave its blessing to *high-brow*, the *Express* to *fence-sitter*, the *News of The World* to *gate-crasher*, and other eminent authorities to *scram*, *hooch* and *lousy*. By the end of the thirties the issue was not in much doubt, and the war gave the *coup de grâce*. By the end of the forties the battle had been lost – or won.

* * *

Film business is a curious amalgam of two diverse elements, a duality which is reflected in its language. On the one hand, on the technical side, the cinema employs the serious language of science, and some knowledge of the more common technical terms is almost a necessity to full enjoyment and understanding of the film-makers art. But at the same time the movies are part of the entertainment business, and the exuberance, the racy, bold, slashing manner affected by the impresarios of show business, is reflected in the lively slang of the cinema. Who could resist a lingo in which a success is not just a success, but far, far more – *snappy*, *torrid*, *hotsy*, *lush*, *red-hot*, a *whammo*, a *sock*, a *boff*, a *blitz* and a *sizzler*!

AWARDS!

An annual review of the year's awards to movies and moviemakers (note also the various Festival Awards mentioned by Peter Cowie in his article.)

Probably the biggest surprise in the awards list this year came with the announcement on April 11 of the year's "Oscar" winners, handed out by the American Academy of Motion Picture Arts and Sciences. Nearly everyone had tipped "Bonnie and Clyde" to more or less sweep the board, but in fact this film gained only two comparatively minor awards.

These were the winners:

Best Actor:

Rod Steiger (for his performance in "In the Heat of the Night").

Best Supporting Actor:

Arthur Kennedy (for his performance in "Cool Hand Luke").

Best Actress:

Katharine Hepburn (for her performance in "Guess Who's Coming to Dinner").

Best Supporting Actress:

Estelle Parsons (for her performance in "Bonnie and Clyde").

Best Direction:

Mike Nichols ("The Graduate").

Best Art Direction – Colour:

John Truscott, Edward Garrere; set decoration: John W. Brown ("Camelot").

Best Cinematography – Colour:

Burnett Guffey ("Bonnie and Clyde").

Best Costume Design:

John Truscott ("Camelot").

Best Film Editing:

Hal Ashby ("In the heat of the Night").

Best Foreign-language Film:

"Closely Watched Trains" (Czechoslovakia).

Best Music Score – Substantially Original:

Elmer Bernstein ("Thoroughly Modern Millie").

Best Music – Adaptation or Treatment:

Alfred Newman and Ken Darby ("Camelot").

Best Song First Used in Eligible Motion Picture:

Leslie Bricusse (for "Talk to the Animals" in "Doctor Dolittle").

Best Picture and Producer:

"In the Heat of the Night" – Walter Mirisch.

Best Sound:

"In the Heat of the Night".

Best Sound Effects:

John Pyner ("The Dirty Dozen").

Best Special Visual Effects:

L. B. Abbott ("Doctor Dolittle").

Best Screenplay – Material from Another Medium:

Stirling Silliphant ("In the Heat of the Night").

Best Story and Screenplay – Written for the Screen:

Willaim Rose ("Guess Who's Coming to Dinner").

Best Documentary Feature:

"The Anderson Platoon" – The French Broadcasting System (Producer: Pierre Schoendorffer).

Best Documentary Short:

"The Redwoods" – King Screen Productions (Producers: Mark Harris, Trevor Greenwood).

Best Short – Live Action:

"A Place to Stand" – A TDF Production for the Ontario Department of Economics and Development, Columbia Pictures (Producer: Christopher Chapman).

Best Cartoon Short:

"The Box" – Murakami Wolf Films, Brandon Films (Producer: Fred Wolf).

* * *

On Thursday, March 28, at the 21st annual *British Film Academy Awards* dinner, the Academy's "Stella" awards for 1967 were announced as follows;

The Film Awards:

Best Film from any Source:

"A Man for All Seasons".

Best British Film:

"A Man for All Seasons".

United Nations Award:

"In the Heat of the Night".

Best Short Film:

"Indus Waters".

Best Specialised Film:

"Energy and Matter".

Best Animated Film:

"Notes on a Triangle".

Robert Flaherty Award:

"To Die in Madrid".

 The Craft Awards:

Best Screenplay for a British Film:

Robert Bolt ("A Man for All Seasons").

Best Cinematography in a British Colour Film:

Ted Moore ("A Man for All Seasons").

Best Cinematography in a British Black and White Film:

Gerry Turpin ("The Whisperers").

Best Art Direction in a British Colour Film:

John Box ("A Man for All Seasons").

Best Costume Design in a British Colour Film:

Elizabeth Haffenden and John Bridge ("A Man for All Seasons").

Best Costume Design in a British Black and White Film:

Jocelyn Rickards ("Mademoiselle").

Performance Awards:

Best British Actress:

Dame Edith Evans (for her performance in "The Whisperers").

Best British Actor:

Paul Scofield (for his performance in "A Man for All Seasons").

Best Foreign Actress:

Anouk Aimee (for her performance in "Un Homme et Une Femme").

Best Foreign Actor:

Rod Steiger (for his performance in "In the Heat of the Night").

Most Promising Newcomer to Leading Film Roles:

Faye Dunaway (for her performance in "Bonnie and Clyde").

* * *

The Writers Guild of Great Britain's annual cinema awards (other awards go to Radio and TV) were announced on Thursday, March 14, 1968, as follows:

Best Documentary or Short Script:

Ronnie Whitehouse (Plaque) for "Dead Safe", and Anthony Short (Merit Scroll) for "Good as Gold".

Best British Comedy Screenplay:

Bill Naughton (Plaque) for "The Family Way", and Frederick Raphael (Merit Scroll) for "Two for the Road".

Best British Original Screenplay:

Edward Boyd, Peter Yates and George Markstein (Team Plaque) for "Robbery", and Frederick Raphael (Merit Scroll) for "Two for the Road".

Best British Screenplay:

Robert Bolt (Plaque) for "A Man for All Seasons", and Harold Pinter (Merit Scroll) for "Accident".

* * *

Made in black basalt, this nine-inch-tall wedgwood figure inscribed in gold was the new British Film Academy Award which this year took the place of the previous "Stella", as the Award is named. Designed by Eric Owen, the wedgwood sculptor, the new statuette was inspired by 18th-century models of mythological figures by John Flaxman.

The American trade paper The Motion Picture Herald *organise an important countrywide popularity poll of star ratings according to their box-office value, and the voters are the people who should know, for they are the cinema owners and managers of the United States. For 1967 this was the order of voting:*

1. Julie Andrews 2. Lee Marvin
3. Paul Newman 4. Dean Martin
5. Sean Connery 6. Elizabeth Taylor
7. Sidney Poitier 8. John Wayne
9. Richard Burton 10. Steve McQueen
11. Jane Fonda 12. James Coburn
13. Jack Lemmon 14. Julie Christie
15. Michael Caine 16. Elvis Presley
17. Cary Grant 18. Sandy Dennis
19. Frank Sinatra 20. Bob Hope
21. Shirley Maclaine 22. Audrey Hepburn
23. Dick Van Dyke 24. Doris Day
25. Jerry Lewis

A similar poll among British exhibitors produced the following results:

1. Sean Connery 2. Lee Marvin
3. Michael Caine 4. Julie Christie
5. John Wayne 6. Hayley Mills
7. Audrey Hepburn 8. Elizabeth Taylor
9. Julie Andrews 10. Richard Burton
11. Norman Wisdom 12. Morcambe & Wise
13. Peter Sellers 14. Burt Lancaster
15. George Peppard 16. James Coburn
17. Vanessa Redgrave 18. Rex Harrison
19. Stanley Baker 20. Cliff Richard
21. Yul Brynner 22. Peter O'Toole
23. Clint Eastwood 24. Steve MacQueen
25. Elvis Presley

Each year U.S. and Canadian exhibitors are asked to select ten players who seem to them to show the most promise for lasting stardon. On this occasion the list they produced was:

1. Lynn Redgrave 2. Faye Dunaway
3. James Caan 4. John Philip Law
5. Michele Lee 6. Michael Sarrazin
7. Sharon Tate 8. Michael York
9. Hywell Bennett 10. David Hemmings

* * *

While it is not possible to give lists of all *the awards of the year, including a considerable number of minor ones, the following are of some special interest:*

New York Film Critics' Circle:

Best Picture:

"In the Heat of the Night".

Best Actor:

Rod Steiger, in "In the Heat of the Night".

Best Actress:

Dame Edith Evans, in "The Whisperers".

Best Director:

Mike Nicols, for "The Graduate".

Best Screenplay:

Robert Benton and David Newman, for "Bonnie and Clyde".

Best Foreign-language Picture:

"La Guerre est Finie".

National Society of U.S. Film Critics:

Best Picture:

"Persona".

Best Actor:

Rod Steiger, in "In the Heat of the Night".

Best Actress:

Bibi Anderson, in "Persona".

Best Supporting Actor:

Gene Hackman, in "Bonnie and Clyde".

Best Supporting Actress:

Marjorie Rhodes, in "The Family Way".

Best Director:

Ingmar Bergman, for "Persona".

Best Screenplay:

Robert Benton and David Newman, for "Bonnie and Clyde".

Best Cinematography:

Haskell Wexler, for "In the Heat of the Night".

The American National Board of Review:

Best Picture:

"Far from the Madding Crowd".

Best Actor:

Peter Finch, in "Far from the Madding Crowd".

Best Actress:

Dame Edith Evans, in "The Whisperers".

Best Supporting Actor:

Paul Ford, in "The Comedians".

Best Supporting Actress:

Marjorie Rhodes, in "The Family Way".

Best Director:

Richard Brooks, for "In Cold Blood".

Best Foreign-language Picture:

"Elvira Madigan".

The biggest money making films in Britain for 1967 were: *The Sound of Music* (now in its third year and past the £12,000,000 mark!) with *Doctor Zhivago* now coming along nicely in second place. But these were "special showing" films; the greatest money-maker on general release was *You Only Live Twice*, and the next eleven, not necessarily in this order, were: *The Blue Max, Bonnie and Clyde, Casino Royale, The Dirty Dozen, El Dorado, The Family Way, The Magnificent Two, My Fair Lady, One Million Years B.C., Press For Time, The Professionals*

* * *

There were, of course, many, many other awards issued during the year, not the least interesting of which was a special one given by the cinema Exhibitors' Association of Britain to *Richard Attenborough* in recognition of his outstanding contribution to the British Cinema.

Claudia Cardinale at Cannes 1967

THE FESTIVAL SCENE

Peter Cowie

The catastrophic and premature end of the Cannes Festival in May has spotlighted the pros and cons of film festivals everywhere. In effect, an extremist group, led by such respected directors as François Truffaut, Jean-Luc Godard, and Claude Lelouch, was able to disrupt an event which for over twenty years had been the major gathering of its kind, a fortnight of screenings, wheelings, and dealings on the Riviera which involved literally millions of dollars.

The precipitate decision to close the festival in the face of threats of violence only underlined what one had always suspected, that every major festival is in fact a national affair. Despite the simultaneous translations into English available to the audience, despite the German journalist's column in the daily festival "Bulletin", and despite the presence of representatives from the press in a score of countries, Cannes proved to be a French manifestation. When the crisis came, the producers and directors from abroad were left in the lurch, their invitations cut short and their means of retreat literally severed (no flights, no trains, no international 'phone calls as a result of the general strike that swiftly paralysed France). One wonders if indeed Cannes will ever be host to a film festival again.

For behind every festival there lurks a subsidy. Producers are not charged massive fees for entering their films, as an outsider might presume, although they are pressed to take stands in the local hotels and to mount lavish receptions, all of which brings money to the municipality concerned, and lends a much needed glamour to the event. Cannes reputedly draws a government subsidy of over £60,000, but such figures are rarely divulged. Festivals in communist countries, such as Moscow and Karlovy Vary, attract invaluable foreign currency as well as serving as excellent cultural propaganda. The power that a government can exert over a film festival was amply demonstrated in 1967 when the Greek junta quashed the international week at the Salonika event, so that it could not be used by the left as a political forum in the presence of delegates from overseas.

The real loss at Cannes was to the people who *make* films – the producers who had booked expensive suites at the hotels along the Croisette and the directors who had worked (like Mai Zetterling) day and night to finish their pictures on time, only to watch them vanish without trace in a non-existent second week. More serious still, the spirit of the festival was crushed. The daily screenings are not the be-all and end-all of a great festival like Cannes. It is the fact that *everyone* is there that really counts – journalists as well as stars, distributors as well as traders, directors as well as publicists, writers as well as technicians. If you have anything to do with the cinema, in any of these capacities, you can obtain accreditation at Cannes, Venice, Berlin, or any of the smaller events. There is (or was!) a "market" in the margins of Cannes where some 150 titles are screened in local cinemas at strange hours of the day, with often no more than half-a-dozen people present. But if those six men are distributors from as many countries, then the projection is probably well worth while. Some companies show a film on the market three or four years in succession. No one seems to mind, and sooner or later that film is sold to even the most difficult of territories. Journalists like the festival circuit because it enables them to travel on expense accounts, or to reap a lucrative harvest of fees for free-lance articles and broadcasts. (One of the more stimulating sights on the last day of Cannes this year was the crush of writers round the telex machines and telephone booths, all trying to make the front page of their papers with the film story of a decade.)

FIAPF (The International Federation of Film Producers) extends recognition to only 24 of the 200-odd festivals, and sanctions awards in even fewer cases. This year, for example, FIAPF had a protracted dispute with Signor Chiarini, the aesthetically-minded chief of the Venice Mostra, because he was tending more and more to reject "official" entries from FIAPF's member countries and to follow his own idiosyncratic taste in choosing films for exhibition at the festival. But I predict that the proliferation of festivals must reach its height in a very short time, and that the enthusiasm behind several of the minor gatherings will wane in the face of ever increasing difficulties in getting new titles. It is the "supermarket" festivals that will survive at one end of the scale, and the specialist events (Oberhausen, Annecy, Pesaro) at the other.

AWARDS

CANNES 1967 (no Awards in 1968)
Grand Prix: *BLOW-UP* (Britain).
Special Jury Prize: *HAPPY GIPSIES* (Yugoslavia), and *ACCIDENT* (Britain).
Best Actor: Odded Kotler in *THREE DAYS AND A CHILD* (Israel).
Best Actress: Pia Degermark in *ELVIRA MADIGAN* (Sweden).
Best Direction: Ferenc Kosa for *TEN THOUSAND SUNS* (Hungary).

BERLIN 1967
Golden Bear: *LE DÉPART* (Belgium).
Silver Bears: *LA COLLECTIONNEUSE* (France), and *ALLE JAHRE WIEDER* (West Germany).
Best Actor: Michel Simon for *THE OLD MAN AND THE CHILD* (France).
Best Actress: Edith Evans for *THE WHISPERERS* (Britain).
Best Direction: Zivojin Pavlović for *THE RATS AWAKE* (Yugoslavia).

VENICE 1967
Golden Lion: *BELLE DE JOUR* (France).
Special Jury Prize: *LA CHINOISE* (France), and *LA CINA E VICINA* (Italy).
Best Actor: Ljubisa Samardzić for *DAWN* (Yugoslavia).
Best Actress: Shirley Knight for *DUTCHMAN* (Britain).
Opera Prima Prize: Edgar Reitz for *MAHLZEITEN* (West Germany).

MOSCOW 1967
Grand Prix: *FATHER* (Hungary), and *THE JOURNALIST* (U.S.S.R.).
Special Jury Prize: *DEVIATION* (Bulgaria), and *ROMANCE FOR CORNET* (Czechoslovakia).
Best Actor: Paul Scofield for *A MAN FOR ALL SEASONS* (Britain).
Best Actress: Sandy Dennis for *UP THE DOWN STAIRCASE* (U.S.A.), and Grynet Molvig for *THE PRINCESS* (Sweden).
Best Comedy: *OPERATION SAN GENNARO* (Italy).

OBERHAUSEN 1968
Best Cartoon: *A FUNNY THING HAPPENED ON MY WAY TO GOLGOTHA* (Belgium).
Best Fiction Short: *WAITING FOR GODOT* (Czechoslovakia).
Best Documentary: *RESPICE FINEM* (Czechoslovakia), and *NEZAPOSLENI LJUDI* (Yugoslavia).
Best National Selection: the Budapest Film School entries.

TOURS 1968
Grand Prix: *YOU'RE HUMAN LIKE THE REST OF THEM* (Britain).
Prix de la Première Oeuvre: *FIRE! FIRE! ANYWAY SOMETHING'S HAPPENING* (Poland).
Special Jury Prize: *JIMMY THE TIGER* (Greece); *WHAT DO YOU THINK?* (Japan); and *THE GAME* (U.S.A.).

FILM FUTURE

To the optimist – and regular moviegoers just *have* to be optimists – the future is always rosier in hue than the present; tomorrow's movies, on paper, always look more exciting than those we're seeing now. Every year, as one glances ahead, the prospect seems more exciting. In fact, with but comparatively slight variations, one year follows the pattern of another, with its high spots, its great bulk of ordinary entertaining movies – and its resounding flops.

Knowing this I always approach the various film companies' production schedules and their glowing promises with reservations. Yet . . . I admit *that* movie sounds wonderful . . . this one *ought* to be great . . . what a cast they've poured into 'x'! . . . they could surely hardly go wrong with a story like *that*? . . . Almost against the will one warms to the promise, one begins to look forward with eagerness to the months to come, so full of – on paper! – cinematically exciting events.

In these pages I have given a necessarily abridged and rather hurried look at the films to come, picking out a few of the many that are now completed, in course of final editing or still in production. For every one selected I've had to omit another – or several. You will admit, I think, that they *look* a likely bunch! So let's just hope – hope that the coming year will be cinematically a vintage one.

* * *

James Coburn and Susannah York in the Martin Manulis Technicolor production *Duffy*. James Fox and James Mason are the other stars of this Columbia picture – a contemporary comedy-drama, produced by Manulis and directed by Robert Parrish.

Barbra Streisand will have her first screen role in the lavishly spectacular *Funny Girl* – adapted from the international stage musical hit. Already she has been acclaimed as one of the brightest star personalities ever to emerge from Hollywood and her starring partnership with Omar Sharif is said to be extraordinarily exciting. *Funny Girl* co-stars Kay Medford, Anne Francis and Walter Pidgeon, as Florenz Ziegfeld. It was produced by Ray Stark and directed by William Wyler and is a Columbia picture.

Opposite page
Harry Secombe as "Mr Bumble" and Mark Lester as "Oliver" in a scene from Lionel Bart's *Oliver*! the most ambitious and spectacular musical drama produced in a British studio. In 70 mm Panavision and Technicolor, it is a Romulus production produced by John Woolf, directed by Carol Reed and released by Columbia. Ron Moody as "Fagin", Oliver Reed as "Bill Sikes" and Shani Wallis as "Nancy" are the other stars, with "The Artful Dodger" played by Jack Wild.

HENRY ARMSTRONG
BLACKSMITH
HORSES SHOD & HAND FORGING

Interlude, the story of a brief, passionate love affair which spans the months of a hot, English summer, stars Oskar Werner with one of Britain's most exciting screen newcomers, Barbara Ferris. In Technicolor, it is a Domino Production released by Columbia, produced by David Deutsch and directed by Kevin Billington.

Richard Attenborough as Robert Blossom, a brassiere manufacturer of international repute, at the Blossom Conference in Paramount's *The Bliss of Mrs Blossom*, a light-hearted comedy – for adults! Shirley MacLaine plays the wife, and James Booth plays the lover the wife keeps hidden in the attic! Produced by Josef Shaftel and directed by Joseph McGrath.

As Nicky (Marcello Mastroanni) stretches forward to pull Honey (Maggie Blye) to safety, he is rewarded with a kiss, in Paramount's *Diamonds for Breakfast*, in which Mastroanni recruits seven young ladies to help him steal the Russian crown jewels while they are on display in an English castle! Rita Tushingham also stars, with Warren Mitchell, Elaine Taylor, Margaret Blye, and Francesca Tu. Directed by Christopher Morahan and produced by Pierre Rouve for Carlo Ponti.

Kirk Douglas and Alex Cord in Paramount's *The Brotherhood*, a story of two brothers – one in America and one in Italy – of a family committed to the Mafia. In spite of their love for each other they become involved in a savage conflict which destroys them both. The film also stars Irene Papas, Luther Adler, Eduardo Cinanelli, Susan Strasberg and Joe de Santis. Produced by Martin Ritt and Kirk Douglas and directed by Martin Ritt.

Jane Fonda as *Barbarella*, the strip cartoon heroine who travels through outer space vanquishing evil and meting out rewards – in her own sexy way – to the men who befriend her. A Paramount film directed by Roger Vadim also starring John Phillip Law and Milo O'Shea with guest David Hemmings. Produced by Dino de Laurentiis.

Yul Brynner (right) plays Pancho Villa, the legendary Mexican revolutionary in Paramount's *Villa Rides*. Robert Mitchum (left) plays an American pilot who enlists in Villa's cause. Produced by Ted Richmond and directed by Buzz Kulik.

Gertrude Lawrence (Julie Andrews) and Noel Coward (Daniel Massey) share a love scene from Coward's 1930 play "Private Lives" in a sequence from *Star!*, the Robert Wise 20th Century-Fox film about the life of Miss Lawrence.

Rex Harrison in 20th Century-Fox's *A Flea in Her Ear*, based on a play by Georges Feydeau and co-starring Rosemary Harris, Louis Jourdan and Rachel Roberts. Directed by Jacques Charon and produced by Fred Kahlmar, with screenplay by John Mortimer.

Michael Caine and Eric Portman in Bryan Forbes' psychological thriller for 20th Century-Fox release, *Deadfall*. Giovanna Ralli and newcomer Carlos Pierre play other characters and Nanette Newman and David Buck contribute other performances.

James Stewart and Dean Martin as brothers in 20th Century-Fox's Western *Bandelero!* which also stars Raquel Welch, George Kennedy and Andrew Prine. Andrew V. McLaglen directed and Robert L. Jacks produced.

Frank Sinatra, portraying a veteran New York detective, pushes his way through newsmen with an accused killer in a scene from his latest film, *The Detective*, an Aaron Rosenberg production for 20th Century-Fox release. Lee Remick and Mia Farrow also star.

Twenty-three-year-old Judy Huxtable plays Sadie, leader of *The Touchables*, London's most switched-on foursome of fearless feminity, in the film of the same title. Robert Freeman directed and John Bryan produced this 20th Century-Fox British film, which also stars Esther Anderson, Kathy Simmonds, Marilyn Rickard, David McBride and Ricky Starr.

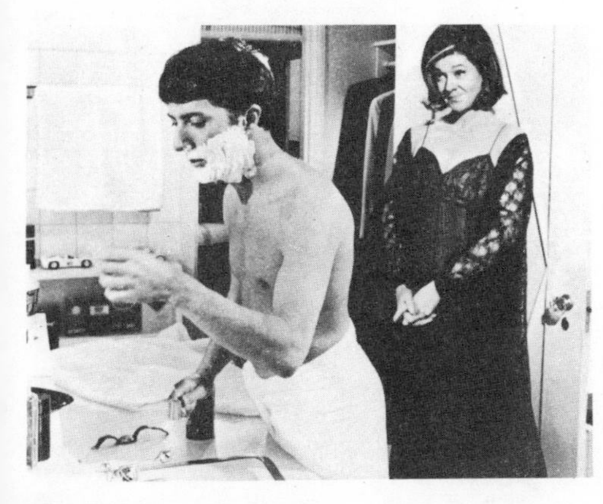

Mrs Robinson (Anne Bancroft) and the son of her husband's business partner whom she has seduced in U.A.'s Oscar-winning *The Graduate* which Mike Nichols directed.

Meet *The One and Only, Genuine, Original Family Band* . . . Left to right in this scene from the new Walt Disney film: (top) Lesley Ann Warren, Kurt Russell, Janet Blair and Buddy Ebsen. Second row, Debbie Smith and Jon Walmsley. Bottom row, Bobby Riha, Pamelyn Ferdin, Smitty Wordes, Heidi Rook and Walter Brennan.

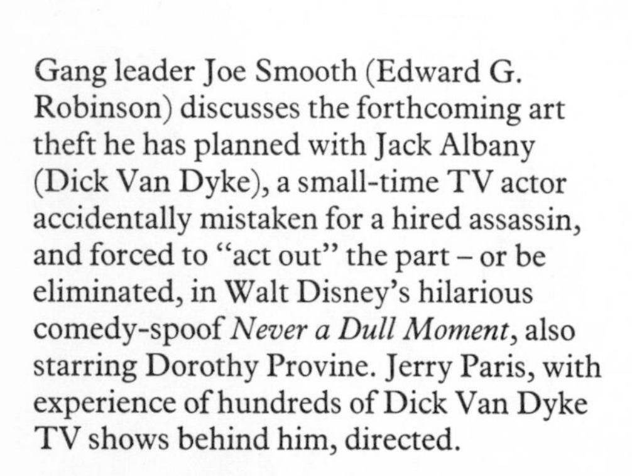

Gang leader Joe Smooth (Edward G. Robinson) discusses the forthcoming art theft he has planned with Jack Albany (Dick Van Dyke), a small-time TV actor accidentally mistaken for a hired assassin, and forced to "act out" the part – or be eliminated, in Walt Disney's hilarious comedy-spoof *Never a Dull Moment*, also starring Dorothy Provine. Jerry Paris, with experience of hundreds of Dick Van Dyke TV shows behind him, directed.

In *Great Catherine*, Warner Bros-Seven Arts screen adaptation of Bernard Shaw's play, Peter O'Toole plays the dashing Captain Charles Edstaston of the Light Dragoons, a young English officer who attracts the attentions of Catherine the Great with devastating results in the St Petersburg at the turn of the century. Also starring are Jeanne Moreau, Zero Mostel and Jack Hawkins. Produced by Jules Buck and directed by Gordon Flemyng.

Fashioned as an exercise in chilling terror and mounting suspense, Warner Bros-Seven Arts *Wait Until Dark* is the screen version of Frederick Knott's international stage hit, the story of a young blind girl in terror of her life from three unscrupulous thugs seeking to wring from her the whereabouts of a doll stuffed with a priceless cache of heroin. Audrey Hepburn plays the blind girl, Efrem Zimbalist is her photographer husband, and the three crooks are played by Alan Arkin, Richard Crenna and Jack Watson. Robert and Jane-Howard Carrington adapted the play for the screen and the drama was produced by Mel Ferrer and directed by Terence Young.

One of the most "explosive" teamings of any year is that of Sean Connery and Brigitte Bardot in Edward Dmytryk's *Shalako*, a Dimitri de Grunwald production, produced by Euan Lloyd. A multi-million-dollar action adventure on an epic scale, *Shalako* is for release in this country by Anglo-Amalgamated through Warner-Pathé. Photographed in Technicolor by Award-winning cameraman Ted Moore.

Produced and directed by actor Paul Newman (his first stint behind the camera in either capacity) *Now I Lay Me Down* stars his wife, Joanne Woodward, as a small-town school teacher who is awakened to life by a summer love affair. Based on a novel by Margaret Laurence – a book which won the Canadian equivalent of a Pulitzer Prize – the screenplay for the Warner Bros-Seven Arts production was written by Steward Stern. Also starring are James Olsen and Estelle Parsons.

A Peter Sellers comedy is always an event, especially when the star in question counts it among the best films he has ever made! Such a claim is for Warner Bros-Seven Arts *I Love You, Alice B. Toklas* in which Sellers, a staid Los Angeles lawyer on the threshold of marriage to a staid, Los Angeles girl, renounces convention to become a "hippy" and join the beat generation. Also starring, Leigh Taylor-Young. Direction by Hy Averback.

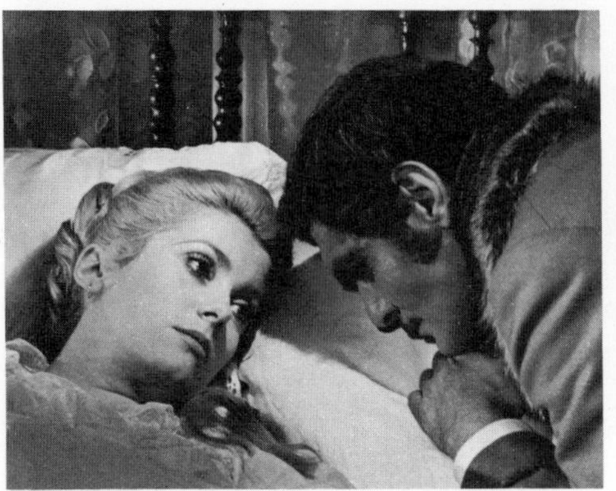

Fashioned as one of the great romantic stories of our time, *Mayerling*, the Associated British Picture Corporation presentation, comes to the screen as a tenderly-observed story which spotlights one of the great tragedies of European royalty – the ill-fated love affair between Prince Rudolf of Austria and the lovely aristocrat Maria Vetsera, a liaison which ended one cold morning at the Hunting Lodge in Mayerling, Lower Austria, when the two lovers were found dead in a love suicide pact. Written, produced and directed by Terence Young, *Mayerling* boasts a cast of stellar international proportions headed by Omar Sharif as Rudolf, Catherine Deneuve as Maria, Ava Gardner as the Empress Elizabeth, James Mason as the Emperor Franz Josef and James Robertson Justice as The Prince of Wales.

Brilliantly created for the screen with all the technical expertise for which he has become famous, Richard Lester brings to Warner Bros-Seven Arts *Petulia* a kaleidoscopic interpretation of the lives of three people living in present-day San Francisco: a kooky young newly-married girl, her sinister neurotic husband and the cynical, world-weary doctor with whom she has an on-off affair. This official 1968 American entry at the Cannes Film Festival, *Petulia* is certain to be one of the year's most-talked-of pictures. Starring Julie Christie, George C. Scott and Richard Chamberlain.

Dick Van Dyke and Sally Ann Howes lead a chorus of dancers through "Toot Sweets", one of the most spectacular production numbers in Albert R. Broccoli's *Chitty Chitty Bang Bang*. Director Ken Hughes set the scene in an Edwardian candy factory – and gave the routine all the flair of the Edwardians, combined with 1968 zing.

Seen so far in London and selected provincial centres, audiences throughout the country can anticipate the release later this year of *Camelot*, that lavish Warner Bros-Seven Arts screen version of the famed musical play. Spectacle-splashed, star-studded and musically-mounted, *Camelot* has Richard Harris as King Arthur, Vanessa Redgrave as Queen Guinevere and handsome Italian star Franco Nero as bold Sir Lancelot. Produced by Jack L. Warner and directed by Joshua Logan.

Betty (Cilla Black) and Van (David Warner) arrive home after their marriage in *Work . . . is a Four-Letter Word*, a Cavalcade Film Production directed by Peter Hall, produced by Thomas Clyde and released by the Rank Organisation and Universal.

Pamela Franklin is held prisoner by Richard Boone (centre) and Marlon Brando in a remote cottage awaiting the ransom money from her father in this scene from Universal's *The Night of the Following Day*, a modern suspense thriller recently made in Paris.

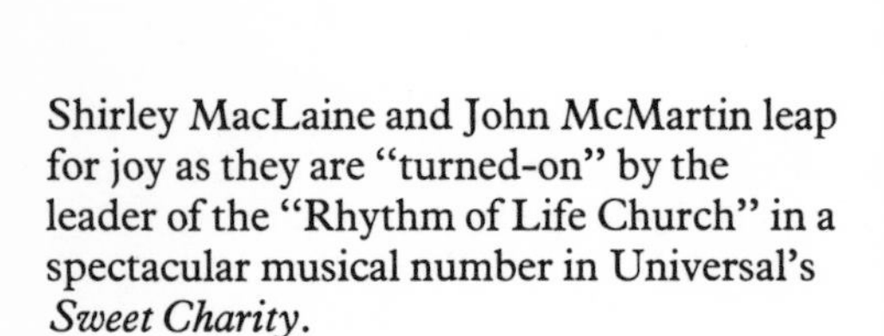

Shirley MacLaine and John McMartin leap for joy as they are "turned-on" by the leader of the "Rhythm of Life Church" in a spectacular musical number in Universal's *Sweet Charity*.

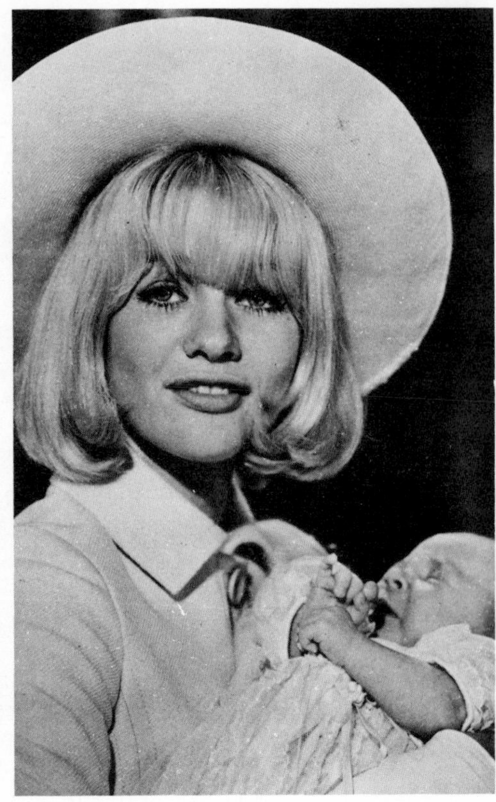

Lovely Judy Geeson becomes a mother in Fox's *Prudence and the Pill* – the moral being that even for teenage girls who switch their mother's birth control pills for aspirin tablets, events do not necessarily work out as planned. Co-stars are Deborah Kerr and David Niven, Robert Coote, Irina Demick, Keith Michell, Edith Evans, Joyce Redman.

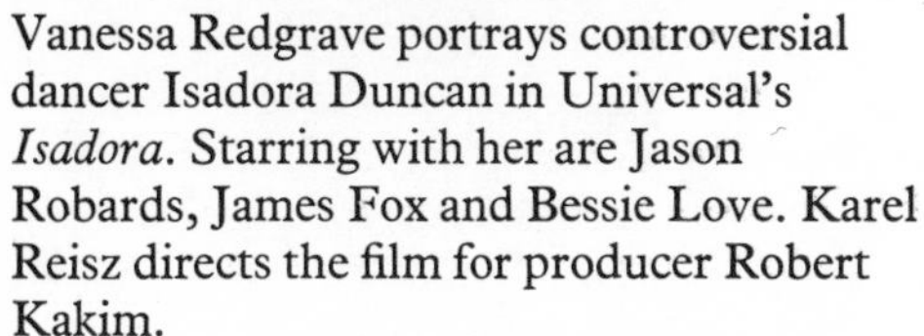

Vanessa Redgrave portrays controversial dancer Isadora Duncan in Universal's *Isadora*. Starring with her are Jason Robards, James Fox and Bessie Love. Karel Reisz directs the film for producer Robert Kakim.

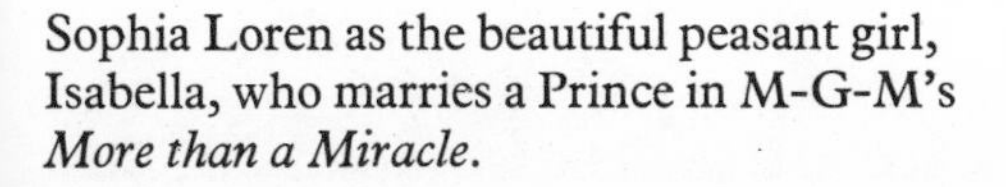

Sophia Loren as the beautiful peasant girl, Isabella, who marries a Prince in M-G-M's *More than a Miracle*.

Again playing a British secret agent, as he did in his British TV series, "Secret Agent", Patrick McGoohan makes his Hollywood film début in Filmways–M-G-M's *Ice Station Zebra*. A Martin Ransohoff Filmways production about a U.S. nuclear submarine's dash under the Arctic icecap and a hidden-from-the-world confrontation between American and Russian task forces at the North Pole. Rock Hudson, Ernest Borgnine, Patrick McGoohan and Jim Brown are starred in the picture, directed by John Sturges.

To sign or not to sign . . . Doris Day can't decide whether or not to sign a movie contract urged on her by Terry-Thomas in this scene from *Where Were You When the Lights Went Out?* Miss Day plays a Hollywood–Broadway star and Terry-Thomas her director in the new M-G-M-comedy, produced by Everett Freeman and Martin Melcher. Hy Haverback directed.

Already premiered in London but still to be seen by wider audiences, Stanley Kubrick's *2001: A Space Odyssey* is one of the most magnificent and imaginative science-fiction films ever made; a tremendously exciting spectacle and at the same time a puzzling problem story which leaves the audience guessing. Though Keir Dullea has the main role of an astronaut, the real stars are the stars.

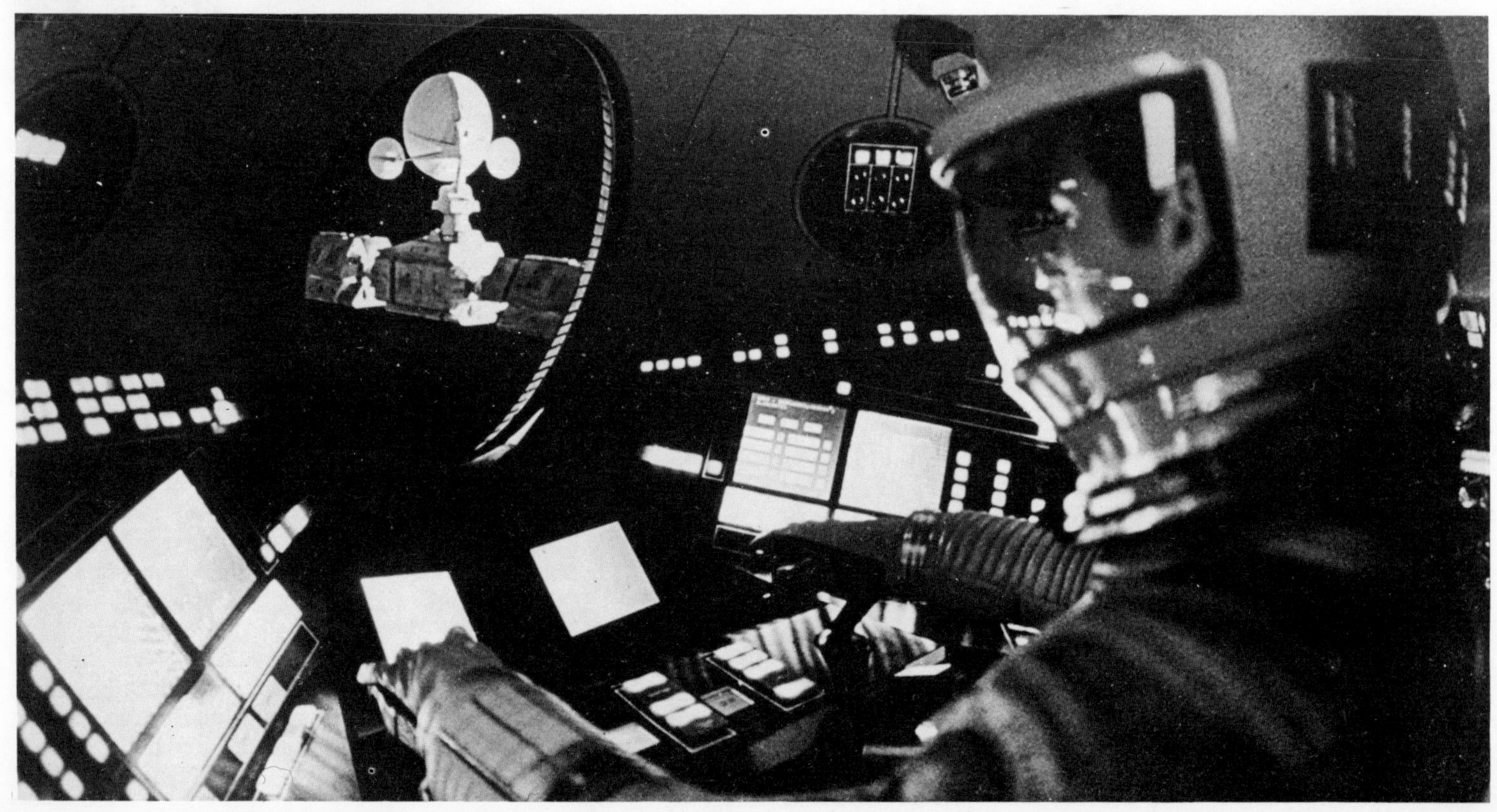

All the old familiar characters are brought back by Gerry and Sylvia Anderson in their second, Slough-made puppet feature *Thunderbird Six*, which David Lane directs from the Anderson's own screenplay. That's the luscious Lady Penelope at the bottom of the ladder!

Ageless, fadeless and as magnificent now as screen entertainment as the year in which it was made, M-G-M's first sound-colossus *Gone With the Wind* returns this year in a new size (it has virtually been re-made frame by frame from the old square ratio to today's more elongated aspect) and with a new stereophonic track. And it's sad to think that many of its stars, including Clark Gable and Vivien Leigh (shown) are now dead.

Peter Sellers as Hrundi V. Bakshi, whose presence at *The Party*, in Hollywood, brings with it the chaos and disaster which follows him everywhere he goes in the U.A. film of that title. With him, Claudine Longet, as one of his very few admirers.

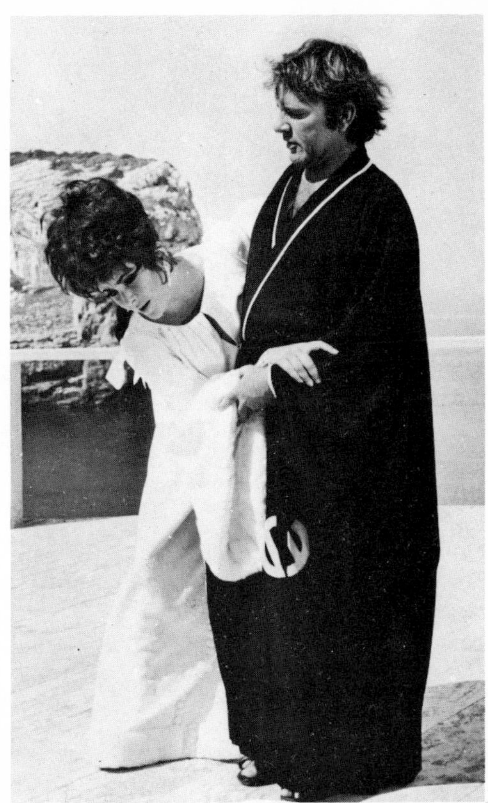

Elizabeth Taylor and Richard Burton are together once more on the screen in Universal's *Go forth*, and Noel Coward co-stars with the Burtons in this Technicolor feature filmed in Sardinia and Rome. Joseph Losey directed from a story and screenplay by Tenessee Williams.

RELEASES OF THE YEARS IN DETAIL

Note: In the following pages certain abbreviations have been made in order to save space. The technical abbreviations are as follows: (T) Technicolor; (C) CinemaScope; (Tech) Technirama; (Total) Totalscope; (M) Metrocolor; (D) Deluxe Colour; (Pan) Panavision. Company names you will find abbreviated as follows: (Anglo) Anglo-Amalgamated; (U.I.) Universal-International; (Lion) British Lion; (Fox) 20th Century-Fox; (U.A.) United Artists

1967–68

The Adventures of Bullwhip Griffin
Walt Disney Western set in the Gold Rush era and telling the story of a family butler who goes thataway to California, becomes accidentally famous for knocking out the town's toughest character, wins a saloon and a girl and doesn't worry too much when he loses the first in a fire! Cast: *Roddy McDowall, Suzanne Pleshette, Karl Malden, Harry Guardino, Richard Haydn, Hermione Baddeley, Bryan Russell, Liam Redmond, Cecil Kellaway, Joby Baker, Mike Mazurki, Alan Carney, Parley Baer, Arthur Hunnicutt, Dub Taylor, Pedro Gonzalez-Gonzalez*. Dir: James Neilson. Pro: Walt Disney. Screenplay: L. S. Hawley. (Disney.) Rel: Dec. 24. (T.) 111 Mins.

Africa Addio
Jacopetti and Prosperi (they made the Mondo Cane films) documentary about modern Africa; a bloody, violent and disturbing view of the dark continent which includes senseless wholesale slaughter of the wild life, revolution, tribal revenge, executions, etc. Conceived, written and directed: Jacopetti & Prosperi. (Golden Era.) Rel: Floating. (Techniscope & T.) 122 Mins.

Africa – Texas Style
Simple, pleasing if on occasions quite unintentionally verbally amusing, colour film, made in East Africa and based on a real idea: the formation of semi-domesticated herds of wild animals in order to assure their future and at the same time provide meat and milk for the hungry Africans. *John Mills* as the Britisher with the idea; *Hugh O'Brian* as the Texas cowboy he imports to do the animal catching; *Tom Nardini* as his Redskin sidekick; and with *Adrienne Corri* as the pretty nurse. Rest of cast: *Nigel Green, Ronald Howard, Charles Malinda, Honey Wamala, Charles Hayes, Stephen Kikumu, Ali Twaha, Mohammed Abdullah*. Dir & Pro: Andrew Marton. Screenplay: A. White. (Ivan Tors–Paramount.) Rel: July 16. (Colour.) 109 Mins.

Albert Carter, Q.O.S.O.
A 3-reel comedy about a roadsweeper, set in London. Dir: Ian Brims. Pro: M. Hayworth. Screenplay: Eric Idle & Ian Brims. (Dormer.) Rel: March 10. 30 Mins.

The Ambushers
Third and one of the liveliest of the Matt Helm series with Matt (*Dean Martin*) assigned the case of the vanishing secret saucer spacecraft, trailing it from a New York brewery to the South American jungle headquarters of a martial-minded villain, where Matt and pretty *Janice Rule*, with the help or hindrance of sundry other lovelies, smash up his plans and pinch back the pinched saucer! Rest of cast: *Senta Berger, James Gregory, Albert Salmi, Kurt Kasznar, Beverley Adams, David Mauro, Roy Jenson, John Brascia, Linda Foster*. Dir: Henry Levin. Pro: Irving Allen. Screenplay: Herbert Baker. (Meadway–Claude–Columbia.) Rel: Jan. 28. (T.) 102 Mins.

Amsterdam Affair
Neat mystery thriller set against a background of the city in the title, with an English writer suspected of having murdered his ex-mistress and actually charged with the crime before the persistent police inspector on the case finds another more likely suspect. . . .Cast: *Wolfgang Keiling, William Marlowe, Catherine Von Schell, Pamela Ann Davy*. Dir: Gerry O'Hara. Pro: George Willoughby. Screenplay: Edmund Ward. (LIP.) Rel: June 2. (E.) 91 Mins.

An Idiot in Paris
Jean Lefebre as the innocent rural half-wit who comes to Paris and finds it very different to what he had imagined it to be, but is smart enough to take a pretty little prostitute back with him to the country, planning to start a farm with her nest-egg cash! Rest of cast: *Dany Carrel, Bernard Blier*. Dir: Serge Korber. (Eagle.) First shown at Cinephone, Feb., 1968. (E.) 89 Mins.

And Now Miguel
The tender, wholesome story of a young Mexican shepherd boy who dreams of the day he will be old enough to be accepted as an adult by his father and allowed to take the flocks to the mountainside for their daily feed. Cast: *Pat Cardi, Michael Ansara, Guy Stockwell, Clu Gulagere, Joe de Santis, Pilar Del Rey, Peter Robbins, Buck Taylor*. Dir: J. B. Clark. Pro: Robt. B. Radnitz. Screenplay: Ted Sherdeman & Jane Klove. (U.I.–Rank.) Rel: Dec. 30. (Colour.) 95 Mins. (Second general release: first was at Dec. 30, 1966.)

Angelique
The first of several films based on the famous risque stories by best-seller Sergeanne Golon. With gorgeous *Michele Mercier* in the title-role. Unabashed action-filled melodrama with some pretty nudity for good measure. Cast: *Robert Hossein, Jean Rochefort, Guiliano Gemma, Francois Maistre, Jacques Toja, Bernard Woringer, Yves Barsacq, Etchika Choureau, Charles Regnier, Jacques Castelot, Claude Giraud, Philippe Lemaire, Robert Porte, Jacques Mignot, Jean Topart, Black Salem, Jean-Pascal Aran, Roberto*. Dir: Bernard Borderie. Pro: Francis Cosne. Screenplay: Claude Brule. (Butchers.) Rel: Floating. (E.) 116 Mins.

The Anniversary
Straightforward adaptation of the Bill MacIlwraith stage play, a wonderful melodramatic star vehicle for *Bette Davis* as the horrible, man-eating momma who keeps her three weak sons under her thumb. Rest of cast: *Sheila Hancock, Jack Hedley, James Cossins, Elaine Taylor, Christian Roberts, Timothy Bateson, Arnold Diamond*. Dir: Roy Ward Baker. Pro & Screenplay: Jimmy Sangster. (Hammer–Warner–Pathe.) Rel: Feb. 18. (T.) 95 Mins.

Aquasex
About a marine biologist in search of some mysterious creatures who turn out to be mermaids, and the crook who arrives at the same spot after pearls, and the way that the two men, after the latter has murdered a mermaid, meet for a final struggle on the sea-bed! Cast: *Gaby Martone, George Rowe, Timothy Carey, Jose Gonzales*. (World Cinema.) Rel: Floating. (E.) 71 Mins.

Arizona Bushwhackers
A Western set in the turbulent period at the end of the Civil War with *Howard Keel* – who is actually a Confederate spy – enlisting in the Union Army which has the job of trying to bring law and order to a largely lawless land and personally succeeding to a large extent in bringing it to the little town of Colton before riding on. . . . Rest of cast: *Yvonne de Carlo, John Ireland, Marilyn Maxwell, Scott Brady, Brian Donlevy, Barton MacLane, James Craig, Roy Rogers, Jun., Reg Parton, Montie Montana, Eric Cody*. Dir: Lesley Selander. Pro: A. C. Lyles. Screenplay: Steve Fisher. (Paramount.) Rel: April 7. 87 Mins.

Assignment K.
Routine spy thriller about a British toy manufacturer who, using his frequent trips between Britain and Germany as cover for his spy ring, becomes suspect and is thereafter involved in lots of intrigue, a murder in Munich and the blowing up of counter-spies in a Harrow house! Cast: *Stephen Boyd, Camilla Sparv, Michael Redgrave, Leo McKern, Jeremy Kemp, Robert Hoffmann, Jane Merrow, Carl Mohner, Vivi Bach, Werner Peters, Dieter Geissler, John Alderton, Jan Werich, David Healy, Ursula Howells, Basil Dignam, Geoffrey Bayldon, Joachim Hansen, Marthe Harell, Traudi Hochfilzer, Friedrich Von Thun, Katharina Von Schell, Herbert Fuchs, Peter Capell, Heinz Leo Fisher, Karl Otto Alberty, Helmut Schneider, Friedrich Von Ledebur, Andrea Allen, Rosemary Reede, Jenny White, Mia Nardi, Olga Linden, Alexander Allerson, Alastair Hunter, Gert Widenhofen*. Dir: Val Guest. Pro: Ben Arbeid & Maurice Foster. Screenplay: V. Guest, Bill Strutton, M. Foster. (Gildor–Columbia.) Rel: Feb. 18. (Techniscope & T.) 98 Mins.

Assignment to Kill
More than usually credible and literate thriller with tough and handsome investigator *Patrick O'Neal* hired to find out the truth of the sinkings of two ships owned by a shady financier. Rest of cast: *Joan Hackett, Herbert Lom, Eric Portman, Peter Van Eyck, Oscar Homolka, John Gielgud*. Dir & Screenplay: Sheldon Reynolds. Pro: Wm. Conrad. (Warner–Pathe.) Rel: May 12. (T & Pan.) 73 Mins.

The Ballad of Josie
Doris Day, a widow accused and acquitted of having murdered her husband, finds it more than a little difficult to become the cattlewoman she would like to be and causes a range war before everything is tidily sorted out. Rest of cast: *Peter Graves, George Kennedy, Andy Devine, William Talman, David Hartman, Guy Raymond, Audrey Christie*. Dir: Andrew V. McLaglen. Pro: Norman MacDonnell. Screenplay: Harold Swanton. (U.I.–Rank.) Rel: May 12. (Colour.) 102 Mins.

Banning
Oddly titled melodrama which tears a few veils off the American Country Club to reveal plenty of corruption beneath: cheating, adultery, blackmail and other quiet pastimes! *Robert Wagner* plays the golf pro who has to pass most of his winnings on, while

instructor *Guy Stockwell* and *James Farentino* (as another ambitious staff member) do a little scene stealing. Rest of cast: *Anjanette Comer, Jill St John, Susan Clark, Mike Kellin, Gene Hackman, Howard St John, Sean Garrison, Logan Ramsey, Edmon Ryan, Oliver McGowan, Lucille Meredith, Bill Cort.* Dir: Ron Winston. Pro: Dick Berg. Screenplay: James Lee. (U.I.–Rank.) Rel: Nov 5. (Techniscope & Colour.) 102 Mins.

Barefoot in the Park
Delicious, witty, consistently amusing comedy – based on the Neil Simon stage success – about an averagely ill-assorted young couple who marry and rent a tiny flat high under the roofs of Manhattan – sans bath, sans heating – and there love, bicker, and find the usual difficulties of living together. Lovely performances by *Jane Fonda, Robert Redford, Miland Natwick, Charles Boyer* and everyone else in the small cast. Rest of cast: *James Stone, Ted Hartley, Mabel Albertson, Fitz Field, Herbert Edelman.* Dir: Gene Saks. Pro: Hal Wallis. Screenplay: Neil Simon. (Paramount.) Rel: July 2. (T.) 105 Mins.

Barrier
The work of a new young Polish director, Jerzy Skolimowski – an obtuse fantasy that examines the gap between the generations in Poland. A mixture of the irritating and the brilliant. Cast: *Jan Nowicki, Joanna Szczerbic, Tadeusz Lomnicki, Zdzislaw Maklakiewicz, Ryszard Pietruski, Maria Malicka, Malgorzata Lorentowics.* Dir & Written: Jerzy Skolimowski. (Kamera, Warsaw–Contemporary.) First shown at Academy, Oct. 1967. 83 Mins.

Beach Red
Cornel Wilde directed, produced and himself stars in this typical story of the war in the Pacific, *c.* 1943, about a group of American combat troops sent to take a Japanese-held island and achieving their object only at considerable bloody cost. And the final incident, when a young American and a young Jap soldier mortally wound each other and are then left together, leaves the final anti-war question hovering in the air: Why? Rest of cast: *Rip Torn, Burr De Benning, Patrick Wolfe, Jean Wallace, Jaime Sanchez, Genki Koyama, Gene Blakely, Norman Pak, Dewey Stringer, Fred Galang, Hiroshi Kiyama, Linda Albertano, Jan Garrison, Michio Hazama, Masako Ohtsuki.* Dir & Pro: C. Wilde. Screenplay: Clint Johnson, D. A. Peters & J. Pascal. (Theodora–U.A.) Rel: May 5. (T.) 101 Mins.

The Beautiful People
Strange little Japanese film about a girl dragged into prostitution by her lover, who himself becomes the victim of his gangster masters and gradually reverts to a position where he is almost his former mistress's servant. Cast: *Miyuki Kuwano, Mikijiro Hira, Keisuke Sonoi, Masuyo Iwamoto, Misako Tominaga, Bunta Sugawara, Isao Kimura.* Dir: Noboru Nakamura. Pro: A. Shimada. Screenplay: T. Gondo. (Shochiku–A. Balch.) First shown at Jacey, Charing X Rd. July 1967. (Scope & E.) 105 Mins.

Bedazzled
TV comics *Peter Cook* and *Dudley Moore's* first large-screen effort. Their own adaptation of the old Faust legend with a devilish Cook tempting whimpy chef Moore to sell his soul in exchange for seven wishes – which with truly devilish ingenuity he manages to spoil as taken! Plenty of fun at the expense of religion, and other jokes in more superior taste, but episodic and too blown-out, with the wit too widely spaced. Rest of cast: *Eleanor Bron, Michael Bates, Raquel Welch, Bernard Spear, Parnell McGarry, Howard Goorney, Alba, Barry Humphries, Daniele Noel, Robert Russell, Peter Hutchins, Max Faulkner, Martin Boddey, John Steiner, Robin Hawdon, Eric Chitty, Michael Trubshawe, Evelyn Moore, Robin Tolhurst, Anna Turner, Lockwood West.* Dir & Pro: Stanley Donen. Screenplay: Peter Cook. (Fox.) Rel: May 12. (Pan & D.) 104 Mins.

Belle de Jour – Day Girl
Luis Bunuel film from a book by Joseph Kessel; about a cold young wife of a doctor who is fascinated by whoredom and becomes the afternoons-only inmate of a brothel, where one day her husband's friend turns up. It all ends in a flash of melodrama: and its all rather flesh-creepingly ugly and unpleasant. But finely photographed and well acted. Cast: *Catherine Deneuve, Jean Sorel, Marcel Piccoli, Genevieve Page, Francisco Rabal, Pierre Clementi, Georges Marchal, Francoise Fabian, Maria Latour, Francis Blanche, Mach a Meril, Muni.* Dir: Luis Bunuel. Pro: R. & R. Hakim. (Curzon.) First shown at Curzon cinema, Nov. 1967. (E.) 100 Mins.

Berserk
Murder thriller against interesting circus background, with *Joan Crawford* the owner whose employees have a habit of meeting violent ends! Rest of cast: *Ty Hardin, Diana Dors, Judy Geeson, Michael Gough, Robert Hardy, Geoffrey Keen, George Claydon, Philip Madoc, Golda Casimir, Sidney Tafler, Ted Lune, Milton Reid, Peter Burton, Miki Iveria.* Dir: Jim O'Connolly. Pro: Herman Cohen. Screenplay: Aben Kandel & H. Cohen. (Cohen. Columbia.) Rel: Nov. 26. (T.) 96 Mins.

The Best Man
Absorbing and convincing screen adaptation of the Gore Vidal play about dirty American politics: the struggle between the two leading candidates for Presidential nomination, a struggle in which one accuses the other of mental instability, against which the accused is urged to use a smear of homosexuality! Hardly reassuring: but biting, amusing and finely played. Cast: *Henry Fonda, Cliff Robertson, Edie Adams, Margaret Leighton, Shelley Berman, Lee Tracy, Ann Sothern, Gene Raymond, Kevin McCarthy, John Henry Faulk, Richard Arlen, Penny Singleton.* Dir: Franklin Schnaffer. Pro: S. Millar & L. Turman. Screenplay: Gore Vidal. (U.A.) Rel: Floating. 102 Mins.

The Bible . . . In the Beginning
Three-hour (plus interval) De Laurentis picturisation, directed by John Huston, of the first chapters of Genesis: the creation of Man, his tempting and expulsion; Cain and Abel's story; Noah and the Flood (the best sequence), etc. Done on a vast scale, with extremely good taste, perhaps too good taste in fact . . . A real all-star cast includes – best – *Huston* himself as Noah, *Michael Parks* (Adam), *Ulla Bergryd* (Eve), *Richard Harris* (Cain). Rest of cast: *Stephen Boyd, Geo. C. Scott, Ava Gardner, Peter O'Toole, Zoe Sallis, Gabrielle Ferzetti, Eleonora Rossi Drago, Franco Nero, Robert Rietty, Grazia Maria Spina, Claudie Lange, Adriana Ambesi, Alberto Lucantoni, Luciana Conversi.* Dir: John Huston. Pro: Dino de Laurentis. Screenplay: Christopher Fry. (Laurentis–Fox.) Rel: Special – March 10. (70mm & D.) 277 Mins. plus interval.

The Big Mouth
Typical *Jerry Lewis* comedy in which he becomes involved with some stolen diamonds, dying frogmen and his own "double". Rest of cast: *H. J. Stone, Susan Bay, Buddy Lester, Del Moore, Paul Lambert Jeannine Riley, Leonard Stone, Charlie Callas, Frank DeVol, Vern Rowe.* Dir, Pro and Screenplay: J. Lewis. (Columbia.) Rel: Dec. 3. (Colour.) 107 Mins.

Billion Dollar Brain
Highly involved and confusing addition to the Harry Palmer series based on Len Deighton stories, with *Michael Caine* again playing that somewhat reluctant Cockney spy Palmer. This time he becomes involved with a Texas millionaire's plan to start a revolution in Latvia and from there with his private army smash the Soviets, a plot neatly foiled by jolly Red espionage chief *Oscar Homolka* and his pretty assistant *Francoise Dorleac*! Beautiful Finnish backgrounds, drawn-out climax spectacle. Rest of cast: *Karl Malden, Ed Begley, Guy Doleman, Vladek Scheybal, Milo Sperber, Mark Elwes, Stanley Caine.* Dir: Ken Russell. Pro: Harry Saltzman. Screenplay: John McGrath. (Saltzman–U.A.) (T & Pan.) Rel: Jan 14. 111 Mins.

Blackbeard's Ghost
Peter Ustinov having – and giving – a high old comedy time in the title role, as the materialised spirit of a bloodthirsty old pirate captain cursed to roam in limbo until a good deed releases him. His efforts to do this, and make the hopeless college athletics team win a triangular match against infinitely superior opponents makes a wonderful slapstick sequence. Grand family fun again from Disney. Rest of cast: *Dean Jones, Suzanne Pleshette, Elsa Lanchester, Joby Baker, Elliott Reid, Richard Deacon, Norman Grabowski, Kelly Thordsen, Michael Conrad, Herbie Faye, George Murdock, Hank Jones, Ned Glass, Gil Lamb, Alan Carney, Ted Markland, Lou Nova, Charlie Brill, Herb Vigran, William Fawcett, Betty Bronson, Elsie Baker, Kathryn Minner, Sara Taft.* Dir: Robt. Stevenson. Pro: Bill Walsh. Screenplay: B. Walsh & Don DaGradi. (Walt Disney.) Rel: April 7. (T.) 107 Mins.

The Blood Beast Terror
Grand guignol thriller about a lovely girl given powers by her experimenting daddy which she starts to use on her own account, turning into a death's head moth –

giant size – in order to kill her victims – which in due course includes her daddy! Cast: *Peter Cushing, Robert Flemyng, Wanda Ventham, Vanessa Howard, David Griffin, Glyn Edwards, William Wild, Russell Napier, John Paul, Roy Hudd, Simon Cain, Leslie Anderson, Mike Mundell, David Lyell, Kevin Stoney, Malcolm Rogers, Kenneth Colley, Robin Wentworth, John Scott Martin, Beryle Cooke.* Dir: Vernon Sewell. Pro: A. Miller. Screenplay: P. Bryan. (Tenser–Tigon.) Rel: May 19. (E.) 88 Mins.

The Bobo
Comedy with uneasy tragic undertones: about a less than brilliant matador who fancies himself as a singer, comes to Barcelona to conquer the city as such, has to woo and win a famous courtesan as a condition of his getting his big chance, woos and wins . . . and then quixotically throws it all away, to return to his old job, as "The Only Blue Singing Matador!" *Peter Sellers* accentuates the melancholy of the story and plays down the comedy; a most interesting performance. Rest of cast: *Britt Ekland, Rossano Brazzi, Adolfo Celi, Hattie Jacques, Ferdy Mayne, Kenneth Griffith, Alfredo Lettieri, John Wells, Marne Maitland.* Dir: Robt. Parrish. Pro: Elliott Kastner & Jerry Gershwin. Screenplay: D. R. Schwartz. (Gina–Warner-Pathe.) Rel: Sept. 10. (T.) 103 Mins.

Bonnie and Clyde
Amusing, bloody and exciting – and most unusual – gangster story based on the facts of a 30's case history about a small gang led by a gay girl and a wild young man (*Faye Dunaway* and *Warren Beatty*) whose small hold-ups led to bigger, bank jobs and the final double-cross and police ambush which wiped them off the crime slate. It has already become a screen classic of its time. Rest of cast: *M. J. Pollard, Gene Hackman, Estelle Parsons, Denver Pyle, Dub Taylor, Evans Evans, Gene Wilder.* Dir: Arthur Penn. Pro: Warren Beatty. Screenplay: D. Newman & R. Benton. (Tatira-Hiller–Warner-Pathe.) Rel: Oct. 1. (T.) 111 Mins.

Carnival of Thieves
Shown in America under the title *The Caper of the Golden Bulls. Stephen Boyd* as the very moral bank robber blackmailed by former luxury-loving confederate *Giovanna Ralli* into taking part in a plan to blast open the vaults of the Bank of Spain during the annual carnival at Pamplona. Rest of cast: *Yvette Mimieux, Walter Slezak, Vito Scotti, Clifton James, Lomax Study, Tom Toner.* Dir: Russell Rouse. Pro: Clarence Greene. Screenplay: Ed Waters & David Moessinger. (Levine–Paramount.) Rel: Dec. 17. (Pathecolour.) 93 Mins.

Carry On Doctor
Typical addition to the "Carry On" series of broad and essentially British comedies. With something less than documentary approach it lifts the lids off medical life and finds it somewhat less than always seriously dedicated! Cast: *Frankie Howerd, Sidney James, Kenneth Williams, Charles Hawtrey, Jim Dale, Barbara Windsor, Hattie Jacques, Joan Sims, Anita Harris, Bernard Bresslaw, Peter Butterworth, June Jago, Dilys Laye, Derek Francis, Peter Gilmore, Dandy Nichols, Valerie van Ost, Julian Orchard, Julian Holloway, Alexandra Dane.* Dir: Gerald Thomas. Pro: Peter Rogers. Screenplay: Talbot Rothwell. (Rogers–Rank.) Rel: April 14. (Colour.) 95 Mins.

Castle of Blood
Thriller based on Edgar Allan Poe's "Dance Macabre" story, about some horrible happenings during a violent night in an old and haunted castle! Cast: *Barbara Steele, George Riviere, Margrete Robsahm, Henry Kruger, Sylvia Sorent, Montgomery Gleen, Paul H. Newman.* Dir: A. Dawson. Pro: R. Belty & W. Sarch. Screenplay: J. Grimaud & G. Wilson Jr. (Columbia.) Rel: Floating. 82 Mins.

A Challenge for Robin Hood
That colourful Sherwood Forest chapter of Olde English life brought to the screen yet again in a jolly re-retelling of the story of Robin Hood, the brave and gallant outlaw, and his Merrie Men. With *Barrie Ingham* as the New Robin. Rest of cast: *James Hayter, Leon Greene, Peter Blythe, Gay Hamilton, Alfie Bass, Jenny Till, John Arnatt, Eric Flynn, John Gugolka, Reg Lye, William Squire, Donald Pickering, Eric Woofe, John Harvey, Douglas Mitchell, John Graham, Arthur Hewlett, Norman Mitchell.* Dir: Pennington Richards. Pro: Clifford Parkes. Screenplay: Peter Bryan. (Hammer–Assoc.–Warner–Pathe.) Rel: Dec. 24. (T.) 96 Mins.

The Champagne Murders
After having been with three girls, each of which is murdered leaving the suspicion of their respective deaths at his door, *Maurice Ronet* decides the only way to escape being finally condemned for the crimes is for himself to find out who the real killer is, and why he is doing it. Rest of cast: *Anthony Perkins, Stephane Audran, Yvonne Furneaux, Suzanne Lloyd, Catharine Sola, Christa Lang, Henry Jones, George Skaff.* Dir: Claude Chabrol. Pro: Raymond Eger. Screenplay: Claude Brule & Derek Prouse. (Chabrol–U.I.–Rank.) Rel: Feb. 4. (T. & Techniscope.) 98 Mins.

A Child is Waiting
A brave Stanley Kramer film which examines some of the human problems involved with mentally defective children and, telling its moving story of a national institution in which the head (*Burt Lancaster*) is trying new methods of treatment and care, actually uses some of the children in the cast, which includes *Judy Garland* as a do-gooder who becomes too deeply involved with one small boy. Rest of cast: *Gena Rowlands, Steven Hill, Bruce Ritchey, Gloria McGehee, Paul Stewart, Elizabeth Wilson, Barbara Pepper, John Morley, June Walker, Mario Gallo, Frederick Draper.* Dir: John Cassavetes. Pro: Stanley Kramer. Screenplay: Abby Mann. (Kramer–U.A.) Rel: Floating. 115 Mins.

Chubasco
Tough adventure melo set among the tuna fishers of San Diego. Cast: *Christopher Jones, Susan Strasberg, Richard Egan, Ann Sothern, Joe de Santis.* Dir & Screenplay: Alan H. Miner. Pro: Wm. Conrad. (Warner–Seven Arts.) Rel: June 16. 76 Mins.

Circus of Fear
Police Inspector *Leo Genn* manfully making his way through a shoal of red-herrings in order to pin the killings on the right one of the many possible murderers in the circus where the main sleuthing takes place. Rest of cast: *Christopher Lee, Anthony Newlands, Heinz Drache, Eddi Arent, Klaus Kinski, Margaret Lee, Suzy Kendall, Cecil Parker, Victor Maddern, Maurice Kaufmann, Lawrence James, Tom Bowman, Skip Martin, Fred Powell, Gordon Petrie, Henry Longhurst, Dennis Blakely, George Fisher, Peter Brace, Roy Scammel, Geoff Silk, Keith Peacock.* Dir: John Moxey. Pro: H. A. Towers. Screenplay: Peter Welbeck. (Anglo–Warner–Pathe.) Rel: Nov. 19. (E.) 83 Mins.

Clambake
Elvis Presley as the rich boy, tired of his riches, who swops places with "ordinary guy", water-ski instructor, *Will Hutchins*, and in this disguise woos and wins *Shelly Fabares* (a girl looking for a rich husband!), also fighting and winning an important motor-boat race! Rest of cast: *Bill Bixby, James Gregory, Gary Merrill.* Dir: A. N. Nadel. Pro: A. Laven, A. Gardner & J. Levy. Screenplay: Arthur Browne, Jun. (U.A.) Rel: June 9. (Colour.) 99 Mins.

Closely Observed Trains
Delightful Czech film about a railway apprentice in a sleepy little Czech town during the war who asserts his masculinity, grows into manhood and dies as a saboteur all within a few hectic hours. Winner of the American Academy Award for best foreign film of 1967. Cast: *Vaclav Neckar, Jitka Bendova, Vladimir Valenta, Libuse Havelkova, Josef Somr, Alois Vachek, Jitka Zelenohorska, Vlastimil Brodsky, Ferdinand Kruta, Nada Urbankova, Kveta Fialova, Jiri Menzel.* Dir: Jiri Menzel. (Curzon.) First shown at the Curzon cinema, May, 1968. 92 Mins.

Cold Days
Hungarian film about the massacre at Novi Sad, in Yugoslavia, in 1942, when the Hungarian troops rounded up everyone in sight on suspicion of revolt and shot them down into holes in the Danube ice. Brilliantly made, with compassion, it uncovers the reasons why some of the soldiers carried out their horrible orders. Cast: *Zoltan Latinovits, Ivan Darvas, Adam Szirtes, Tibor Szilagyi, Margit Bara, Eva Vas, Mari Szemes, Iren Psota.* Dir & Screenplay: Andras Kovacs. (Mafilm–Contemporary.) First shown at Academy Three. Sept. 1967. 101 Mins.

The Comedians
Smooth, long, generally faithful, well acted and directed Graham Greene adaptation of his novel, which is a strong indictment of the dictatorial, brutal regime in Haiti. A story about a few foreigners there including the British hotelier in love with the American Ambassador's wife (*Richard Burton* and *Elizabeth Taylor* as the couple; *Peter Ustinov* as the husband), the crooked British Major Jones (*Alec Guinness*) and the

vegetarian missionary couple from America: *Paul Ford* and *Lillian Gish*. Rest of cast: *Georg Stanford Brown, Roscoe Lee Browne, Gloria Foster, James Earl Jones, Zaeks Mokae, Raymond St. Jacques, Douta Seck, Cicely Tyson*. Dir & Pro: Peter Glenville. Screenplay: Graham Greene. (Glenville–M-G-M). Rel: March 3. (Pan & Metrocolor.) 160 Mins.

Cool Hand Luke
Brutal American Chain Gang drama with *Paul Newman* as the "beheader" of parking-meters who is sentenced and brought to rebellion by the treatment by the guards, and his mother's death, a rebellion that leads him to escape again and again until the final, desperate bid for freedom with its tragic ending. Rest of cast: *George Kennedy, J. D. Cannon, Lou Antonio, Robert Drivas, Strother Martin, Jo Van Fleet, Clifton James, Morgan Woodward, Luke Askew, Marc Cavell, Richard Davalos*. Dir: Stuart Rosenberg. Pro: Gordon Carroll. Screenplay: D. Pearce & F. R. Pierson. (Warner–Seven Arts.) Rel: Dec. 31. 127 Mins.

Coppelia
Wholly delightful Spanish-American ballet film, with endless melody, fine dancing, gorgeous colour and an amusing performance by ballerina *Claudia Corday*. Rest of cast: *Walter Slezak, Caj Selling, Eileen Elliott, Luis Prendes, Milorad Miskovitch, Carmen Rojas, Veronica Kusmin* and the *Ballet of the Gran Teatro del Liceo of Barcelona* and *International Cine Ballet*. Dir & Written: Ted Kneeland. Pro: Frank Hale. (Gala.) First shown at Royalty Theatre, London, March, 1968. (E & C.) 97 Mins.

Cosa Nostra An Arch Enemy of the F.B.I.
Quite slick cops and robbers piece which rather jerkily tells the story of a member of the crooked Cosa Nostra who tries to get out but finds he's in too deep to achieve release. Cast: *Walter Pidgeon, Efrem Zimbalist Jr., Celeste Holm, Telly Savalas, Susan Strasberg, Philip Abbott, Stephen Brooks, Robert Drivas, Robert Duvall, Anthony Eisley, Ken Lynch, Wesley Addy, Ted Knight*. Dir: Don Medford. Pro: Charles Larson. Screenplay: Norman Jolley. (Quinn Martin–Warner-Pathe.) Rel: Sept. 10. (T.) 79 Mins.

Counterpoint
Famous American conductor (*Charlton Heston*) trapped by the Germans during the war with his whole 70-piece symphony orchestra and in spite of the open mass grave dug for them refusing to give a concert to a Nazi music-lover (*Maximilian Schell*). Rest of cast: *Kathryn Hays, Leslie Nielsen, Anton Diffring, Linden Chiles, Pete Masterson, Curt Lowens, Neva Patterson, Cyril Delevanti, Gregory Morton, Parley Baer, Dan Drazer, Ed Peck*. Dir: Ralph Nelson. Pro: Dick Berg. Screenplay: James Lee & Joel Oliansky. (U.I.–Rank.) Rel: May 26. (T.) 99 Mins.

Countdown
Double-dealing and dastardly doings among the American astronauts scheduled to make an "instant" Moonflight in order to beat the Russians, (who are already on the way there). Cast: *James Caan, Joanna Moore, Robert Duvall, Barbara Baxley, Charles Aidman, Steve Ihrat, Michael Murphy, Ted Knight, Stephen Coit, John Rayner, Charles Irving, Bobby Riha Jr*. Dir: Robt. Altman. Pro: Wm. Conrad. Screenplay: Loring Mandel. (Warner.) Rel: Floating. (T. & Pan.) 73 Mins.

A Country Coyote Goes Hollywood
Half-hour Walt Disney Western which switches things a little by making a Coyote the hero and the humans the villains of the piece! He escapes a posse, ends up in Hollywood Hills (where a band of city-bred brothers show him a thing or two) and then flees from the fire which swept through 6,000 Los Angeles acres in 1961. A True Life Adventure. Pro: W. Disney with Winston Hibler as associate. Screenplay: Jack Spiers. (Disney.) Rel: Nov. 5. (T.) 37 Mins.

Cry in the Wind
Film about two young people who become outcasts from a small, closed community living to their ancient code of law on a small island off the coast of Greece. Made entirely on location on Skyros. Cast: *Flora Robson, Yannis Voglis, Dimitra Kasma, Takis Emanouil*. Dir: Leonard Schach & Anthony Heller. Pro: A. Heller Screenplay: A. Heller & George St. George. (Contemporary.) First shown at the Paris–Pullman, Jan. 1968. 87 Mins.

Cuckoo Patrol
Little comedy with music to star and exploit the talents of the pop group *The Dreamers*, with their leader *Freddie*. Rest of cast: *Kenneth Connor, Victor Maddern, John Le Mesurier, Arthur Mullard, Ernest Clarke, Basil Dignam, Michael Brennan, Neil McCarthy, Jack Lambers, Joe Gibbont, Vic Wise, Dominic Pye, Bill Turney, Roger Avon, Anthony Buckingham, John Ross, Victor Platt, Dan Cornwall, Lew Marco*. Dir: Duncan Wood. Pro: Maurice J. Wilson. Screenplay: Lew Schwarz. (Grand National.) Rel: July 16. 76 Mins.

Custer of the West
Very long, giant-scale Western about the famous General from the time he victoriously concluded his Civil War career until, still hungry for glory, he allowed himself to be lured into a trap by the Redskins at Little Big Horn and massacred – that famous "General Custer's Last Stand". Made in Spain, finely photographed and with a grand performance by *Robert Shaw* in the title role. Rest of cast: *Mary Ure, Jeffrey Hunter, Ty Hardin, Charles Stalnaker, Robert Hall, Lawrence Tierney, Kieron Moore, Marc Lawrence, Robert Ryan*. Dir: Robt. Siodmak. Pro: I. Lerner. Screenplay: B. Gordon & J. Halevy. (Louis Dolivet/Philip Yordan–Security–Cinerama Int.) First shown in Cinerama at Casino, Nov., 1967. Rel: May 26. (Colour.) 144 Mins.

Dancing the Sirtaki – Diplopenies
Delightfully simple and unpretentious little Greek musical, with plenty of dancing and exciting bouzoukia playing against sunny backgrounds of the port of Piraeus. All about a handsome housepainter, *Dimitri Papamichael*, who becomes a cabaret star; and his lovely and jealous young wife, *Alice Vouyouklaki*, who also makes the grade in the same profession. Rest of cast: *Rica Dialyna, Dionyses Papayannopoulo, Vassali Avlonitis*. Dir: George Scalenakis. Screenplay: Alecos Sakellarios. (Gala.) First shown at the Continentale, Aug. 1967. 77 Mins.

A Dandy in Aspic
Somewhat gloomy and certainly incredible espionage piece which presents *Laurence Harvey* as a double-spy presented by his British masters with the difficult assignment of rubbing out his other, Russian spy half and getting no help from his Russian masters when they judge he's of no more use to them. Rest of cast: *Tom Courtenay, Mia Farrow, Lionel Stander, Harry Andrews, Peter Cook, Per Oscarsson, Barbara Murray, Norman Bird, Michael Trubshawe, Richard O'Sullivan, Geoffrey Denton, Geoffrey Lumsden, James Cossins, Calvin Lockhart, Geoffrey Bayldon, John Bird, Michael Pratt, Monika Dietrich, Lockwood West, Arthur Hewlett, Vernon Dobtcheff, Paulene Stone*. Dir & Pro: Anthony Mann – who died while working on the film on location in Berlin, star Harvey stepping in to finish it. Screenplay: Derek Marlowe. (Columbia.) Rel: April 28. (Pan & T.) 108 Mins.

Danger Route
Highly complicated espionage piece with *Richard Johnson* as the ex-Commando British agent who gets a bit tired of rubbing out various people for his M.I.5 bosses but is always persuaded by fair means, or foul, to carry on. Rest of cast: *Carol Lynley, Barbara Bouchet, Sylvia Syms, Diana Dors, Harry Andrews, Gordon Jackson, Maurice Denham, Sam Wanamaker, David Bauer, Julian Chagrin, Reg Lye*. Dir: Seth Holt. Pro: Max J. Rosenberg & Milton Subotsky. Screenplay: Meade Roberts. (U.A.) Rel: Dec. 17. (D.) 92 Mins.

Dark Nights in St. Pauli
German film set largely in that district of Hamburg and concerned with the police efforts to track down a gang of drug runners and white slavers. (Amanda.) First shown at Jacey–Tatler, May, 1968.

Day of the Evil Gun
Western: *Glenn Ford* (ex-husband) and *Arthur Kennedy* (would-be husband) reluctantly combining forces in order to get pretty *Barbara Babcock* and her two daughters back from the Indians who have kidnapped her and then sold her to another tribe. Rest of cast: *Dean Jagger, John Anderson, Paul Fix, Nico Mibardos, Dean Stanton, Pilar Pellicer, Parley Baer, Royal Dano, Ross Elliott, James Griffith*. Dir & Pro: Jerry Thorpe. Screenplay: C. M. Warren & E. Bercovici. (M-G-M.) Rel: May 5. (Pan & Metrocolor.) 90 Mins.

Days of Desire – Ils Sont Nus
French shock sex film about a strange family who live in poverty in a disused old hut on the shores of the sea and the desire and death that go hand-in-hand in the dunes. Cast: *Catherine Ribeiro, Alain Saury, Jacques Normand, Gerard Dessalles-Isabelle, Rita Maiden*.

Dir: Claude Pierson. (Schulman.) First shown at Cameo, Victoria. (C.) 90 Mins.

Dead Heat on a Merry-Go-Round
Pretty wild but sometimes wonderful and always firmly director-writer-stamped comedy from Bernard Girard which relates the story of a super-con man who wins a bank (by stealing its content) but loses a larger, easier fortune (which after he has left her comes to the girl he married for convenience). Cast: *James Coburn, Camilla Sparv, Aldo Ray, Nina Wayne, Robert Webber, Rose Marie, Todd Armstrong, Marian Moses, Michael Strong, Severn Darden, James Westerfield, Philip E. Pine, Simon Scott, Ben Astar, Michael St Angel, Lawrence Mann, Alex Rodine, Albert Nalbandian, Tyler McVey, Roy Glenn.* Dir & Written: Bernard Girard. Pro: Carter DeHaven. (DeHaven–Girard–Columbia.) Rel: Dec. 3. (T.) 108 Mins.

The Deadly Bees
Whodunnit thriller about a bee-keeper who breeds a swarm of winged killers that sting to his orders and what happens when he starts to put them to work. Cast: *Suzanna Leigh, Frank Finlay, Guy Doleman, Catherine Finn, John Harvey, Michael Ripper, Anthony Bailey.* Dir: Freddie Francis. Pro: Max J. Rosenberg & Milton Subotsky. Screenplay: R. Bloch & A. Marriott. (Paramount.) Rel: Dec. 10. (T.) 83 Mins.

Deadly Roulette
Intricate espionage mystery with *Robert Wagner* fighting his way through a haze of strange happenings which lead him to think he holds the secret of some mysterious and deadly organisation. Rest of cast: *Peter Lawford, Lola Albright, Walter Pidgeon, Jill St. John, Michael Ansara, Len Lesser, Alberto Morin, Ralph Smiley, Tiger Joe Marsh, Joni Webster, Lyn Peters, Asher Dann, Peter Camlin, Frank Delfino, Francisco Ortega, Victor Dunlop, Horst Ebersberg, Peter Pascal, Rolf Sedan.* Dir: Wm. Hale. Pro: Jack Laird. Screenplay: Gene Kearney. (U.I.–Rank.) Rel: March 3. (T.) 90 Mins.

The Defector
Complicated espionage story with the late *Montgomery Clift* (this was his last film) as the unwilling American agent in East Germany apparently trying to help a Soviet scientist to defect to the West and finding that in fact the whole set of plots and counter-plots are far more tangled than he at first imagines. Rest of cast: *Hardy Kruger, Macha Meril, Roddy McDowall, David Opatoshu, Christine Delaroche, Hannes Messemer, Karl Leiffen.* Dir & Pro: Raoul Levy. Screenplay: R. Guenette & R. Levy. (P. E. C. F. Rhein Main Film–Warner–Pathe.) Rel: Oct. 1. 106 Mins.

The Dirty Dozen
Good, well-handled war story about a company of U.S. rapers and killers who are given the opportunity to expiate their crimes by volunteering to train for and take part in a desperate pre-D-Day Commando raid behind the German lines in France. Cast: *Lee Marvin, Ernest Borgnine, Charles Bronson, Jim Brown, John Cassavetes, Richard Jaeckel, George Kennedy, Trini Lopez, Ralph Meeker, Robert Ryan, Telly Savalas, Donald Sutherland, Clint Walker, Robert Webber, Tom Busby, Ben Carruthers, Stuart Cooper, Robert Phillips, Colin Maitland, Al Mancini.* Dir: Robt. Aldrich. Pro: Kenneth Hyman. Screenplay: Lukas Heller & Nunnanly Johnson. (Hyman–M-G-M.) Rel: Oct. 22. (Repeat Gen Rel: Jan. 7). (70mm & Metrocolor.) 150 Mins.

Divorce, American Style
A cynical, satirical celluloid examination of wedded bliss and ex-wedded poverty in the United States, where the law takes so much from the husband at divorce he is driven to desperately strive to marry off his ex-wife so that he can be freed of the burden of the enormous alimony and start to live again. Illustrated by the story of *Dick Van Dyke* and *Debbie Reynolds*, who lightly dissolve their 19-year-old marriage and then find the horrors that lie beyond the moment of legal freedom. A serious problem amusingly and wittily stated. Rest of cast: *Jason Robards, Jean Simmons, Van Johnson, Joe Flynn, Shelley Berman, Martin Gabel, Lee Grant, Pat Collins, Tom Bosley, Emmaline Henry, Dick Gautier, Tim Matthieson, Gary Goetzman, Eileen Brennan, Shelley Morrison, Bella Bruck, John J. Anthony.* Dir: Bud Yorking. Written & Pro: Norman Lear. (Tandem–Columbia.) Rel: Sept. 10. (T.) 109 Mins.

Doctor Faustus
The Oxford University Dramatic Society's production of the Christopher Marlowe play, written in 1588, about a learned professor whose thirst for ever more erudition (and, more especially, fair women!) leads him into making a bargain with the devil, exchanging his soul for more knowledge – and a wordless *Elizabeth Taylor*. *Richard Burton* as the doctor and *Andreas Teuber* brilliant as Mephistopheles. Colourful, magical, and with touches of sheer pantomime! Rest of cast: *Ian Marter, Elizabeth O'Donovan, David McIntosh, Jeremy Eccles, Ram Chopra, Richard Carwardine, Richare Heffer, Hugh Williams, Gwydion Thomas, Nicholas Loukes, Richard Durden-Smith, Patrick Barwise, Adrian Benjamin, Jeremy Chandler, Angus McIntosh, Ambrose Coghill, Anthony Kaufmann, Julian Wontner, Richard Harrison, Nevil Coghill, Michael Menaugh, John Sandbach, Sebastian Walker, R. Peverello, Maria Aitken, Valerie James, Bridget Coghill, Petronella Pulsford, Susan Watson, Jacqueline Harvey, Sheila Dawson, Carolyn Bennitt, Jane Wilford.* Dir: R. Burton & Nevill Coghill. Pro: R. Burton & R. McWhorter. Screenplay: N. Coghill. (Burtons–Columbia.) Rel: Floating (T.) 93 Mins.

Don't Look Now . . . we're being shot at!
French-made, English-dubbed comedy about the crew of an English bomber who bail out over Paris during the war and are sheltered and helped to escape back to Britain, in a whirlwind comic way, by *Bourvil, Louis de Funes* and *Marie Dubois*. Rest of cast: *Terry-Thomas, Benno Sterzenbach, Mike Marshall, Claudio Brook, Andrea Parisy, Marie Marquet, Colette Brosset.* Dir & Written: Gerard Oury. Pro: R. Dorfmann. (Rank.) Rel: June 2. (E & Pan.) 116 Mins.

Don't Make Waves
Loosely jointed, pretty crazy comedy about marital meanderings in California, where *Tony Curtis* is a fast-buck maker and *Claudia Cardinale* his femme fatale. Rest of cast: *Robert Webber, Joanna Barnes, Sharon Tate, David Draper, Mort Sahl, Dub Taylor, Ann Elder, Chester Yorton, Reg Lewis, Marc London, Douglas Henderson, Sarah Selby, Mary Grace Canfield, Julie Payne, Holly Haze, Edgar Bergen, Paul Barselow, George Tyne, David Fresco, Gil Green, Eduardo Tirella.* Dir: Alexander Mackendrick. Pro: Martin Ransohoff & John Calley. Screenplay: Ira Wallach & Geo Kirgo. (Ransohoff–M-G-M.) Rel: Aug. 27. (Pan & Metrocolor.) 85 Mins.

The Doomsday Flight
Drama on board a jet air-liner when it is revealed there is a bomb on board! While the search for the time-bomb goes on, search is made, too, for the criminal who has placed it there and is now demanding a hundred thousand dollar ransom to divulge the hiding place! Cast: *Jack Lord, Van Johnson, Edmond O'Brien, Katherine Crawford, John Saxon, Richard Carlson, Tom Simcox, Michael Sarrazin, Malachi Throne, Edward Faulkner, Jan Shepard, Edward Asner, Don Stewart, Robert Pickering, Gregg Morris, David Lewis, Howard Caine, John Kellogg, Bernadette Hale, Celia Lovsky, Dee Pollock, J. Wilbanks.* Dir: Wm. Graham. Pro: Frank Price, Screenplay: Rod Serling. (U.I.–Rank.) Rel: April 14. (T.) 97 Mins.

Double Trouble
Elvis Presley sings, fights and laughs his way through his usual mixture: nine songs and a light-hearted story about his discovery that while apparently the target for some unpleasant happenings, the real intended victim is the young English girl who is romantically chasing him. Rest of cast: *Annette Day, John Williams, Yvonne Romain, The Wiere Brothers, Chips Rafferty, Norman Rossington, Monty Landis, Michael Murphy, Leon Askin, John Alderson, Stanley Adams, Maurice Marsac, Walter Burke, Helene Winston.* Dir: Norman Taurog. Pro: Judd Bernard & Irwin Winkler. Screenplay: Jo Heims. (M-G-M.) Rel: Aug. 13. (Pan & Colour.) 90 Mins.

Dutchman
Screen adaptation of the Leroi Jones stage play about a little white trollop who excites, tempts and reviles to the edge of madness her little negro co-traveller on a New York subway train. It has all sorts of significance if you care to see it. Quite magnificently acted by *Shirley Knight* as the girl (she won the Best Actress Award at the Venice Festival for this performance) and *Al Freeman Junior* as the boy. Dir: Anthony Harvey. Pro: Gene Persson. (Planet.) First shown at Academy Two, Nov. 1967. 57 Mins.

Eight on the Run
Bob Hope, with his seven children and a dog, fleeing from justice when he suspects that the bank he works at suspects him of embezzling $50,000! After him, detective *Jonathan Winter* and romantically inclined *Shirley Eaton*. Rest of cast: *Phyllis Diller, Jill St. John,*

Stacey Maxwell, Kevin Brody, Robert Hope, Glenn Gilger, Avis Hope, Debi Storm, Michael Freeman, Austin Willis, Peter Leeds. Dir: George Marshall. Pro: Bill Lawrence. Screenplay: Bob Fisher, Arthur Marx, A. E. Lewin & Burt Styler. (U.A.) Rel: June 9. (Colour.) 106 Mins.

El Dorado
Classical, large-scale Western about a gunfighter, craggy, tough, but basically honest (*John Wayne*) who, about to take up a job with a bad range baron, decides on the advice of his Texas ex-Army buddie, now sheriff (*Robert Mitchum*) to turn it down and support the opposing side (the law) in a bitter range war for the water the baron wants in order to expand his Empire. It all ends with a wonderful showdown battle between the crippled pals and their frail support and the hired army of gunmen on the other side. Superbly acted. Rest of cast: *James Caan, Charlene Holt, Michele Carey, Arthur Hunnicutt, R. G. Armstrong, Edward Asner, Paul Fix.* Dir & Pro: Howard Hawks. Screenplay: Leigh Brackett – based on the novel, "The Stars in their Courses". (Paramount.) Rel: Aug. 6. (T.) 127 Mins.

Elvira Madigan
Beautiful Swedish film – directed by Bo Widerberg – based on the true story of an Army officer who fell madly in love with a pretty tight-rope walker, took her off to Denmark and there spent an idyllic few months before the inevitably tragic ending. Apart from the perfect atmosphere of passion, the director has used colour with outstanding brilliance and achieved an unforgettable picture with only a few flaws. Cast: *Thommy Berggren, Pia Dagermark.* Dir & Written: Bo Widerberg. (Academy.) First shown at Academy One, March, 1968. (Colour.) 102 Mins.

The Empty Canvas
An adaptation of the Alberto Moravia novel, about a young artist's struggles against the great physical attractions of a quite lovely but utterly immoral artist's model, something his possessive mother can't overcome though she's pretty horrified when she walks into one of her rooms one day and finds her son covering his nude mistress with paper money! Cast: *Bette Davis, Horst Bucholz, Catherine Spaak, Isa Miranda, Lea Padovani, Daniela Rocca, Georges Wilson, Leonida Repaci, Luigi Giuliani, Denny Parsi, Daniela Calvino.* Dir: Damiano Damiani. Screenplay: D. Damiani, T. Guerra & U. Liberatore. Pro: Carlo Ponti. (J. Levine–Planet.) Rel: Floating. 118 Mins.

The Endless Summer
A feature-film about the pleasures of surf riding as experienced round the world by two experts. With *Mike Hynson* & *Robert August*. Dir & Pro (and narrated by): Bruce Brown. (Columbia.) Rel: Floating. (T.) 92 Mins.

Every Young Man
Amusing two-part comedy by one of the gifted new crop of young Czech directors, which with observation and warm humour follows the adventures of two young soldiers whiling away a day in a boring small town and then returning to the even more boring routine of the garrison. Cast: *Hana Ruzickova, Pavel Landovsky, Ivan Vyskocil.* Dir & Written: Pavel Juracek. (Contemporary.) First shown at Cameo Poly, Sept. 1967. 85 Mins.

Eye of the Devil
Highly incredible, purply-melodramatic story about a noble French family whose living head is sacrificed in a black magic ritual every time that the vines fail three years in a run! This time it is Marquis *David Niven* who's for "the chop", to the sorrow of his frantically worried wife *Deborah Kerr*. Well, well! Rest of cast: *Donald Pleasence, Edward Mulhare, Flora Robson, Emlyn Williams, Sharon Tate, David Hemmings, John Le Mesurier, Suky Appleby, Donald Bissett, Robert Duncan, Michael Miller.* Dir: J. Lee Thompson. Pro: John Calley & Martin Ransohoff. Screenplay: R. Estridge & D. Murphy. (Filmways–M-G-M.) Rel: March 31. 90 Mins.

The Fabulous Adventures of Marco Polo
Spectacular relating of the famous travels of Venetian Polo (*Horst Bucholz*), who set out one November morning in the year 1271 and travelled through the Holy Land and Asia to Mongolia and China and the great Emperor Kublai Khan (*Anthony Quinn*). Rest of cast: *Omar Sharif, Elsa Martinelli, Akim Tamiroff, Gregoire Aslan, Robert Hossein, Orson Welles, Massimo Girotti, Folco Lulli, Lee Sue Moon, Bruno Cremer, Jacques Monod, Mica Orlovic, Mansoureh Rihai.* Dir: Denys de la Patelliere & Noel Howard. (Golden Era.) Rel: Floating. (Francoscope & E.) 115 Mins.

Far from Vietnam
A compilation, protest film in which six directors try to prick the moviegoers' conscience; only occasionally effective but honest, and finally fairly successful in its aim. Dir: Alain Resnais, William Klein, Joris Ivens, Agnes Varda, Claude Lelouch, Jean-Luc Godard. (Contemporary.) First shown at Paris–Pullman, Dec. 1967. 115 Mins.

The Fastest Guitar Alive
Light, musical Western with *Roy Orbison*, playing one of two Confederate spies (other, *Sammy Jackson*) who with a Medicine Wagon and load of pulchitrude, plans to steal the South's gold from the Bank in 'Frisco. And Roy's guitar is a new secret weapon – it not only produces music, but it can in a tight spot spit bullets as well! Rest of cast: *Maggie Pierce, Joan Freeman, Lyle Bettger, John Doucette, Patricia Donahue, Ben Cooper, Ben Lessy, Douglas Kennedy, Len Hendry, Iron Eyes Cody, Sam the Sham, Wilda Taylor, Victoria Carroll, Maria Korda, Popee Gamin.* Dir: Michael Moore. Pro: Sam Katzman. Screenplay: R. E. Kent. (Four-Leaf–M-G-M.) Rel: Feb. 25. (Metrocolour.) 87 Mins.

Fathom
Wild, light-hearted and pretty weird thriller set in Spain and centred around the considerable physical charms of *Raquel Welch*, who plays a sky-diver who becomes involved in espionage and crime and gets pretty confused as to who is who and which is which; a feeling you'll probably share. Rest of cast. *Tony Franciosa, Ronald Fraser, Greta Chi, Richard Briers, Tom Adams, Clive Revill, Reg Lye, Ann Lancaster, Elizabeth Ercy, Tutte Lemkow.* Dir: Leslie Martinson. Pro: John Kohn. Screenplay: Lorenzo Semple Jr. (Fox.) Rel: Oct. 1. (D.) 99 Mins.

Firecreek
Western. *James Stewart* as the easy-going farmer and part-time sheriff who is suddenly confronted with a gang of badmen led by the wily *Henry Fonda* and forced into a struggle to the death in order to rouse the community to resist the gang's intention to take over and run the place. Rest of cast: *Gary Lockwood, Dean Jagger, Ed Begley, Jay C. Flippen, Jack Elam, James Best, Barbara Luna, Jacqueline Scott, Brooke Bundy, J. Robert Porter, Morgan Woodward, John Qualen, Louise Latham, Athena Lorde, Harry "Slim" Duncan, Inger Stevens.* Dir: Vincent McEveety. Pro: P. Leacock. Screenplay: Calvin Clements. (Warner–Pathe.) Rel: April 21. (Pan & T.) 104 Mins.

The First Teacher
The struggle of a largely illiterate teacher to bring some sort of light to a small and wholly illiterate Russian village in the 1920's. Cast: *Natalia Arinbasarova, Bolot Beishenaliev.* Dir: Andrei Konchalovsky. Written: C. Aytmatov & B. Dobrodeyev. (Kirghizfilm Mosfilm–Contemporary.) First shown at Paris–Pullman, Sept. 1967. 98 Mins.

Fitzwilly Strikes Back
Dame Edith Evans as a delightfully dotty old lady whose good deeds and financial contributions to charity are underwritten by the crooked and devious plans of her faithful butler *Dick Van Dyck* and his loyal staff, all of whom are in league to prevent the truth of her present pennilessness percolating through to her. Newcomer, secretary *Barbara Feldon*, and a budding romance between her and the butler nearly ruins everything – but a fairy story chance brings a happy ending. Rest of cast: *John McGiver, Harry Townes, John Fiedler, Norman Fell, Cecil Kellaway, Stephen Strimpell, Anne Seymour, Helen Kleeb, Sam Waterston, Paul Reed, Albert Carrier, Nelson Olmstead, Dennis Cooney, Noam Pitlik, Antony Eustrel, Laurence Naismith, Karrin Norris, Patience Cleveland, Lew Brown, Monroe Arnold, Bob Williams, Billy Halop.* Dir: Delbert Mann. Pro: Walter Mirisch. Screenplay: Isobel Lennart. (Mirisch–U.A.) Rel: June 23. (D & Pan.) 102 Mins.

Five Golden Dragons
Bob Cummings as the American playboy type who comes to Hong Kong and is immediately involved in a top-brass smuggling ring, in murder and girls! Rest of cast: *Rupert Davies, Margaret Lee, Maria Perschy, Kalus Kinski, Maria Rohm, Sieghardt Rupp, Brian Donlevy, Dan Duryea, Christopher Lee, George Raft.* Dir: J. Summers. Pro: H. A. Towers. Screenplay: P. Welbeck. (Anglo–Warner–Pathe.) Rel: Jan. 28. (T. & Techniscope.) 70 Mins.

Follow That Camel
One of the Peter Rogers "Carry On" style comedies. It, not uproariously, lampoons the Foreign Legion, where *Kenneth Williams* as a clipped-haired Commandant steals most of the fun. Rest of cast: *Phil Silvers, Jim Dale, Peter Butterworth, Charles Hawtrey, Anita Harris, Joan Sims, Bernard Bresslaw, Angela Douglas, John Bluthal, Larry Taylor, William Hurndell, Gertan Klauber, Peter Gilmore, Julian Orchard, William Mervyn, Julian Holloway, Vincent Ball, David Glover*, Dir: Gerald Thomas. Pro: Peter Rogers. Screenplay: Talbot Rothwell. (Rogers–Rank.) Rel: Jan. 7. (Colour.) 95 Mins.

For a Few Dollars More
The second in the series of European (a Spanish-Italian-German collaboration: made in Spain) Westerns about the Bounty Hunter, The Man-With-No-Name (*Clint Eastwood*). This time he teams up with another head-hunter, *Lee Van Cleef*, to bring in the high-priced mad killer (*Gian Maria Volonte*) and his robber gang. Brutal, cliché-ridden, but wonderfully visual, finely directed and fascinating to watch. Well acted, too, by the three main characters. Rest of cast: *Josef Egger, Rosemary Dexter, Mara Krup, Klaus Kinski, Aldo Sambrell, Luigi Pistilli, Benito Stefanelli.* Dir: Sergio Leone. Pro: Alberto Grimaldi. Screenplay: Luciano Vincenzoni. (U.A.) Rel: Oct. 22. (E.) 128 Mins.

Fortunat
A restrained, impressive Bourvil – as the bibulous poacher of the title – who during the war is recruited into the Resistance and assigned the task of squiring well-born refugee *Michele Morgan* and her children to Toulouse, where they try to settle down. Rest of cast: *Rosy Varte, Teddy Bilis, Frederic Robert, Patrick Millow, Gaby Morlay.* Dir & Written (with Pierre Corti): Alex Joffe. (Cinetel–Contemporary.) First shown at Cameo–Poly, Sept. 1967. 120 Mins.

40 Guns to Apache Pass
Western, with *Audie Murphy* as the Cavalry Captain struggling, against war-pathing Indians and his own traitorous men, to get the guns though, the arrival of which alone can save the situation. Rest of cast: *Michael Burns, Kenneth Tobey, Laraine Stephens, Robert Brubaker, Michael Blodgett, Michael Keep, Kay Stewart, Kenneth MacDonald, Byron Morrow, Willard Willingham, Ted Gehring, James Beck.* Dir: Wm. Witney. Pro: Grant Whytock. Written: W. & M. Willingham. (Admiral–Columbia.) Rel: Jan. 28. (T.) 96 Mins.

The Fox
Sensitive screen treatment of the D. H. Lawrence novella about two girls who work and live together on a remote Canadian farm whose relationship is sharpened and smashed by the advent on the scene of a young man who falls in love with one of them. Cast: *Sandy Dennis, Keir Dullea, Anne Heywood.* Dir: Mark Rydell. Pro: Raymond Stross. Screenplay: L. J. Carlino & Howard Koch. (Warner–Seven Arts.) Rel: June 16. 110 Mins.

Frozen Alive
Drama about a scientist trying a "deep-freeze" experiment, using himself as "guinea-pig". When the police arrive to ask questions about his wife's mysterious death they find their prime suspect frozen, and his pretty assistant unable to revive him. Cast: *Mark Stevens, Marianne Koch, Delphi Lawrence, Joachim Hansen, Walter Rilla, Wolfgang Lukschy, Helmuth Weiss, John Longden, Albert Bessler, Sigurd Lohde, Wolfgang Gunther.* Dir: Bernard Knowles. Pro: A. Brauner & Ronald Rietti. Screenplay: Evelyn Frazer. (Butchers.) Rel: July 16. 63 Mins.

The Further Perils of Laurel and Hardy
Compilation film of extracts of some of the funniest sequences from old Laurel and Hardy movies. Great, classic comedy. Pro. (& Screenplay) Robt Youngson. (Fox.) Rel: June 16. 99 Mins.

The Game is Over–La Curée
Roger Vadim's adaptation of the Zola novel about a young man who falls in love with his beautiful young stepmother: all this updated to the Paris of today. Cast: *Jane Fonda, Peter McEnery, Michel Piccoli, Tina Marquand, Jacques Monod, Simone Valere, Germaine Montero.* Dir: Roger Vadim. Screenplay: Jean Cacau, R. Vadim, & B. Frechtman. (Marceau–Cocinor–Columbia.) Rel: Floating. (Pan & T.) 95 Mins.

Games
Odd little story about a bored and rich young couple whose twisted idea of fun leads them to carry out a series of cruel practical jokes which develop into a clever murder plot. Cast: *Simone Signoret, James Caan, Katharine Ross, Don Stroud, Kent Smith, Estelle Winwood, Marjorie Bennett, Ian Wolfe, Antony Eustrel, Eloise Hardt, George Furth, Carmen Phillips, Peter Brocco, Florence Marly, Carl Guttenberger, Pitt Herbert, Stuart Nisbet, Kendrick Huxham, Richard Guizon.* Dir: Curtis Harrington. Pro: Geo. Edwards. Screenplay: Gene Kearney. (U.I.–Rank.) Rel: March 31. 100 Mins.

The Ghost Goes Gear
Feature pop musical woven around the talents of the *Spencer Davis Group*: with a whispy story about a beat group trying to establish a "Stately Home". Rest of cast: *Nicholas Parsons, Sheila White, Lorne Gibson, Arthur Howard, Acker Bilk and the Paramount Jazz Band, Lorne Gibson Trio, Dave Berry, The M.6., The Three Bells, St. Louis Union, etc.* Dir: Hugh Gladwish. Pro: Harry Field. Screenplay: Roger Dunton & Hugh Gladwish. (Assoc.–Warner-Pathe.) Rel: Sept. 17. 41 Mins.

The Gnome-Mobile
Typical Disney whimsy about a Canadian Redwoods tycoon (*Walter Brennan*) and his grandchildren ("Mary Poppins" youngsters *Matthew Garber* and *Karen Dotrice*) and the way they meet and become friendly with a two-foot-tall gnome, for whom they all go off seeking a suitable feminine companion! Rest of cast: *Richard Deacon, Tom Lowell Sean McClory, Ed Wynn, Jerome Cowan, Charles Lane, Norman Grabowski, Gil Lamb, Maudie Prickett, Ellen Corby, Frank Cady, Cami Sebring, Pamela Gail.* Dir: Robt. Stevenson. Pro: James Algar. Screenplay: Ellis Kadison. (Disney.) Rel: July 23. (T.) 84 Mins.

Go With Matt Monro
Half-hour musical which moves from London to Rome and back, against which backgrounds he, and guests *Roy Castle* and *Marian Montgomery*, sing a few songs and have some laughs. Dir: Bertram Tyrer. Pro: Harry Field. (Assoc. British–Warner-Pathe.) Rel: July 2. (E.) 27 Mins.

The Gospel According to St. Matthew
Pasolini's milestone in screened biblical history: a comprehensive life of Christ told with humility and self-confidence, resulting in a sense of total reality never previously achieved in a film. There is an unflinching look at the Agony in the Garden and the journey to the Crucifixion; and an interested onlooker's view at Pilate's mock trial. With *Enrique Irazoqui* as Jesus suggesting purposefulness, deliberation and, finally, resignation. Rest of cast: *Margherita Caruso, Susanna Pasolini, Marcello Morante, Mario Socrate, Settimio di Porto, Otello Sestili, Ferruccio Nuzzo, Giacomo Morante, Alfonso Gatto, Enzo Siciliano, Giorgio Agamben, Guido Cerretani, Luigi Barbini, Marcello Galdini, Elio Spaziani, Rosario Migale, Rodolfo Wilcock, Alessandro Tasca, Amerigo Bevilacqua, Francesco Leonetti, Paola Tedesco, Franca Cupane, Rossana Di Rocco, Eliseo Boschi, Natalia Ginzburg.* Dir: Pier Paolo Pasolini. Pro: Alfredo Bini. (Arco Films, Rome–Compton.) First shown at Paris–Pullman, June 1967. 135 Mins.

Grand Prix
John Frankenheimer's large-scale motor racing film, bringing to the great Cinerama screen all the thrills of driving a car at 180 m.p.h. along the Monza track. The year's Grand Prix meetings are the background for a slim little story about some of the drivers and the women in their lives, with *Eva Marie Saint* giving a wonderful performance as the American girl in love with "tired" Ferrari ace *Yves Montand* – also superb. Rest of cast: *James Garner, Toshiro Mifune, Brian Bedford, Jessica Walter, Antonio Sabato, Francoise Hardy, Adolfo Celi, Claude Dauphin, Enzo Fiermonte, Genevieve Page, Jack Watson, Donal O'Brien, Jean Michaud, Albert Remy, Rachel Kempson, Ralph Michael, Alan Fordney, Anthony Marsh, Tommy Franklin, Phil Hill, Graham Hill, Bernard Cahier.* Dir: John Frankenheimer. Pro: Edward Lewis. Screenplay: Robert Alan Aurthur. (M-G-M.) Rel: Nov. 12. (Super-Pan & Metrocolor.) 169 Mins.

Grand Slam
Neat crime melodrama about an austere old professor (*Edward G. Robinson*) who retiring after thirty years of teaching decides with the help of his criminal friends to pull off a ten million dollar diamond robbery! And just how, after having seen it all going to plan, including the double-crossing among the crooks, there occurs the final humiliating hitch! Rest of cast: *Janet Leigh, Adolfo Celi, Klaus Kinski, George Rigaud, Robert Hoffman, Riccardo Cucciolla Jussara.*

Dir: Giuliano Montaldo. Pro: H. Colombo & Geo. Papi. Screenplay: Mino Roli. (Jolly–Paramount.) Rel: June 23. 120 Mins.

The Greatest Story Ever Told
George Stevens' serious, more than usually literary telling of the Christ story in terms of Cinerama-cinema. Based on both New and Old Testaments, on the Fulton Oursler book and sundry other sources, it took five years and eight million pounds in cash to make, it is utterly anti-De-Mille in its general austerity and avoidance of anything like sensation or spectacle for their own sakes. And the Christ is played, finely, by *Max von Sydow*. Rest of cast: *Dorothy McGuire, Robert Loggia, Charlton Heston, Martin Landau, Nehemiah Persoff, Joseph Schildkraut, Victor Buono, Robert Busch, John Crawford, Russell Johnson, John Lupton, Abraham Sofaer, Chet Stratton, Ron Whelan, Donald Pleasence, Jose Ferrer, Claude Rains, Richard Conte, Frank De Kova, Joseph Sirola, John Abbott, Rodolfo Acosta, Cyril Delevanti, Mark Lenard, Frank Silvera, Michael Ansara, Philip Coolidge, Dai Jenkins, Joe Perry, Marian Seldes, Michael Anderson, Jun., Robert Blake, Burt Brinckerhoff, John Considine, Jamie Farr, David Hedison, Peter Mann, David McCallum, Roddy McDowall, Gary Raymond, Tom Reese, David Sheiner, Ina Balin, Janet Margolin, Michael Tolan, Sidney Poitier, Joanna Dunham, Carroll Baker, Pat Boone, Van Heflin, Sal Mineo, Shelley Winters, Ed Wynn, John Wayne, Telly Savalas, Angela Lansbury, Johnny Seven, Paul Stewart, Harold J. Stone.* Dir & Pro: Geo. Stevens. Screenplay: J. L. Barrett & G. Stevens. (Stevens–U.A.) Rel: Special Floating. First shown at Casino, April, 1965. (T & Ultra Pan 70.) 201 Mins.

Guess Who's Coming to Dinner
Polished, balanced and superbly acted Stanley Kramer film about racial prejudice which has historical significance in that in it *Spencer Tracy*, who died soon after the movie was completed, gives his last performance: a masterly portrait of a liberal-minded, colour-equality campaigning newspaper editor suddenly confronted by his young daughter with the negro she has decided to marry! Rest of cast: *Sidney Poitier, Katharine Hepburn, Katharine Houghton, Cecil Kellaway, Beah Richards, Roy E. Glenn Sr., Isabell Sanford, Virginia Christine, Alexandra Hay, Barbara Randolph, D'Urville Martin, Tom Heaton, Grace Gaynor, Skip Martin, John Hudkins.* Dir & Pro: S. Kramer. Screenplay: Wm. Rose. (Columbia.) Rel: March 24. (T.) 108 Mins.

A Guide for the Married Man
Neatly and wittily directed – by Gene Kelly – story about the lessons in sophisticated infidelity that practised deceiver *Robert Morse* gives his innocent but willing pupil *Walter Matthau* – lessons which fall down flat when the teacher is himself caught red-handed. Rest of cast: *Inger Stevens, Sue Anne Langdon, Claire Kelly, Linda Harrison, Elaine Devry, Michael Romanoff, Jason Wingreen, Fred Holliday, Pat Becker, Lucille Ball, Jack Benny, Polly Bergen, Joey Bishop, Sid Caesar, Art Carney, Wally Cox, Jayne Mansfield, Hal March, Louis Nye, Carl Reiner, Phil Silvers, Terry-Thomas, Ben Blue, Ann Morgan Guilbert, Jeffrey Hunter, Marty Ingels.* Dir: Gene Kelly. Pro: Frank McCarthy. Screenplay: Frank Tarloff (Fox.) Rel: Sept. C. (Pan & D.) 96 Mins.

Gunn
Quite good, thick-ear detection melodrama with the tough, somewhat mysterious trouble-shooter of the title (*Craig Stevens*) seeking out the killer of the gangster big-shot who once saved his life. All very complicated and difficult to unravel but gripping. Rest of cast: *Laura Devon, Edward Asner, Sherry Jackson, Helen Traubel, Albert Paulsen, Marion Marshall, J. Pat O'Malley, Regis Toomey, Dick Crockett, Charles Dierkof, Jerry Douglas, Ken Wales, George Murdock, Frank Kreig.* Dir: Blake Edwards. Pro: Owen Crump. Screenplay: B. Edwards & W. P. Blatty. (Blake Edwards–Paramount.) Rel: Nov. 26. (T.) 94 Mins.

Guns for San Sebastian
Anthony Quinn in the outsize part of an 18-century outlaw who returns a kindly old priest's succour and shelter by taking on the man's mantle and defending the villagers of San Sebastian against the Injun hordes! Rest of cast: *Anjanette Comer, Charles Bronson, Sam Jaffe, Silvia Pinal, Jorge Martinez de Hoyos, Jaime Fernandez, Rosa Furman, Jorge Russek, Leon Askin, Jose Chavez, Ivan Desny, Fernand Gravet, Pedro Armendariz, Jun., Aurora Clavel, Julia Aldama, Ferrusquilla, Pancho Cordova, Enrique Lucero, Chano Urueta, Noe Murayama, Guillermo Hernandez, Francisco Reiguera, Carlos Berriochea, Armando Acosta, Guy Fox, Rico Lopez.* Dir: Henri Verneuil. Pro: Jacques Bar. Screenplay: James R. Webb. (M-G-M.) Rel: April 28. (Franscope & Metrocolour.) 111 Mins.

The Happening
About a gang of teenage layabouts who suddenly find their joke kidnapping has become deadly serious and has turned horribly sour on them: with the kidnapped (*Anthony Quinn*) being disillusioned during the operation and planning his own special kind of revenge. Rest of cast: *George Maharis, Michael Parks, Robert Walker, Martha Hyer, Faye Dunaway, Milton Berle, Oscar Homolka, Jack Kruschen, Clifton James, Eugene Roche, James Randolph Kuhl, Luke Askew.* Dir: Elliot Silverstein. Pro: Jud Kinberg. Screenplay: F. R. Pierson, J. D. Buchanan & R. Austin. (Sam Spiegel–Columbia.) Rel: Nov. 26. (T.) 91 Mins.

Happy Gipsies . . . .!
Ironically titled Yugo-Slavian prize-winner about the Gipsies living in that country; buying goose feathers from the peasants and re-selling them at a profit, arguing over which territory belongs to who, drinking, beating up their wives, and sometimes fighting to the death over a woman. And the backgrounds are mistily cold, grey-washed and muddy: superbly atmospherically photographed. With music and dancing, too. Cast: *Bekim Fehmiu, Olivera Vučo, Bata Zivojinović, Gordana Jovanović, Mija Aleksić, Rahela Ferari, Severin Bijelić, Etelka Filipovski, Milorad Jovanović, Milivoje Djordjević,* Dir & Written: Aleksandar Petrovic. (Rocee–Schulman & Sen.) First shown at the Cameo Poly, Feb., 1968. (Colour.) 90 Mins.

The Helicopter Spies
That intrepid UNCLE duo Robert – Solo – Vaughn and David – Illya – McCallum in a quick-moving, bright but highly ludicrous adventure in which they chase a new and deadly "thermal prism" weapon which passes from the hands of its not very nice Persian inventor into the even less unscrupulous hands of a would-be world dominator. Rest of cast: *Carol Lynley, Bradford Dillman, Lola Albright, Leo G. Carroll, John Dehner, John Carradine, Julie London, H. M. Wynant, Roy Jenson, Arthur Malet, Kathleen Freeman, Robert Karnes, Barbara Moore, Sid Haig, Lyzanne Ladue, Thordis Brandt.* Dir: Boris Sagal. Pro: Anthony Spinner. Screenplay: Dean Hargrove. (Arena–M-G-M.) Rel: Feb. 25. (Metrocolour.) 93 Mins.

Her Private Hell
The story of a young girl who arrives in town with the hopes of becoming a fashion model, but suddenly finds, after the photographer has seduced her, that she's been used for pornographic pictures. Cast: *Lucio Modunio, Terry Skelton, Pearl Catlin, Daniel Ollier, Jeanette Wild, Mary Land, Robert Creudson.* Dir: Norman J. Warren. Pro: Bachoo Sen. (Piccadilly–Richard Schulman Entertainments.) Rel: Floating. 84 Mins.

Here We Go Round the Mulberry Bush
Clive Donner's with-it, swinging comedy about a young man's sex-searching, disillusion, fulfilment and – once more – sex-searching! Delightfully visual and ironically amusing in parts; less, "poppily", successful at others. Some nice performances from some nice little dollies and a good one by newcomer *Barry Evans*, at his best when least cockney. Rest of cast: *Judy Geeson, Angela Scoular, Sheila White, Adrienne Posta, Vanessa Howard, Diane Keen, Moyra Fraser, Michael Bates, Maxine Audley, Denholm Elliott, Christopher Timothy, Nicky Henson, Allan Warren, Roy Holder, George Layton, Gareth Robinson, Oliver Cotton, Andrew Hamilton, Sally Avory, Erika Raffael, Cavan Kendall, Trevor Jones, Gillie Austin, Christopher Mitchell, Pauline Challoner, Mary Griffiths, Stella Kemble, Angela Pleasence, The Spencer Davis Group.* Dir & Pro: Clive Donner. Screenplay: Hunter Davies. (U.A.) Rel: Feb. 25. (T.) 94 Mins.

The Heroin Gang
Taking time off from UNCLE and sparring partner Solo, *David McCallum* becomes the ace agent from the American Government's Narcotics bureau and as Sol Madrid breaks a Mafia plan for a 25 million-dollar profit on a heroin deal! And David wins and loses, tragically, pretty mobster's moll *Stella Stevens*. Rest of cast: *Telly Savalas, Ricardo Montalban, Rip Torn, Pat Hingle, Paul Lukas, Michael Ansara, Perry Lopez, Michael Conrad, Robert Rockwell, Merritt Bohn, Madge Cameron, Shep Sanders, Henry Escalante, George Sawaya, Ken Del Conte, Robert McNamara.* Dir: Brian C. Hutton. Pro: Hall Bartlett. Screenplay: D. Karp.

(M-G-M.) Rel: March 31. (Pan & Metrocolor.) 89 Mins.

Hondo and the Apaches
A Western introducing to the screen Louis L'Amour's colourful literary character Hondo Lane (*Ralph Taeger*). It's all about a mine-owner (*Robert Taylor*) suddenly confronted by a son (*Randy Boone*) he has never seen. Rest of cast: *Kathie Browne, Michael Rennie, Noah Beery, Gary Clarke, Gary Merrill, John Smith, Buddy Foster, Michael Pate, Victor Lundin, Jim Davis, Steve Marlo, John Pickard, William Bryant*. Dir: Lee H. Katzin. Pro & Written: A. J. Fenady. (M-G-M.) Rel: Aug. 13. (Metrocolor.) 85 Mins.

The Honey Pot
Polished, smoothly-acted film about a very spry and wealthy Englishman (*Rex Harrison*) living in splendour in Venice who gets an idea from a performance of "Volpone" to invite three of his ex-mistresses to visit him on the pretext of his approaching death and watch their reactions to the situation. But when one of the three is murdered the whole thing takes a sudden ugly whodunnit turn. Rest of cast: *Susan Hayward, Cliff Robertson, Capucine, Edie Adams, Maggie Smith, Adolfo Celi, Herschel Bernardi, Hugh Manning, David Dodimead*. Dir, Pro & Screenplay: J. L. Mankiewicz. (Feldman–U.A.) Rel: June 25. (T.) 150 Mins.

Hostile Guns
Western. U.S. Marshal *George Montgomery* taking a prison wagon, with a killer, a couple of thieves and a woman who has shot her lover, back to the far-off penitentiary, and finding it a pretty tough going, what with the killer's ambushing relatives and his own wavering deputy. Rest of cast: *Yvonne de Carlo, Tab Hunter, Brian Donlevy, John Russell, Leo Gordon, Robert Emhardt, Pedro Gonzalez Gonzalez, James Craig, Richard Arlen, Emile Meyer, Donald Barry, Fuzzy Knight, William Fawcett, Joe Brown, Reg Parton, Read Morgan, Eric Cody*. Dir: R. G. Springsteen. Pro: A. C. Lyles. (Paramount.) Rel: Feb. 11. 77 Mins.

Hot Nights in Frankfurt
A story of the vice rings in the German city, which springs into gang warfare following the killing of one well-known prostitute and the beatings up of girls working for the different organisations. Cast: *Vera Tschechowa, Barbara Valentin, Marisa Fiori, Erik Schumann, Richard Munch*. Dir: Marc Danton. (S. F. Film Dist.) Rel: Floating. 77 Mins.

Hour of the Gun
John Sturges Western in which he carries on where his previous (1957) film "Gunfight at the O.K. Corral" left off, with the battle between the Earps and the Clantons. Wyatt, with his brothers killed or crippled, sets out on a grim crusade of revenge, using the law as a cover for his vendetta. Cast: *James Garner, Jason Robards, Robert Ryan, Albert Salmi, Charles Aidman, Steve Ihnat, Michael Tolan, Frank Converse, Sam Melville, Austin Willis, Richard Bull, Larry Gates, Karl Swenson, Bill Fletcher, Robert Phillips, William Schallert, John Voight, Lonnie Chapman, Monte Markham, William Windom, Edward Anhalt, Walter Gregg, David Perna, Jim Sheppard, Jorge Russek*. Dir & Pro: John Sturges. Screenplay: Edward Anhalt. (Mirisch–U.A.) Rel: Dec. 17 (Pan & D.) 101 Mins.

House of a Thousand Dolls
Vincent Price as an evil illusionist who, with the help of his lovely assistant *Martha Hyer*, uses his act as a "front" for his real job of white slaving, storing his "vanishing ladies" in a well-guarded house until the moment of sale! Pity – for him – that he ever decides to add *George Nader's* wife *Ann Smyrner* to his collection, for George, with police help, spoils his whole set-up! Rest of cast: *Wolfgang Kieling, Sancho Gracia, Maria Rohm, Louise Rivera, Jose Jaspe, Juan Olaguivel, Herbert Fuchs, Yelena Samarina, Diane Bond*. And the Dolls: *Andrea Lascelles, Jill Echols, Kitty Swan, Ursula Janis, Loli Munoz, Karin Skarreso, Monique Aime, Lara Lenti, Carolyn Coon, Marisol Anon, Sandra Petrelli, Francoise Fontages*. Dir: Jeremy Summers. Pro: H. A. Towers. Screenplay: Peter Welbeck. (Planet.) Rel: Floating. (T & Techniscope.) 97 Mins.

How I Learned to Love Women
Loosely constructed, lavishly produced and mildly amusing Italian film (actually a Franco–Spanish–Italian production) about a young man, for some reason the oldest pupil at his school, being initiated into the pleasures of sex by the headmaster's young wife, being chased by her maid and thereafter tasting here and tasting there until the young lady who long ago has set her eye on him, pounces and pops him into matrimony. Cast: *Nadja Tiller, Michele Mercier, Elsa Martinelli Anita Ekberg, Romina Power, Zarah Leander, Robert Hoffman*. Dir: Luciano Salce. Pro: Alfonso Sansone & Enrico Chroscicki. Sub-titled. (Eagle.) First shown at Cameo Royal, Feb., 1968. (E.) 109 Mins.

How I Won the War
A lampoon on war in general and war films in particular, an odd mixture of farce, satire and bloody horror, heavy-hammeringly hitting home the ludicrousness of fighting. Gimmicky and without any clearly discernible story. Cast: *Michael Crawford, John Lennon, Roy Kinnear, Lee Montague, Jack MacGowran, Michael Hordern, Jack Hedley, Karl Michael Vogler, Ronald Lacey, James Cossins, Ewan Hooper, Alexander Knox, Robert Hardy, Sheila Hancock, Charles Dyer, Bill Dysart, Paul Danemas, Peter Graven, Jack May, Richard Pearson, Pauline Taylor, John Ronane, Norman Chappell, Bryan Pringle, Fanny Carby, Dandy Nichols, Gretchen, Franklin, John Junkin, John Trenaman, Mick Dillon, Kenneth Colley*. Dir & Pro: R. Lester. Screenplay: Chas. Wood. (U.A.) Rel: Floating (Colour.) 110 Mins.

How to Live with a Neurotic Dog
Half-hour comedy film based on Stephen Baker's American best-seller book about dog's best friend – Man! (Baim–U.A.) Rel: Oct. 22.

How to Save Your Marriage and Ruin Your Life
Comedy about mistaken identities with *Dean Martin* rushing to the rescue of his pal being sued for divorce, and getting mixed up with the mistresses and the misunderstandings. Rest of cast: *Stella Stevens, Eli Wallach, Anne Jackson, Betty Field, Jack Albertson*. Dir., Pro & co-screen played (with Nate Monaster): Stanley Shapiro. (Columbia.) Rel: June 30. (Colour.) 108 Mins.

Hugs and Kisses – Puss Och Kram
Delightfully amusing Swedish comedy from a new young director which takes the old situation of husband, wife, and lodger, and gets quite a lot of fresh fun out of it. Cast: *Sven-Bertil Taube* (hubbie), *Agneta Ekmanner* (wife), *Hakam Serner* (lodger–lover), *Lena Granhagen*. Dir & Screenplay: Jonas Cornell. (Contemporary.) First shown at Paris–Pullman, March, 1968. 94 Mins.

The Human Dutch–Alleman
Bert Haanstra's brilliant, multi-prize-winning documentary which stylishly and with perfect use of the hidden camera captures an illuminating and amusing but also warmly sympathetic picture of the Dutch and their country. Directed and narrated in English by Haastra. (Contemporary.) First shown at the Paris–Pullman, March, 1968. 83 Mins.

Hunger
Strange Scandinavian film based on the Knut Hamsun novel about a young author whose pride and hunger are the main things in life as he struggles for recognition in Oslo in 1890. For his performance in the role *Per Oscarsson* won the Best Actor Award at the Cannes Film Festival. Rest of cast: *Brigitte Federspiel, Sigrid Horne-Rasmussen, Oswald Helmuth*. Dir. & Screenplay: Henning Carlsen. Pro: Bertil Ohlsson. (Scandinavian co-production/Curzon.) First shown at Academy Three, Nov. 1967. 110 Mins.

Hurry Sundown
Otto Preminger film, a straightforward, strong drama of racial intolerance, and greed punished, set against a background of the deep American South, where *Michael Caine*, bounder, tries by fair means and – soon – foul, to remove the two small farmers, one white and one black, who stand in the way of a grandiose land improvement scheme which will bring his wife, and him, a great deal of money. Full of incident, with a number of delightful cameo performances. Rest of cast: *Jane Fonda, John Phillip Law, Diahann Carroll, Rex Ingram, Madeleine Sherwood, Burgess Meredith, Loring Smith, Peter Goff, George Kennedy, Luke Askew, Robert Hooks, Beah Richards, Donna Danton, Frank Converse, William Elder, Steve Sanders, Faye Dunaway, Dawn Barcelona, David Sanders, Michael Henry Roth, Gladys Newman, Joan Parks, John Mark, Doro Merande, Robert C. Bloodwell, Charles Keel, Gene Rutherford, Bill Hart, Dean Smith, Kelly Ross, Ada Hall Covington, Robert Reed, Jim Backus*. Dir & Pro: Otto Preminger. Screenplay: T. C. Ryan & H. Foote. (Paramount.) Rel: Sept. 24. (Pan & T.) 142 Mins.

I'll Never Forget What's 'Isname
Oliver Reed as the advertising exec. who decides to opt

out of the rat race which is his business, forego the comforts and complications of a wife and three mistresses and return to a simple life – but finds it isn't all that simple! Lovely work by *Orsen Welles* and a decidedly promising one by *Carol White*. Rest of cast: *Harry Andrews, Michael Hordern, Wendy Craig, Marianne Faithfull, Norman Rodway, Frank Finlay, Harvey Hall, Ann Lynn, Lyn Ashley, Veronica Clifford, Edward Fox, Stuart Cooper, Roland Curran, Peter Graves, Mark Burns, Mark Eden, Josephine Rueg, Mona Chong, Robert Mill, Terence Seward*. Dir & Pro: M. Winner. Screenplay: Peter Draper. (Scimiter–U.I.) Rel: Feb. 4. (T.) 97 Mins.

In Like Flint
Another in the series of Bond-like espionage comedy-thrillers with Derek Flint – engagingly portrayed by *James Coburn* – officially engaged to destroy a feminine plot to take over the world, and uncovering a plot behind that plot to take over the world from them! Good fun. Rest of cast: *Lee J. Cobb, Jean Hale, Andrew Duggan, Anna Lee, Hanna Landy, Totty Ames, Steve Inhat, Thomas Hasson, Mary Michael, Diane Bond, Jacki Ray, Herb Edelman, Yvonne Craig, Buzz Henry, Henry Wills, Mary Meade French, Erin O'Brien, Ginny Gan, Eve Bruce, Inge Jaklyn, Kaye Farrington, Thordis Brandt, Inga Neilsen, Marilyn Hanold, Pat Becker, Lyzanne La Due and Nancy Stone, W. P. Pear, Sr.* Dir: Gordon Douglas. Pro: Saul David. Screenplay: Hal Fimberg. (Saul David–Fox.) Rel: July 30. (C & D.) 115 Mins.

In the Heat of the Night
Whodunnit with racial undercurrents: set in a steaming hot Mississippi small town, where the local police chief, a moody, irritable, not too bright a character, with an unwelcome murder on his hands, grows to lean on and finally like the despised "nigger" who, arrested as the first suspect, turns out to be an intelligent, patient and brilliant homicide expert from Philadelphia who follows the leads, sifts the suspects and finally comes up with all the right answers. Cast: *Sidney Poitier, Rod Steiger, Warren Oates, Quentin Dean, James Patterson, William Schallert, Lee Grant, Scott Wilson, Matt Clark, Anthony James, Larry Gates, Kermit Murdock, Khalil Bezaleel, Bea Richards, Peter Whitney, William Watson, Timothy Scott, Arthur Malet*. Dir: Norman Jewison. Pro: Walter Mirisch. Screenplay: Stirling Silliphant. (Mirisch–U.A.) Rel: Oct. 8. (D.) 110 Mins.

Inside North Vietnam
Feature-length documentary report by Felix Greene, of the C.B.S. and "San Francisco Chronicle", of the three and a half months he spent in that country. (Contemporary.) First shown at Academy Two, Feb. 1968. (Colour.) 81 Mins.

Jack of Diamonds
The last exploit of a trio of expert thieves (*George Hamilton, Joseph Cotten* and *Marie Laforet*) who, having successfully pulled off the job of the Zarahoff diamonds, have to return them in order to gain the freedom of the captured Cotten and promise that they will now all happily retire from the trade! Rest of cast: *Maurice Evans, Wolfgang Preiss, Carroll Baker, Zsa Zsa Gabor, Lilli Palmer*. Dir: Don Taylor. Pro: S. Howard & H. Jedele. Screenplay: J. Dewitt & S. Howard. (Harris Assoc.–Bavaria Atelier Munich–M-G-M.) Rel: Oct. 15. (Pan & Metrocolor.) 90 Mins.

Jack the Giant Killer
Fairy-tale telling the Cornish fable about Pendragon, Prince of Witches, whose efforts to capture the throne are thwarted by a fine young Cornish farmer. Cast: *Kerwin Mathews, Judi Meredith, Torin Thatcher, Walter Burke, Roger Mobley, Barry Kelley, Don Beddoe, Drayton Lummis, Anna Lee, Helen Wallace*. Dir: Nathan Juran. Pro: Edward Small. Screenplay: O. H. Hampton & N. Juran. (Small-Tigron.) Rel: Floating. (T.) 91 Mins.

Jeu de Massacre – Comic Strip Hero
Amusing Alain ("Life Upside Down") Jessua film which seems to put forward the suggestion that maturity brings, or should bring, a philosophy which says that even the small things of today richly savoured – a good cigar, a fine glass of wine, a warm woman! – is better than dreams biting at a dubious tomorrow: the story of an author who comes across a wild, eccentric young man who claims to be the hero the author has created and eventually teams up with the writer's wife and his own mother as the producers of a successful comic strip! Cast: *Jean-Pierre Cassel, Claudine Auger, Michel Duchaussoy, Eleanore Hirt, Anna Gaylor, Guy Saint-Jean, Nancy Holloway*. Dir & Written: A. Jessua. Pro: Rene Thevenet. (A. Balch.) First shown at Cinephone, Dec. 1967. (E.) 95 Mins.

The Jokers
Mildly amusing comedy about a "joke" planned by two brothers for the sake of the notoriety they feel they need; a neat if elaborate plot to steal the Crown Jewels from the Tower of London, a jape which turns sour when, having stolen them, one of the two double-crosses the other and allows him to be sent to prison for the crime. Cast: *Michael Crawford, Oliver Reed, Harry Andrews, James Donald, Daniel Massey, Michael Hordern, Gabriella Licudi, Lotte Tarp, Frank Finlay, Warren Mitchell, Rachel Kempson, Peter Graves, Ingrid Brett, Brian Wilde, Edward Fox, Michael Goodliffe, William Devlin, William Mervyn, William Kendal, Kenneth Colley, Charlotte Curzon, Mark Burns, Brook Williams, Brian Peck, Basil Dignam, John Kidd, Freda Jackson, Nan Munro*. Dir: M. Winner. Pro: M. Foster & Ben Arbeid. Screenplay: Dick Clement & Ian La Frenais. (Gildor–Scimitar–U.I.–Rank.) Rel: July 9. 94 Mins.

Jules Verne's Rocket to the Moon
Wholly delightful and amusing pseudo-science-fiction film about the – finally abortive – efforts of Barnum (*Burl Ives*) to promote the building of a giant rocket which will go to the moon. Rest of cast: *Troy Donahue, Gert Frobe, Terry-Thomas, Hermione Gingold, Daliah Lavi, Lionel Jeffries, Dennis Price, Stratford Johns, Graham Stark, Jimmy Clitheroe, Edward de Souza, Joachim Tege, Joan Sterndale Bennett, Judy Cornwell, Renata Holt, Dan Cressy, Tony Woodruff, Hugh Walters, Audrey Nicholson, Don Bisset*. Dir: Don Sharp. Pro: H. A. Towers. Screenplay: Dave Freeman. (Anglo–Warner-Pathe.) Rel: July 23. (Pan & E.) 101 Mins.

The Jungle Book
Walt Disney's delicious cartoon feature based on Kipling's Mowgli stories, about a small boy's adventures in the jungle, where he has been brought up by the wolves who decide on his tenth birthday he should be returned to the nearest man-village! Wonderfully amusing and entertaining; often visually as well as verbally witty in its caricatures of animals with recognisable human characters and characteristics. The voices of: *Phil Harris* (the Bear), *Sebastian Cabot* (Panther), *Louis Prima* (King Ape), *George Sanders* (Tiger), *Sterling Holloway* (Snake), *J. Pat O'Malley* (Elephant), *Bruce Reitherman* (Boy), *Verna Felton, Clint Howard, Chad Stuart, Lord Timothy Hudson, John Abbott, Ben Wright, Darleen Carr*. Dir: Wolfgang Reitherman. Pro: Walt Disney. (Disney.) Rel: Dec. 24. (T.) 78 Mins.

The Karate Killers
Those two intrepid men from UNCLE, *Robert Vaughn* and *David McCallum*, daring all sorts of danger in order to stop THRUSH getting the murdered professor's recipe for making gold out of seawater! Rest of cast: *Joan Crawford, Curt Jurgens, Herbert Lom, Telly Savalas, Terry-Thomas, Leo G. Carroll, Kim Darby, Diane McBain, Jill Ireland, Danielle De Metz, Irene Tsu, Jim Boles, Philip Ahn, Arthur Gould-Port, Rob Okazaki, Maria Lennard, Lindsay Workman, Rick Traegar, Frank Arno, Julie Ann Johnson, William Burnside, Gloria Neil, William Bryant, Jason Wincreen, Grant Woods, Sharyn Hillyer, Dick Crockett, Paul Bailey, Jerry Summers, Fred Stromsor*. Dir: Barry Shear. Pro: Norman Felton. Screenplay: Norman Hudis. (Arena–M-G-M.) Rel: Aug. 27. 92 Mins.

Khartoum
Vast, Cinerama-ed, chapter of history; telling with sweeping spectacle (several enormously staged battles; great desert panoramas) and a number of performances large and good enough to match the background, the story of General Gordon of Khartoum, his despatch to defend the Sudanese city; his undercover fight with dogged politician Gladstone; his final losing struggle against the fanatical Mahdi; and his martyr's death. *Charlton Heston* as Gordon. Rest of cast: *Laurence Olivier, Richard Johnson, Ralph Richardson, Alexander Knox, Johnny Sekka, Nigel Green, Michael Hordern, Zia Mohyeddin, Hugh Williams, Douglas Wilmer, Edward Underdown, Alec Mango, Jerome Willis, Peter Arne, Alan Tilvern, Michael Anthony, Marne Maitland, Leila, Ronald Leigh Hunt, Ralph Michael*. Dir: Basil Dearden. Pro: Julian Blaustein. (Blaustein–U.A.) Rel: Aug. 13. (Cinerama–Ultra Panavision-Technicolor.) 130 Mins.

Kill a Dragon
Jack Palance and *Fernando Lamas* as two rival tough

characters, junk owners, earning a dubious living along the waterside and on the sea in the Hong Kong district, and fighting for possession of a cargo of Nitra-2 explosives. Rest of cast: *Aldo Ray, Alizia Gur, Kam Tong, Don Knight, Hans Lee, Judy Dan*. Dir: Michael Moore. Pro: Hal Klein. Screenplay; Geo. Svhenck & Wm. Marks. (Schenck–U.A.) Rel: March, 17. (T.) 75 Mins.

Kwaidan – Three Ghost Stories
A collection of three short films – there was originally a fourth as well – which though diverse are all concerned with the supernatural. (*a*) **Black Hair.** About a man who dreams he has found his beloved wife only to wake to find he is clutching a corpse. Cast: *Michiyo Aratama, Misako Watanabe, Rentro Mikuni*. (*b*) **In a Cup of Tea.** About a blind performer who is haunted by a 12th-century battle. Cast: *Kanyemon Nakamura, Noborn Nakaya*. (*c*) **The Story of Hoichi.** A concise and ironic piece of necromacy. Cast: *Katsuo Nakamura, Takashi Shimura, Renatro Mikuni, Joichi Hayashi*. Dir: Masaki Kobayashi. Pro: S. Watasuki. Screenplay: Yoko Mizuki. (TOHO–Orb.) First shown at Cameo–Poly, July 1967. (Tohoscope & E.) 120 Mins.

La Marseillaise
The more or less complete, reconstructed 1937 Jean Renoir classic: a patriotic pageant of history, seen with humanity and balance and, now, a revelation in the sense that in its style, construction and general plan it was years ahead of its time. Cast: *Louis Jouvet, Pierre Renoir, Lise Delamare, Aime Clarion, Irene Joachim, Carette, Gaston Modot, Alibert, Andrex, Ardisson*. Dir: J. Renoir. (Contemporary.) First shown at the Paris–Pullman, Nov. 1967. 130 Mins.

La Nuit Infidel – The Unfaithful Night
A story of dreaming passion and sensuality seen against a background of the Camargue one hot Spring night. *Christiane Minazzoli, Andre Oumansky*. Dir: Antoine d'Ormesson. (New Realm.) First shown at the Cameo, Victoria, May, 1968.

La Religieuse
Jacques Rivette's long banned adaptation of 18th century Diderot story about the misadventures of a young girl shunted into a nunnery; her initial suffering, her later efforts to avoid a too-kind Mother Superior, her escape into the world with a very dubious monk and her discovery of the vice outside. Cast: *Anna Karina, Liselotte Pulver, Micheline Presle, Francine Berge, Christine Lenier, Francisco Rabal, Wolfgang Reichmann, Catherine Diamant, Yori Bertin*. Dir (& written, with Jean Ginalt) Jacques Rivette. (Gala.) First shown at the Cambridge Theatre, Sept. 1967. (E.) 140 Mins.

Lady in a Cage
Brutal, terrible (but legitimately so in view of the film's aim to prove that within every gracious lady there's an animal waiting to spring out!) thriller about a woman trapped in her own elevator and having to watch her house pillaged and one of the pillagers murdered. Then herself taunted and attacked, and driven over the edge, she fights back with ruthless violence. A fine piece of screen Grand Guignol, with *Olivia de Havilland* brilliant as the trapped woman. Rest of cast: *Ann Sothern, Jeff Corey, James Caan, Jennifer Billingsley, Rafael Campos, William Swan, Charles Seel, Scat Man Cruthers*. Dir: Walter Grauman. Pro & Written: Luther Davis. (Davis–Gala.) First shown at Royalty, June 1967. Rel: Floating. 93 Mins.

The Last Safari
Stewart Granger as the white hunter who hates the changes that are coming to the dark continent and sets out on his final safari with the idea of killing the rogue elephant which killed his pal and has come to obsess him. Rest of cast: *Kaz Garas, Gabriella Licudi, Johnny Sekka, Liam Redmond, Eugene Deckers, David Munya, John de Villiers, Wilfred Moore, Jean Parnell, Bill Grant, John Sutton, Kipkoske, Labina*. Dir & Pro: Henry Hathaway. Screenplay: John Gay. (Paramount.) Rel: Dec. 17. (T.) 99 Mins.

Le Depart
Modern, amusing, and technically interesting comedy by promising young Polish director Skolimowski, made in Brussels and about a young man whose love for cars hides his budding love for women. Cast: *Jean-Pierre Leaud, Catherine Duport, Jacqueline Bir, Paul Roland, Leon Dony*. Dir: Jerzy Skolimowski. (Contemporary.) First shown at Paris–Pullman, Jan., 1968. 91 Mins.

Le Vieil Homme et L'Enfant – The Two of Us
Completely winning, lyrical little French film which tells, beautifully, a slight story about a small Jewish boy sent to the country for safety during the war and there winning the heart of the old couple – the husband a wonderful old reactionary and Jew-hater – with whom he stays. Warm, wonderful and with a magnificent performance by *Michel Simon* in the leading role. Rest of cast: *Alain Cohen, Luce Fabiola, Roger Carel, Paul Preboist, Charles Denner, Aline Bertrand, Sylvine Delannoy, Zorica Lozice*. Dir: Claude Berri. Pro: Paul Cadeac. Screenplay: C. Berri & G. Brach. (Gala.) First shown at Gala Royal, Mar., 1968. 87 Mins.

Lenin in Poland
The reconstructed story of the famous Soviet figure from early days to his exile and eventual return to his homeland. Cast: *Maxim Straukh, Anna Lissianskaya, Antonina Pawlyczewa, Ilona Kusmerskaya*. Dir: Sergei Yutkevich. Script: Eugeny Gabrilovich & S. Yutkevich. (Contemporary.) First shown at Paris–Pullman, Nov. 1967. 97 Mins.

Lilith
Warren Beatty as the handsome (ex-Army) occupational therapist who becomes entranced with one of his own lovely patients, dubiously moralled Lilith (*Jean Seberg*), who gradually disillusions him. Technically admirable, variably acted, a little pretentious in the final count but showing a lot of the late Robert Rossen's considerable talent. Rest of cast: *Peter Fonda, Kim Hunter, Anne Meacham, James Patterson, Jessica Walter, Gene Hackman, Robert Reilly, Rene Auberjenois, Lucy Smith, Maurice Brenner, Jeanne Barr, Richard Higgs, Elizabeth Bader, Alice Spivak, Walter Arnold, Kathleen Phelan, Cecilia Ray, Gunnar Peters, L. Jerome Offutt, W. Jerome Offutt, Robert Jolivette, Jason Jolivette, Jeno Mate, Ben Carruthers, Dina Paisner, Pawnee Sills*. Dir, Pro & Screenplay: R. Rossen. (Centaur–Columbia.) Rel: Floating. 114 Mins.

A Lion's Holiday
Utterly captivating Russian colour cartoon film about a clever, kindly circus lion who persuades the circus master to let him go for a holiday with his grandma in Africa, where he soon becomes involved in entertaining the local darkie children. Dir: Fedor Hitrouk. (Contemporary.) Rel: Floating. 20 Mins.

The Long Duel
Elaborate, simple, visually pleasing story – based on a true one it appears – set in India in the 20's and about the way that a rather reluctant *Trevor Howard*, as a cop specially assigned to the task, eventually solves the problem of outlaw Dacoit leader *Yul Brynner* and his gang, a struggle which brings mutual respect and even a certain friendship between the enemies. Rest of cast: *Harry Andrews, Andrew Keir, Charlotte Rampling, Virginia North, Laurence Naismith, Maurice Denham, Imogen Hassall, Paul Hardwick, Antonio Ruiz, David Sumner, Rafiq Anwar, George Pastell, Shivendra Sinha, Zohra Segal, Norman Florence, Kurt Christian, Dino Shafeek, Terry Yorke, Tommy Reeves, Jimmy Lodge, Patrick Newell, Jeremy Lloyd, Terence Alexander, Marianne Stone, Edward Fox, Bakshi Prem, Toni Kanal, Ramon Serrano, Ben Tatar, Aldo Sanbrel, Monisha Bose, Naseem Khan, Shymala Devi, Shirley Sen, Guptha, Jamila Massey*. Dir & Pro: Ken Annakin, Screenplay: Peter Yeldham. (Rank.) Rel: Aug. 27. (Colour & Pan.) 115 Mins.

The Long Hair of Death
Ghoulie-thriller set in the late 15th century and telling a tale of terrible revenge exacted by a mother burned for a witchcraft murder of which she is innocent. Cast: *Barbara Steele, George Ardisson, Halina Zalewska, Robert Rains, Laureen Nuyen, Jean Rafferty, John Carey, Jeffrey Darcey*. Dir: Anthony Dawson. Pro: F. T. Gay. Screenplay: R. Bohr. (Butchers.) Rel: Floating. 96 Mins.

The Loved One
Evelyn Waugh's famous satire on "the American way of death", adapted by Terry Southern and Christopher Isherwood. It's a peep at the cynical unctuousness and false sentimentality of a Californian funeral parlour and cemetery, which may give offence to some, but is brilliantly done – except for a mild romance that doesn't quite fit. Cast: *Robert Morse, Jonathan Winters, Anjanette Comer, Rod Steiger, Dana Andrews, Milton Berle, James Coburn, John Gielgud, Tab Hunter, Margaret Leighton, Liberace, Roddy McDowall, Robert Morley, Lionel Stander, Ayllene Gibbons, Bernie Kopell, Asa Maynor, Alan Napier*. Dir: Tony Richardson. Pro: Martin Ransohoff. (Filmways–M-G-M.) Rel: Floating. 116 Mins.

Lust in the Swamps
Sex-and – suspense story about a girl with a mysterious metal box who is lost and found in the dense swamplands, where her finders, two brothers, desire her and they are all chased by the man from whom she has fled – the owner of that box! Dir: Giannis B. Ionnidis. (Amanda.) First shown at the Jacey–Tatley, May, 1968. 85 Mins.

"M"
A re-presentation of the 1931 Fritz Lang thriller about a child murderer who becomes the object of a hunt of a whole town, one of the greatest screen thrillers ever made, with *Peter Lorre* giving the performance of his lifetime as the killer. Dir: Fritz Lang. (Gala.) Rel: Floating. 99 Mins.

Madchen, Madchen – Girls, Girls
German film about a young girl who upon leaving Remand School meets and falls in love with the son of the man responsible for her original seduction. But her continuation of her affair with the father breaks up the romance and she ends without anyone as father and son try to reach a new relationship. Cast: *Helga Ander, Jurhen Junge, Hellmut Lange, Renate Grosser, Monika Zinnenberg*. Dir: Robt. Fritz. (Amanda.) First shown at Jacey-Tatler, May, 1968. 102 Mins.

Madigan
The story of a few hectic, worrying and tragic hours in one of New York's police districts, with the Commissioner pre-occupied with a number of looming problems and two of his detectives completely obsessed with having to bring in a dangerous murderer and cop-killer within a few hours or else! Cast: *Richard Widmark, Henry Fonda, Inger Stevens, Harry Guardino, James Whitmore, Susan Clark, Michael Dunn, Steve Ihnat, Don Stroud, Sheree North, Warren Stevens, Raymond St. Jacques, Bert Freed, Harry Bellaver, Frank Marth, Lloyd Gough, Virginia Gregg, Henry Beckman Woodrow Parfrey, Dallas Mitchell, Lloyd Haines, Ray Montgomery, Seth Allen, Kay Turner*. Dir: Don Siegel. Pro: F. P. Rosenberg. Screenplay: H. Simoun & A. Polonsky. (U.I.–Rank.) Rel: March 31. (T.) 101 Mins.

The Magnificent Two
In their third screen comedy *Eric Morecambe* and *Ernie Wise* play a couple of travelling salesman caught up in a South American revolution, won by Ernie's knowledge of toy soldiers (well, he sells them for a living) and lovely *Margit Saad's* nubile Army! Rest of cast: *Virgilio Texera, Cecil Parker, Isobel Black, Martin Benson, Michael Godfrey, Sue Sylvaine, Henry Beltran, Tyler Butterworth, Sandor Eles, Andreas Malandrinos, Victor Maddern, Michael Gover, Charles Laurence, Larry Taylor, David Charlesworth, Hugo De Vernier, Sara Luzita, Bettine Le Beau, Aubrey Morris, Carlos Douglas, Anna Gilchrist, Catherine Griller*. Dir: Cliff Owen. Pro: Hugh Stewart. Screenplay: S. C. Green & R. M. Hills with M. Pertwee & P. Blackmore. (Stewart–Rank.) Rel: Aug. 6. (Colour.) 100 Mins.

Mahanagar – Big City
Another quiet Satyajit Ray screen classic, a sedate, beautifully composed picture of contemporary Indian life set in Calcutta and showing the growing emancipation of women, the difficulty of understanding between old and new generations and the triumph of honesty and moral principles. A brilliant performance by the lovely *Madhabi Mukherjee* as the working wife who turns down a promising commercial future because her Anglo-Indian friend is the victim of her boss's prejudices. Rest of cast: *Anil Chatterjee, Haradhan Banerjee, Haren Bannerjee, Vicky Redwood, Jaya Bhaduri*. Dir, Pro, written and with music by S. Ray. (Contemporary.) First shown at Paris-Pullman, May, 1968. 131 Mins.

The Man Outside
Superior thriller with a good script, a portrait in depth in the leading role (supplied by *Van Heflin*), good supporting performances and direction that holds the tension tinglingly tight! *Heflin*, sacked by his CIA bosses for not reporting the suspicions he has had of one of his team, becomes involved in London with a complicated series of double-crosses, plots and counter-plots and general espionage chicanery. Rest of cast: *Heidelinde Weis, Pinkas Braun, Peter Vaughan, Charles Gray, Paul Maxwell, Ronnie Barker, Linda Marlowe, Gary Cockrell, Bill Nagy, Larry Cross, Archie Duncan, Willoughby Gray, Christopher Denham, Rita Webb, Carole Ann Ford, Carmel McSharry, John Sterland, Alex Marchevsky, Paul Armstrong, Hugh Elton, Derek Baker, Frank Crawshaw, Roy Sone, Harry Hutchinson, Gabrielle Drake, Carol Kingsley, Martin Terry, Anna Willoughby, Suzanne Owens*. Dir & Written: Samuel Gallu. Pro: Wm. Gell. (London Ind. Producers–Trio Group W.) Rel: June 9. (T & Techniscope.) 97 Mins.

Martyrs of Love
Highly individual, charming Czech film which beautifully captures the world of dreams in its three episodes. The first, "The Temptations of a White Collar Worker" is about a finally frustrating fling by a frustrated office worker; the second is about the dreams of fair masculine men by a train restaurant waitress – "Nattenska's Reveries" and the third, "Orphan Rudolph's Adventure" is about a man who meeting and promising to return at night to a girl then finds he just can't recall exactly where he met her . . . three episodes poetically taking you into a crazy, illogical and frustrating world of dreams! Cast: (A) *Peter Kopriva, Marta Rubisova*. (B) *Hana Kuberova, Karel Gott, Vladimir Preclik*. (C) *Josef Konicek, Denisa Dvorakova*. Dir: Jan Nemec. Written: J. Nemec & Esther Krumbachora. (Contemporary.) First shown at Jacey, Piccadilly, Jan., 1968. 73 Mins

Masculin – Feminin
Typically slap-happy, self-indulgent Jean-Luc Godard movie which with a ragbag of interviews, set-ups, asides, etc., attempts to present a picture of youth in general and Parisian youth in particular. Cast: *Chantal Goya, Jean-Pierre Leaud, Marlene Jobert, Michel Debord, Isabelle Duport, Eva Britt Standberg, Birger Malmsten*. Dir & Script: Jean-Luc Godard. (Argos–Sandrews–Gala.) First shown at Cameo–Royal and Cameo, Victoria, June 1967. 104 Mins.

Massacre for an Orgy
Sensational, ambiguous French film which, originally shown at Cannes, caused a sensation when the police were called to confiscate the movie. A skit on all sex and violence films which goes further than most of the films it parodies! Still refused a showing in France, it has been shown in America and here after a severe censorsial pruning which has cut out most of the orgy and left much of the violence! Dir: Jean-Loup Grosdard (no comment!) (Balch.) First shown at Cameo–Moulin, Nov. 1967.

The Mercenaries
A violent film about violence seen against Congo backgrounds; a story of a desperate mission undertaken by a small company of soldiers, commanded by Mercenary officers, to fight their armoured train through enemy territory to a distant town where there are a crowd of refugees and a pile of diamonds, the latter needed by the President in order to carry on the war. Brutal, bloody and exciting, with a lightly hinted moral undertone. Cast: *Rod Taylor, Yvette Mimieux, Peter Garsten, Jim Brown, Kenneth More, Andre Morell, Olivier Despax, Guy Deghy, Bloke Modisane, Calvin Lockhart, Alan Gifford, Davie Bauer, Murray Kash, John Serret, Danny Daniels*. Dir: Jack Cardiff. Pro: George Englund. Screenplay: Q. Werty & A. Spies. (Englund–M-G-M.) Rel: March 17, (Pan & Metrocolor.) 100 Mins.

Midsummer's Night in Sweden
Two young girls, with and without their clothes, enjoy the pleasures of Stockholm and a yachting cruise on that festival few hours of the midnight sun. English commentary. Dir & Pro: Werner Kunz. (Miracle.) Rel: Floating. (E.) 18 Mins.

The Million Dollar Collar
The adventures of an amazingly clever airedale dog who is always able to outwit the human villains during his wanderings in Spain and Portugal in the period he is forcibly separated from his rightful, loving owner. Cast: *Guy Stockwell, Craig Hill, Eric Pohlmann*. Dir: Vincent McEveety. Pro: Walt Disney. Screenplay: L. S. Hawley. (Disney.) Rel: July 23. (T.) 64 Mins.

Mini Weekend
About the young chap who just hasn't got the knack with the birds! But he tries again and again – in a Mini-skirted, swinging London. Cast: *Anthony Trent, Liza Robers, Veronica Lang, Connie Frazer, Vicky Hodge, Jane MacIntosh, Patti Bryant, Avril Gaynor, Rossalind Elliot, Kathleen Southern, Maria Hauffer, Lucy Swain, Eve Aubrey, Anna Palk, Karon Leslie, Nina Dwyer, Valarie Stanton*. Dir: Georges Robin. Pro: Tony Tenser. Script: G. Robin & T. Tenser. (Tigon–Global.) Rel: Floating. 79 Mins.

Misunderstood
A delightful Italian, English-speaking film which tells a story about a British Consul in Florence who, when

his greatly loved wife dies and leaves him with two small sons, favours the younger one sometimes at the expense of the elder who, lacking the love he needs, goes his own way and meets a tragic end. Though sad and moving, the film is also amusing and gay in its insight into youthful action and expression. Cast: *Anthony Quayle, John Sharp, Stefano Colograndе, Simone Giannozzi, Adriana Facchetti, Rino Benini, Silla Bettini, Graziella Granata, Giorgia Moll*. Dir: Luigi Comencini. Pro: Nello Meniconi. Screenplay: L. Benvenuti & Piero de Bernardi. (Rizzoli–Golden Era.) Rel: Floating. (T.) 105 Mins.

The Monster of London City.
Thriller: during a staging of a play about Jack the Ripper in London the series of horrific murders start all over again and the police begin to suspect that the actor playing the part may also be doing the real thing when he gets a chance. Cast: *Hansjorg Felmy, Marianne Koch, Dietmar Schonherr, Hans Nielson, Charilkia Baxevanos, Fritz Tillman, Walter Pfeil, Peter Schmidt, Kurd Pierritz, Elsa Wagner, Adelheid Hinz, Gerda Blisse, Kai Fischer*. Dir: E. Zbonek. Pro: A. Brauner. Screenplay: B. E. Wallace. (Golden Era.) Rel: Floating. (Scope.) 90 Mins.

Mouchette
Robert Bresson returns to the author who gave him one of his greatest screen successes, Georges Bernanos ("The Diary of a Country Priest"). A story about a young teenager living in poverty and squalor in a remote French village who, when her mother dies and she is raped by the local alcoholic-epileptic, decides death cannot be as painful as living and rolls her way to suicide in the local lake. A cool, uncompromisingly non-involved and anti-sentimental account which adds up to a moving and deeply human document. Brilliantly acted – or, if you like, non-acted – by *Nadine Nortier* as the girl. Rest of cast: *Marie Cardinal, Paul Hebert, Jean Viment, J. C. Guilbert. Marie Susini, Liliane Princet, Raymond Chabrun*. Dir & Scripted: Robt. Bresson. Pro: Anatole Dauman. (Parc–Argos–Contemporary.) First shown at Academy Three, March. 1968. 90 Mins.

Munsters Go Home
The popular TV monster family make their comedy debut on the large screen in a typical story about their inheriting one of England's (once) Stately Homes and the efforts of their English cousins, including *Terry-Thomas* and *Hermione Gingold*, to scare them off. Rest of cast: *Fred Gwynne, Yvonne de Carlo, Al Lewes, Butch Patrick, Debbie Watson, Jeanne Arnold, Robert Pine, Maria Lennard, Arthur Malet, Richard Dawson, John Carradine, Bernard Fox, Diane Chesney*. Dir: Earl Bellamy. Pro: Joe Connelly. (U.I.–Rank.) Rel: Aug. 6. (Colour.) 96 Mins. (Second general release: first was at Dec. 30, 1966.)

My Love and I – The Royal Track
Fascinating Swedish film which tells the story of a man who re-walks the mountain track of the title ten years after he walked it with his girl-friend whose nude flirtation with the Laps and consequent jealousy and passion parted them. Now as he retraces his steps he looks for her – and finds her – or does he? It ends in ambiguity. Cast: *Mathias Henrikson, Maude Adelson, Lars Lind, Guy de la Berg*. Dir. (& Written with Bosse Gustafson) Gunnar Hoglund. (Schulman & Sen.) First shown at Cameo-Poly, June 1967. 106 Mins.

My Name is Pecos
Italian Western in which *Robert Woods*, as Pecos, eventually revenges the killing of his family by the villain and his gang who have taken over the town. Rest of cast: *Peter Carsten, Lucia Modugno, Norman Klark, Cristina Josani, Max Dean*. Dir: Maurizio Lucidi. (Golden Era.) Rel: Floating. (T & Techniscope.) 83 Mins.

My Way Home
Superbly visual, almost hypnotically fascinating Miklos Jansco film which tells a simple, almost ambiguous story about a Russian soldier and a Hungarian student who for a short while become friends in Hungary at the end of the war. A strange, essay-like, setting of the scene, with great images of grassy slopes rising to the skyline, vast skyscapes full of the sounds of singing larks, mysteriously ruined and empty palaces: and puzzling touches such as the constantly appearing light airplane. A beautifully artistic and stylised film but without any real warmth. Cast: *Andras Kozak* (the young Hungarian), *Sergei Nikonenko* (the young Russian). Dir: Miklos Jansco. (Contemporary.) 82 Mins.

The Mystery of Thug Island
Adventure melo in which a British Army Captain, and the young snake hunter who has fallen in love with the girl, smash the thugs and rescue a pretty 18-year-old Ceremonial Virgin, the captain's daughter kidnapped by the sect some fifteen years previously. Cast: *Guy Madison, Inge Schoner, Giacomo Risso Stuart, Ivan Desny, Giulia Rubini, Nando Poggi, Peter Van Eyck*. Dir: L. Capuano. Pro: N. Battiferri. Screenplay: D. R. Arpad & O. Poggi. (Columbia.) Rel: Floating. (T.) 87 Mins.

Naked Hearts – Les Coeurs Verts
A documentary-style film about young layabouts in Paris who spend their lives in cafés, on wasteground and generally idle their time away, slipping into crime at every opportunity. Especially the story of two of them, friends; one (the weak one) ends up by being dragged back to jail while the other (stronger) manages to pin down a job, goes in for training and pulls himself up towards future respectability. Extremely well acted by an amateur cast of Paris youths. Dir & Written: Edouard Luntz. (Contemporary.) First shown at the Cameo-Poly, Nov. 1967. 93 Mins.

The Naked Runner
Good spy thriller in the new, cynical tradition: with *Frank Sinatra* the victim of a complicated, intricate and confusing British espionage plot to kill a man who has defected to the East. Rest of cast: *Peter Vaughan, Derren Nesbitt, Nadia Gray, Toby Robins, Inger Stratton, Cyril Luckham, Edward Fox, J. Dubin-Berhmann, Michael Newport*. Dir: Sidney J. Furie. Pro: Brad Dexter. Screenplay: Stanley Mann. (Warner–Pathe.) Rel: Aug. 20. (Techniscope & T.) 102 Mins.

New Face in Hell
Tough Private Eye thriller with *George Peppard*, the hard-up thick-ear-type of 'tec hired by unscrupulous business tycoon *Raymond Burr*, ostensibly as body-guard to his mistress but, in reality it turns out, as a sitting-duck victim for a nasty murder plot. Rest of cast: *Gayle Hunnicutt, Coleen Gray, Susan Saint James, Jason Evers, Wilfrid Hyde-White, Severn Darden, H. Jane Van Duser, George Furth, Brock Peters, Herbert Edelman, Bert Freed, Ken Lynch, Kay Farrington, Lennie Bremen, Arte Johnson*. Dir: John Guillermin. Pro: E. J. Montagne. Screenplay: P. Reisman, Jun. (U.I.–Rank.) Rel: May 19. (T.) 106 Mins.

The Night Caller
First-rate, often amusing S. F. thriller about a fellow who comes from outer space pinching our pretty dollies in order to re-populate his de-populated planet! Cast: *John Saxon, Maurice Denham, Patricia Haines, Alfred Burke, John Carson, Jack Watson, Stanley Meadows, Warren Mitchell, Marianne Stone, Aubrey Morris, Geoffrey Lumsden, Ballard Berkeley, Barbara French, Anthony Wagner, Tom Gill, David Gregory, Vincent Harding, Douglas Livingstone, Romo Gorrara, John Sherlock, Robert Crewdson*. Dir: John Gilling. Pro: Ronald Liles. Screenplay: Jim O'Connolly. (Armitage–Butcher's.) Rel: Feb. 18. 82 Mins.

Night of the Big Heat
Science-fiction thriller about some unpleasant visitors from Outer Space who start to heat up the island of Bara and burn up any stray humans they find around . . . creating a long night of terror. Cast: *Christopher Lee, Peter Cushing, Patrick Allen, Sarah Lawson, Jane Merrow, William Lucas, Kenneth Cope, Jack Bligh, Thomas Heathcote, Sidney Bromley, Percy Herbert, Anna Turner, Barry Halliday*. Dir: Terence Fisher. Pro: Tom Blakely. Screenplay: Ronald Liles. (Planet.) Rel: Dec. 10. (E.) 94 Mins.

Night Scandal in Japan
Sad little story about a good-natured orphan from out of town, who is raped by her millionaire boss's son, loses her future husband as a result and when she tells the son she is pregnant is almost murdered. So she turns on her seducer and kills him. Cast: *Mayumi Ogawa, Mako Midori, Hizuru Takachino, Tatsuo Umemiya, Ken Mitsuta, Haruko Sugimura*. Dir: Yusuke Watanabe. Pro: Toei Co. (Orb–Nat Miller.) Rel: Floating. (Toeiscope.) 87 Mins.

No Orchids for Lulu
An adaptation of two Wedekind plays with *Nadja Tiller* as Lulu, the girl who appears to immediately enslave every man she meets; and ends up as one of Jack the Ripper's victims. All very German. Rest of cast: *O. E. Hasse, Hildegarde Neff, Rudolf Forster*. Dir: Rolf Thiele. (New Realm.) First shown at Cinephone, 91 Mins.

No Way to Treat a Lady
Rod Steiger as the mentally disturbed killer who plays it all as a game, telephoning the detective who's after him but being just that little bit too clever to be caught until he makes the final slip. Rest of cast: *Lee Remick, George Segal, Eileen Heckart, Murray Hamilton, Michael Dunn, Martine Bartlett, Barbara Baxley, Irene Dailey, Doris Roberts, Ruth White, Val Bisoglio, David Doyle, Kim August*. Dir: Jack Smight. Pro: Sol C. Siegel. Screenplay: John Gay. (Paramount.) Rel: June 9. 108 Mins.

Nobody's Perfect
Light comedy about a couple of always-in-trouble U.S. Naval types (*Doug McClure* and *David Hartman*) and their tough old skipper with a heart of gold (*James Whitmore*): their escapades and the final typhoon which blows everything into cosy shape. Rest of cast: *James Shigeta, Nancy Kwan*. Dir: Alan Rafkin. Pro: Howard Christie. Screenplay: J. D. F. Black. (U.I.–Rank.) Rel: May 19. (Colour.) 103 Mins.

The Oldest Profession
Five-part portmanteau picture presenting peeps at prostitution during the centuries, from prehistoric times to today! 1: Prehistoric Times. How woman learned to sell herself! Cast: *Michele Mercier, Enrico Maria Salerno, Gabriel Tinti*. Dir: Franco Indovina. Screenplay: Ennio Flaiano. 2: Roman Nights. Caesar and his wife learn a thing or two about themselves and each other in a brothel where they meet. Cast: *Elsa Martinelli, Gaston Moschin*. Dir: Mauro Bolognini. 3: Mademoiselle Mini. How an artful young man during the French Revolution convinces Mademoiselle that as a condemned aristocrat he should have her services for free. Cast: *Jeanne Moreau, Jean-Claude Brialy, Jean Richard*. Dir: Phillippe de Broca. Screenplay: Daniel Boulanger. 4: The Gay Nineties. In Vienna in the 1890's a courtesan proves a match for a banker and marries him. Cast: *Raquel Welch, Martin Held*. Dir: M. Pfleghar. Screenplay: Georges & Andre Tabet. 5: Present Day. About two prostitutes who pick up a cop. . . .! Cast: *Nadia Gray, France Anglade, Jacques Duby, Dalio, Francis Blanche*. Dir: Claude Autant-Lara. Screenplay: Jean Aurenche. (Miracle.) First shown at the Cameo Royal, Oct. 1967. 120 Mins.

Once Before I Die
Rather odd little *John Derek* film (he directed, produced and himself stars) about a company of mixed Phillipine and American cavalry trying to make their way to Manilla after the surprise Jap attack, and the girl who tags along with them, surviving all of them to herself kill a Jap at the fade-out. Nice colour; strange stop-motion sequences. Rest of cast: *Ursula Andress, Richard Jaeckel, Rod Lauren, Ronald Ely, Vance Skarstedt, Allen Pinson, Andress Centenera, Gregg Martin, Renato Robles, Fred Galang, Nello Nayo, Mario Taquibulos, Rob Francisco, Eva Vivar, Lola Boy, Armando Lucero*, Dir & Pro: J. Derek. Screenplay: V. Skarstedt. (Seven Arts–Rive.) Rel: Floating. 96 Mins.

One Born Every Minute
Released as "The Flim-Flam Man" in America, this is the story of a wily old "Con" man making his crooked way, with his young apprentice (a soldier on the lam!), across the Southern American States. Genial home-spun humour. Cast: *George C. Scott, Sue Lyon, Michael Sarrazin, Harry Morgan, Jack Albertson, Alice Ghostley, Albert Salmi, Slim Pickens, Strother Martin, George Mitchell, Woodrow Parfrey, Jesse L. Baker*. Dir: Irvin Kershner. Pro: L. Turman. Screenplay: Wm. Rose. (Fox.) Rel: Nov. 19. (Pan & D.) 104 Mins.

Only When I Larf'
Amusing comedy about the confidence tricksters finally caught up and cheated by their own tricks! Cast: *Richard Attenborough, David Hemmings, Alexandra Stewart, Nicholas Pennell, Melissa Stribling, Terence Alexander, Edric Connor, Clifton Jones, Calvin Lockhart, Brian Grellis, David Healy, Alan Giford*. Dir: Basil Dearden Pro: Len Deighton & Brian Duffy. (Paramount–British.) Rel: June 30. (E.) 105 Mins.

Operation Kid Brother
Neil Connery, Sean's real-life brother, in a Junior League adventure melo with Bondish allusions about some sort of secret organisation called THANATOS, whose strictly nefarious object is to pinch half the world's gold! Rest of cast: *Daniela Bianchi, Adolfo Celi, Agata Flori, Bernard Lee, Anthony Dawson*. Dir: Alberto Demartino. Pro: Dario Babtello. Screenplay: Paul Levi & Frank Walker. (U.A.) Rel: May 5. (Techniscope & Colour.) 104 Mins.

The Other Sex
Swedish film about an eventful weekend spent by a group of teenagers who go camping and are caught up in some unpleasant sexual revelations. Cast: *Britt Monstad, Per Christensen, Didi Grimsgaard, Egil Asman, Guri Heitmann Muller, Lauritz Falk*. Dir & Written: Nils R. Muller (E. J. Fancey). First shown at Jacey–Tatler, Jan., 1967. 69 Mins.

The Other World of Winston Churchill
Jack Le Vien's documentary about Sir Winston – artist! Based on his book, "Painting as a Pastime". Featuring *F. M.Vis. Montgomery, Paul Maze, Merle Oberon, Lady Birley and Sian Phillips*; and *Patrick Wymark* speaks for Churchill when no suitable recordings of his voice are available. Dir: Lou Stoumen. Pro: Jack Le Vien. Narrated by Paul Scofield. Script: Caryl Brahms. (Gala.) Rel: Floating. (Colour.) 51 Mins.

Our Mother's House
Grim and even macabre Jack Clayton film about a family of children who, when their mother dies, fear the orphanage and separation enough to bury the body in the garden and carry on as usual; then one of the boys writes to their no-good dad, whose return leads inevitably to the final sad little tragedy. The children: Cast: *Margaret Brooks, Pamela Franklin, Louis Sheldon Williams, John Gugolka, Mark Lester, Sarah Nicholls, Gustav Henry, Parnum Wallace*. Rest of cast: *Yootha Joyce, Claire Davidson, Anthony Nicholls, Annette Carell, Gerald Sim, Edina Romay, Diana Ashley, Garfield Morgan, Faith Kent, John Arnatt, Jack Silk*. Dir & Pro: Jack Clayton. Screenplay: Jeremy Brooks & Haya Harareet. (Filmways–M-G-M.) Rel: Oct. 15. (Colour.) 105 Mins.

Paris in August
French comedy about the romance of a shop assistant who during his family's August holidays picks up an English girl, shows her the Pantheon, and falls in love with her. Cast: *Charles Aznavour, Susan Hampshire, Michel de Re, Daviel Ivernel, Alan Scott, Jacques Marin, Etchika Choreau*. Dir: Pierre Granier-Deferre. Screenplay: R. M. Arlaud & P. G. Deferre. (Contemporary.) First shown at Cameo, Victoria, Nov. 1967. (Totalvision.) 100 Mins.

Payment in Kind
"Scales of Justice" episode: about a young woman who, running into debt and refusing to square the account with her own body, accidentally kills the man who demands this payment in kind! Cast: *Justine Lord, Maxine Audley, Brian Haines, Derrick Sherwin, Gwen Cherell, Peter Bathurst, Henry McGee, Nicola Riley*. Dir: Peter Duffell. Pro: Jack Greenwood. Screenplay: John Roddick & P. Duffell. (Anglo–Warner.) Rel: Sept. 3. (E.) 30 Mins.

The Penthouse
Quite brilliantly achieved, though always creepingly unpleasant, film about two young men who break into a penthouse love nest, tie up the lover, torture him and rape the girl. Cast: *Terence Morgan, Suzy Kendall*, Martine *Beswick, Tony Beckley, Norma Rodney*. Dir & Written: Peter Collinson. Pro: Harry Fine (Tahiti–Paramount.) Rel: Floating. (Colour.) 97 Mins.

The Perils of Pauline
A rather crazy comedy based, loosely on the old silent serials with which the name of Pearl White is so completely associated. *Pamela Austin* is the new Pauline. Rest of cast: *Pat Boone, Terry-Thomas, Edward Everett-Horton, Hamilton Camp, Doris Packer, Kurt Kasznar, Vito Scotti, Leon Askin, Aram Katcher, Rick Natoli*. Dir: H. B. Leonard & J. Shelley. Pro: H. B. Leonard. Written: A. Beich. (U.I.–Rank.) Rel: Dec. 31. (T.) 98 Mins.

The Persecution and Assassination of Jean-Paul Marat as Performed by the Inmates of the Asylum of Charenton under the Direction of the Marquis de Sade
This film with the dubious honour of having the longest title ever, is a straightforward adaptation of the Royal Shakespeare Company's stage production of the play of the same title with little or no concession to the change of medium. A flesh-creeping, blood-curdling horror about a play put on by lunatics which ends in a murder and a revolting riot as the players attack their audience. With the stage cast: *Clifford Rose, Brenda Kempner, Ruth Baker, Michael Williams, Freddie Jones, Hugh Sullivan, Jonathan Burn, Jeannette Landis, Robert Lloyd, Glenda Jackson, Ian Richardson, Susan Williamson, Patrick Magee, John Steiner, Mark Jones, Morgan Sheppard, James Mellor, Ian Hogg, Henry Woolf, John Hussey, John Harwood, Leon Lissek, Carol*

Raymont, Mary Allen, Maroussia Frank, Sheila Grant, Lyn Pinkney, Tamara Fuerst, Michael Farnsworth, Guy Gordon, Michael Percival, Heather Canning, Jennifer Tudor, Timothy Hardy, Stanford Trowell, Patrick Gowers, Richard Callinan, Michael Gould, Nicholas Moes, Rainer Schuelein, Paul Hiley. Dir: Peter Brook. Pro: Michael Birkett. Written: Peter Weiss. (Marat Sade–U.A.) Rel: Special – Floating. (D.) 116 Mins.

Persona
Ingmar Bergman's most fined-down film yet; within eighty minutes he tells a story of an actress who "dries up" in the middle of a line on the stage and does not speak again, and the young nurse who is assigned to look after her during a convalescent stay in the former's seaside cottage, a stay during which gradually the nurse becomes the patient and breaks down, watched with interest by the actress, as she tries to divest herself of her guilt and sex complexes. A little gimmicky, even with a hint of occasional pretentiousness, but wholly fascinating all the same. Cast: *Liv Ullmann, Bibi Andersson, Margaretha Krook, Gunnar Bjornstrand*. Dir & Written: I. Bergman. (Svensk Filmindustri–U.A.) First shown at Academy Two, Sept. 1967. 81 Mins.

The Phantom of Soho
How Scotland Yard chief *Hans Sohnker* and mystery writer girl-friend *Barbara Rutting* work out the identity of the killer of the title from among the several strip-teasing suspects! Rest of cast: *Dieter Borsche, Peter Vogel, Elga Sommerfield, Werner Peters, Hans Nielson, Elisabeth Flickenschildt*. Dir: Ladislos Foder. (CCC Films–Golden Era.) Rel: Floating 93 Mins.

The Pink Jungle
James Garner as a professional photographer in South America on an assignment with lovely model girl *Eva Renzi* becomes involved in explosive local politics and ruthless plots to steal some hidden diamonds. Rest of cast: *George Kennedy, Nigel Green, Michael Ansara, George Rose, Fabrizio Mioni, Vincent Beck, Val Avery, Victor Millan*. Dir: Delbert Mann. Pro: Stan Margulies. Screenplay: Chas. Williams. (U.I.–Rank.) Rel: May 26. 93 Mins.

Planet of the Apes
A lavishly produced screen adaptation of the Pierre Boulle science-fiction story about a rocketship which travels some 4,000 years into the future and then crashes on to a planet on which the ape–man relationship has been reversed, a story which carries what turns out to be a rather amusing twist in the tail, solving a puzzle which builds up right through the story. *Charlton Heston* as the leading astronaut who escapes his companions' fates (one, the girl, dies of sudden old age, another has his memory taken away by the experimenting apes, and a third gets stuffed!) to survive, win a mate and his freedom to search beyond the forbidden zones to try and find a new life! Rest of cast: *Roddy McDowall, Kim Hunter, Maurice Evans, James Whitmore, James Daly, Linda Harrison, Robert Gunner, Lou Wagner, Woodrow Parfrey, Jeff Burton, Buck Kartalian, Norman Burton, Wright King, Paul Lambert*. Dir: F. J. Schaffner. Pro: Arthur P. Jacobs. Screenplay: M. Wilson & R. Serling. (Apjac–fox.) Rel. April 21. (Pan & D.) 112 Mins.

The Plank
Comedy which amusingly exhausts just about every new and old comedy angle of a man with a plank in London. Cast: *Eric Sykes, Tommy Cooper, Jimmy Edwards, Roy Castle, Stratford Johns, Jim Dale, Graham Stark, Jimmy Tarbuck, Hattie Jacques, Rex Garner, Libby Morris, John Lunkin, Joan Young, Barney Gilbraith, Clovissa Newcombe, Dermot Kelly, Anna Carteret, Thomas Gallagher, Howard Douglas, Tricia de Dulin, Bill Oddie, Kenny Lynch, Ronnie Brody, Dave Freeman, Johnny Speight, Ian Wilson, Dennis Golding*. Dir & Written: Eric Sykes. Pro: Jon Pennington. (Assoc. London Films–Rank.) Rel: Floating. 54 Mins.

Point Blank
Lee Marvin, sold down the river by his wife and her crime syndicate friends (who frame him on a robbery charge and leave him for dead) takes his jail medicine and comes out determined to track down and kill, kill, kill every one of them. Rest of cast: *Angie Dickinson, Keenan Wynn, Carroll O'Connor, Lloyd Bochner, Michael Strong, John Vernon, Sharon Acker, James Sikking, Sandra Warner, Roberta Haynes, Kathleen Freeman, Victor Creatore, Lawrence Hauben, Susan Holloway, Sid Haig, Michael Bell, Priscilla Boyd, John McMurtry, Ron Walters, George Strattan, Nicole Rogell, Rico Cattani, Roland LaStarza*. Dir: John Boorman. Pro: Judd Bernard & Robt. Chartoff. Screenplay: Alexander Jacobs, David Newhouse & Rafe. (Bernard–M-G-M–Winkler) Rel: Feb. 4. 92 Mins.

Poor Cow
A raw and boldly presented slice of low life which in a series of incidents tells the story of a girl who marries the man who makes her pregnant – a professional burglar – then goes off with one of his mates when he is sent to jail, subsequently leading a loose and sordid life when he in turn is caught in the thieving act. All rather unpleasant but enlivened by *Carol White*'s warm and wonderfully real performance as the girl – the poor cow! Rest of cast: *Terence Stamp, John Bindon, Kate Williams, Queenie Watts, Geraldine Sherman, James Beckett, Billy Murray, Ellis Dale, Gerald Young, Paddy Joyce, Gladys Dawson, Ron Pember, Malcolm McDowell*. Dir: Kenneth Loach. Pro: J. Janni. Screenplay: Nell Dunn & Kenneth Loach, from the former's novel. (Janni–Anglo–Warner–Pathe.) Rel: Jan. 21. (E.) 101 Mins.

The Power
George Pal science-fiction film about a team of space scientists, one of whom discovers that another, unknown, team-mate possesses a strange and terrible power over the minds of other men which he uses to systematically kill them, and knows that unless he can find out who it is – and quickly – and stop him, will himself be erased. Cast: *George Hamilton, Suzanne Pleshette, Richard Carlson, Yvonne De Carlo, Earl Holliman, Gary Merrill, Barbara Nichols, Arthur O'Connell, Nehemiah Persoff, Beverly Powers, Aldo Ray, Michael Rennie*. Dir: Byron Haskin. Pro: G. Pal. Screenplay: John Gay. (Pal–M-G-M.) Rel: May 6. (Pan & Metrocolor.) 99 Mins.

Prehistoric Valley
Screen version of Jules Verne's "Career of a Comet", about a couple of duellists who are suddenly swept away on to another, passing planet and there find a civilisation like our own earth had in its most primitive period! Cast: *Cesare Danova, Sean McClory, Joan Stanley, Danielle de Metz, Gregg Martell, Gil Perkins, I. Stanford Jolley, Michael Lane, Roger Til, Mark Dempsey, Jerry Sunshine, Dolly Gray*. Dir: Edward Bernds. Pro: Byron Roberts. (ZRB–Columbia.) Rel: Floating. (Monstascope.) 81 Mins.

Pretty Polly
Long and leisurely romantic comedy with travelogue trimmings, set in Singapore, where within the space of a few days Polly (*Hayley Mills*) loses her guardian (*Brenda de Banzie*, who dies of overeating) and her virginity and, listening a little to wise old Uncle Bob (*Trevor Howard*), grows up! Rest of cast: *Shashi Kapoor, Dick Patterson, Kalen Lui, Peter Bayliss, Patricia Routledge, Dorothy Alison*. Dir: Guy Green. Pro: G. W. George & F. Granat. Screenplay: Willis Hall & Keith Waterhouse. (George/Granat–U.I.–Rank.) Rel: Nov. 12. 102 Mins.

Primitive Love
Jayne Mansfield's last film; she plays an anthropologist (!) who proves her point that man is still primitive, by doing a strip-tease and converting a sceptical professor into a wild man. Dir: Luigi Scattini. (Orb.) Rel: Floating. (Colour.) 70 Mins.

The Private Right
Very odd little Michael Papas film which divides itself into three only slightly connected sequences: fighting and torture at the start (including the controversial scenes where a British officer watches a Greek cypriot tortured to near death); a sort of "La Dolce Vita" party with lovers-in-bed interlude tacked on; and a final, ghastly but wonderfully organised chase in which the tortured chases torturer – both now in London – and finally murders him. Often wonderfully effective visually. Cast: *Dimitris Andreas, George Kafkaris, Tamara Hinchco, Christos Demetriou, Charlotte Selwyn, Seraphim Nicola, John Brogan, Nana Georgiou, Takis Theophanous, Joanna Farber, Philip Haralambous, John Harris, Hareclia Kleanthous, Sandra Kington, Lakis Sideras*. Dir, Pro & Written: Michael Papas. (Onyx–London Independent Producers.) First shown at Cameo, Victoria, Dec. 1967. 82 Mins.

Privilege
Peter Watkins (he made "The War Game") directed this incredible, somewhat hysterical story of a pop-singing idol harnessed by some future British government to bring the teenagers to political and religious conformity. Very TV in technique. *Paul*

Jones as the somewhat glum singer-masochist; *Jean Shrimpton* as his girl-friend. Rest of cast: *Mark London, Max Bacon, Jeremy Child, William Job*. Dir: Peter Watkins. Pro: John Heyman. (U.I.–Rank.) Rel: Floating. (T.) 103 Mins.

The Professionals
First-class, near-classic Western set in Mexico against magnificent backgrounds of rock and desert country and telling the story of four men picked by an American tycoon to go across the Mexican border and rescue his wife, being held there by a bandit chieftain. The four men, specialists all, reach their goal (to find their first surprise), achieve their object and return with the girl only to . . . which is the twist in the tale. Apart from one patch of philosophising, a superbly visual, gripping, tremendously exciting movie. Cast: *Burt Lancaster, Lee Marvin, Robert Ryan, Jack Palance, Claudia Cardinale, Ralph Bellamy, Woody Strode, Joe De Santis, Rafael Bertrand, Jorge Martinez De Hoyos, Marie Gomez, Jose Chavez, Carlos Romero, Vaughn Taylor*. Dir & Written: Richard Brooks. (Columbia.) Rel: Aug. 20. (Pan & T.) 117 Mins.

Promenade
Donovan Winter's featurette about a revived romance, between a promenade artist and a girl who was his mistress, seen against a background of Brighton in the spring. Full of colours, quick cuts and topical with-it style. Cast: *Kate O'Mara, Robert Morris, Richard Leech, Margo Cunningham*. Dir, Pro & Written: D. Winters. (Fox.) Rel: April 21. (E.) 40 Mins.

The Pussycats
About a gang of young men who arrange for a number of young girls to be photographed in compromising situations so that their parents can be blackmailed with the negatives. A mixture of sex, goonery, kinky happenings, crime and comedy! Cast: *Pascale Cori Deville, Joel Barbouth, Dominique Erlanger, Ghislaine Paulou*. Dir: J. L. Bastid. (Anthony Balch Films.) First shown at Jacey, Piccadilly, July 1967. 64 Mins.

Quatermass and the Pit
Basically ridiculous (in the sense that most S.F. thrillers are) but well produced and nicely acted ghoulie thriller about a strange, antedeluvian space-craft dug up in London during tube extensions, which, the Professor (*Andrew Keir*) guesses, was one of a regular service once plying between Earth and Mars. When opened it releases a great deal of evil spirit – and finally the devil himself! Rest of cast: *James Donald, Barbara Shelley, Julian Glover, Duncan Lamont, Bryan Marshall, Peter Copley, Edwin Richfield, Grant Taylor, Maurice Good, Robert Morris, Sheila Steafel, Hugh Futcher, Hugh Morton, Thomas Heathcote, Noel Howlett, Hugh Manning, June Ellis, Keith Marsh, James Culliford, Bee Duffell, Roger Avon, Brian Peck, John Graham, Charles Lamb*. Dir: Roy Ward Baker. Pro: Anthony Nelson Keys. Screenplay: Nigel Kneale. (Hammer–Assoc. British. – Warner–Pathe.) Rel: Nov. 19. (T.) 97 Mins.

Rapture
Strange, rather attractive but finally not convincing enough, French-made, English-speaking film which deals with a house overshadowed by an atmosphere of doom and in which a strange trio live, to be sparked off into tragedy with the arrival of an escaped prisoner. Cast: *Melvyn Douglas, Patricia Gozzi, Dean Stockwell, Gunnel Lindblom, Leslie Sands, Murray Evans, Sylvia Kay, Peter Sallis*. Dir: John Guillermin. Pro: Christian Ferry. Screenplay: Stanley Mann. (Fox.) Rel: Sept. 3. (C.) 104 Mins.

Rebellion
Slow starting, violent ending Japanese film, set in the feudal Japan of 240 years ago and relating a story of the way that the local lord's dictatorial command over his subjects finally forces one ill-used family into revolt. Cast: *Toshiro Mifune, Takeshi Kato, Yoko Tsukasa, Tatsuyoshi Ebara, Michiko Otsuka, Tatsuo Matsumura, Masao Mishima, Shigeru Koyama, Isao Yamagata, Tatsuya Nakadai*. Dir: Masaki Kobayashi. Pro: T. Tanaka. Screenplay: S. Hashimoto. (Nat Miller–Orb.) First shown at the new Essoldo, Chelsea, Jan., 1968. 120 Mins.

Reflections in a Golden Eye
Screen adaptation of the Carson McCullers novel about a most unpleasantly odd little group of people living on an Army post in Georgia, where the ox-like major (*Marlon Brando*), having lost all physical interest in his wife, pursues a dour private who appears to spend his days riding naked in the woods and his nights surreptitiously at the foot of the bed of the major's honestly sensual wife (*Elizabeth Taylor*), sniffing her underclothes! The wife, by the way, is having an affair with the major's worried superior (*Brian Keith*), and he's worried because his wife (*Julie Harris*) is far enough round the bend to try and mutilate her breasts and keeps as a constant companion a revoltingly pansy-like Phillipino servant. Rest of cast: *Zorro David, Gordon Mitchell, Irvin Dugan, Fay Sparks, Robert Forster*. Dir: John Huston. Pro: Ray Stark. Screenplay: Chapman Mortimer & Gladys Hill. (Warner–Seven Arts.) Rel: May 12. (Pan & T.) 109 Mins.

The Reward
Beautifully photographed, initially gripping but finally disintegrating Mexican Western about an American adventurer who crashes his plane and through this unexpectedly meets a fugitive he recognises as a man with $50,000 on his head, and so starts out with the local police captain and his posse to bring him in and collect the cash, a pursuit which ends in disaster and death for nearly all concerned. Cast: *Max von Sydow, Yvette Mimieux, Effrem Zimbalist*, Jun., *Gilbert Roland, Emilio Fernandez, Nino Castelnuovo, Henry Silva, Rodolfo Acosta, Julian Rivero, Rafael Lopez*. Dir: Serge Bourguignon. Pro: Aaron Rosenberg. Screenplay: S. Bourguignon & Oscar Millard. (Fox.) Rel: Floating. (C & D.) 91 Mins.

Ringo and his Golden Pistol
Mexican-Western about Ringo, the deadly young bounty hunter who ruthlessly hunts down and kills any man with a price on his head. Cast: *Mark Damon, Valeria Fabrizi, Franco Derosa, Ettore Manni*. Dir: Sergio Corbucci. Pro: Joseph Fryde. (Sanson–M-G-M.) Rel: Dec. 24. 88 Mins.

Rings Around the World
Don Ameche as a writer, John Shawcross, records his personal experiences and stories of the circus, its history, its people and its traditions: filmed in circuses all over the world and with many of its internationally famous stars. Cast: *The Flying Armors, Rudy Cardenas, The Francesco Clowns, The Four Titos, Grey Arrow and Zuni, Fredy Knie Horses, Carl Sembach Krone, Frieda Sembach Krone, Marco, Two Mascotts, Mendez and Seitz, Pablo Noel, Pauline Schumann, Tarzan, Sahib and Boy, The Tongas, Gunther Gebel Williams, Lilly Yokoi*. Dir & Pro: Gil Cates. Written: Victor Wolfson. (Columbia.) Rel: Floating. (T.) 98 Mins.

The Road to St. Tropez
So-called anti-travelogue made in French with English commentary spoken by *Fenella Fielding*, written, directed and produced by Mike Sarne. With *Melissa Stribling, Udo Kier, Gabriella Licudi*. (Fox.) Rel: July 30. (Colour.) 31 Mins.

Robbery
Stanley Baker's film. He set-up, fought for (through a jungle of legal difficulties) produced and himself stars in this meticulous reconstruction of *A* if not *The* Great Train Robbery! Exciting and credible, the message is that while crime may not pay so well for the little fellows it pays big for the big 'uns. Rest of cast: *James Booth, Frank Finlay, Barry Foster, William Marlowe, Clinton Greyn, Joanna Pettet, George Sewell, Michael McStay, Patrick Jordan*. Dir: Peter Yates. Pro: S. Baker & M. Deeley. Screenplay: P. Yates, Geo. Markstein & E. Boyd. (Levine–Paramount.) Rel: Nov. 5. (E.) 114 Mins.

Rosie
Comedy-drama dominated by *Rosalind Russell's* portrait of a millionairess whose determination to enjoy life after the death of her husband leads her to a mental asylum, to where she is committed by her furious family, who don't like to see the fortune dwindling. Luckily there's handsome lawyer *Brian Aherne* to defend her in the subsequent court action and prove her sanity. Rest of cast: *Sandra Dee, Audrey Meadows, James Farentino, Vanessa Brown, Leslie Nielsen, Margaret Hamilton, Reginald Owen, Juanita Moore, Virginia Grey, Dean Harens*. Dir: David Lowell Rich. Pro: Jacque Mapes. Screenplay: Samuel Taylor (based on Ruth Gordon's adaptation of a French play: "A Very Rich Woman"). (Ross Hunter–U.I.–Rank.) Rel: May 12. (Colour.) 98 Mins.

Rough Night in Jericho
First-class, non-complicated, Western with the novelty angle of having *Dean Martin* as the villain – an ex-lawman who has turned to town-terrorising and gets his come-uppance from hero *George Peppard*. Rest of cast: *Jean Simmons, John McIntire, Slim Pickens, Don*

Galloway, Brad Weston, Richard O'Brien, Carol Anderson, Steve Sandor, Warren Vanders, John Napier. Dir: Arnold Laven. Pro: Martin Rackin. Screenplay: S. Boehm & Marvin H. Albert. (U.I.–Rank.) Rel: Nov. 5. (T.) 102 Mins.

Ruddigore
Halas and Batchelor's animated feature cartoon based on the Gilbert and Sullivan comic opera, with the chorus of the D'Oyly Carte Opera Company doing the singing and the Royal Philharmonic Orchestra (under the direction of James Walker) providing the musical background. The voices: *John Reed, Ann Hood, David Palmer, Peggy Ann Jones, Kenneth Sandford, Donald Adams, Gillian Knight, George Cook, Jennifer Toye.* Dir: Joy Batchelor. (Gala.) Rel: Floating. (E.) 54 Mins.

The Sailor from Gibraltar
Jeanne Moreau as the girl who steals *Ian Bannen* away from mistress *Vanessa Redgrave* and takes him on a Mediterranean search for a former lover who may be real or just her ideal male. . . . and very unreal and high-flown. Rest of cast: *Orson Welles, Hugh Griffith, Umberto Orsini, Erminio Spalla, Eleanor Brown, Gabriella Pallotta, Arnoldo Foa, Claudio De Renzi, Fausto Tozzi, Zia Moyheddin, John Hurt.* Dir: Tony Richardson. Pro: Oscar Lewenstein. Screenplay: C. Isherwood, Don Magner & T. Richardson. (Woodfall–U.A.) Rel: Sept. 24. 89 Mins.

The St. Valentine's Day Massacre
A true story of Chicago in the late 20's, when the Al Capone–Bugs Moran gangwar for control of the city's vice led to a series of killings culminating in the wholesale slaughter which stirred the city into belated action. Made in a semi-documentary manner, it becomes a hair-raising indictment, especially in its casual suggestion that the gangs, though more sophisticated, are now in fact more powerful and wealthy than ever! Cast: *Jason Robards, George Segal, Ralph Meeker, Jean Hale, Clint Ritchie, Frank Silvera, Joseph Campanella, Richard Bakalyan, David Canary, Bruce Dern, Harold J. Stone, Kurt Kreuger, Paul Richards, Joseph Turke, Milton Frome, Mickey Deems, John Agar, Celia Lovsky, Tom Reese, Jan Merlin, Alex D'Arcy, Reed Hadley, Gus Trikonis, Charles Dierkop, Tom Signorelli, Rico Cattani, Alex Rocco, Leo Gordon.* Dir & Pro: Roger Corman. Screenplay: Howard Browne. (Fox.) Rel: Nov. 19. (Pan & D.) 99 Mins.

Sallah
Warm, quite charming, simple comedy with comedian *Topol* as the Oriental Jew in Israel coming up against and defeating his more "advanced" cousins, as he struggles to establish himself – without working – in his new home. Rest of cast: *Geula Noni, Gila Almogor, Arik Einstein, Shraga Friedman, Zaharira Marifai, Nathan Meisler, Shaika Levi, Esther Greenberg, Mordecai Arnon.* Dir & Written: Ephraim Kishon. Pro: Menachem Golan. (Gala.) First shown at Royalty, London, June 1967. 104 Mins.

The Sand Pebbles
Gargantuan David Wise production of the Richard McKenna novel which tells the story of an American gunboat sited on the Yangtze river during the Chinese ferment of the 1920's, and of some of the members of the crew: with implications, if you care to find and then to see them, about today's American Asian policies! A mixture of spectacle, blood, sentimental interludes. Cast: *Steve McQueen, Richard Attenborough, Richard Crenna, Candice Bergen, Marayat Andriane, Mako, Larry Gates, Charles Robinson, Simon Oakland, Ford Rainey, Joe Turkel, Gavin MacLeod, Joseph di Reda, Richard Loo, Barney Phillips, Gus Trikonis, Shepherd Sanders, James Jeter, Tom Middleton, Paul Chinpae, Tommy Lee, Stephen Jahn, Jay Allan Hopkins, Steve Ferry, Ted Fish, Loren Janes, Glenn Wilder.* Dir & Pro: Robt. Wise. Screenplay: Robt. Anderson. (Argyle–Solar–Fox.) Rel: June/July 1967. (D & Pan.) 182 Mins. (ex. interval).

The Scalp Hunters
Good, amusing Western with Trapper *Burt Lancaster* grimly tracking down first the Indians and then the renegade white scalphunters who have stolen his winter's work of furs, and being helped and hindered by an escaped black slave given him in exchange by the redskins. Tough but not needlessly brutal, and lightened by some good touches of light relief. Rest of cast: *Ossie Davis, Shelley Winters, Telly Savalas, Armando Silvestre, Dan Vadis, Dabney Coleman, Paul Picerne, Nick Cravat, John Epper, Jack Williams, Tony Epper, Chuck Roberson, Agapito Roldan, Gregorio Acosta, Marco Antonio Arzate,* etc. Dir: Sidney Pollack. Pro: Jules Levy, Arthur Gardner & Arnold Laven. Screenplay: Wm. Norton. (U.A.) Rel: March 17. (D & Pan.) 103 Mins.

The Scorpio Letters
All about agent *Alex Cord's* efforts to infiltrate and smash a large-scale blackmailing racket led by a former French Resistance chief, who uses his knowledge to wipe out the opposition. *Shirley Eaton* as a pretty agent with the same aim. Rest of cast: *Laurence Naismith, Oscar Beregi, Lester Matthews, Arthur Malet, Barry Ford, Emile Genest, Antoinette Bower, Vincent Beck, Ilka Windish, Laurie Main, Andre Philippe, Harry Raybould, Danielle de Metz.* Dir & Pro: R. Thorpe. Screenplay: Adrian Spies & Jo Eisinger. (M-G-M.) Rel: April 28. (Metracolor.) 80 Mins.

Sebastian
Technically excellent, rigidly unromantic, highly incredible story about one of Britain's best brains not yet lost down the U.S. drain who heads our thriving, brilliant, mini-skirted Ministry of Decoding. Falling in love and quickly into bed with one member of the staff, he resigns when another, trusted left-winger, is found to be passing on secret information to you-know-where. But he comes back to crack Russia's latest, most difficult satelite code and does so with the help of his own child's rattle! And that's just a sketched outline of the busy plot. Cast: *Dirk Bogarde, Susannah York, Lilli Palmer, Sir John Gielgud, Janet Munro, Margaret Johnston, Nigel Davenport, Ronald Fraser, John Roxane, Susan Whitman, Ann Beach, Ann Sidney, Veronica Clifford, Jeanne Roland, Lyn Pinkney, Louise Pernell.* Dir: David Greene. Pro: H. Brodkin & M. Powell. Screenplay: Gerald Vaughan-Hughes. (Paramount.) Rel: April 7. (T.) 99 Mins.

The Second Sin
A sort of whodunit – murder, jewel thefts etc. – seen against South African backgrounds. Only at the end, in a cable car on the way to Table Mountain, is it revealed who killed the jewel craftsman and stole the necklace he was working on. Cast: *Annabelle Linder, Max Angorn, Arthur Swemmer, John Whiteley, Olive Bodill, James White, Clive Parnell, Gert Van Den Bergh, John Hayter, Willia Van Rensburg, Louif Ife, Siegfried Mynhardt, Ann Rudnick, Kerry Jordan, Melody O'Brian.* Dir: David Millin. Pro: Hyman Kirstein. Screenplay: Ivan Goff & Ben Roberts. (Killarney–U.A.) Rel: Floating. (C.) 85 Mins.

Seconds
Brilliant in part, wholly interesting and unusual Frankenheimer film of the macabre David Ely novel about a man given a second chance in life but only at a horrible cost. Cast: *Rock Hudson, Salome Jens, John Randolph, Will Geer, Jeff Corey, Richard Anderson, Murray Hamilton, Karl Swenson, Khigh Dhiegh, Frances Reid, Wesley Addy, John Lawrence, Elisabeth Fraser, Dody Heath, Robert Brubaker, Dorothy Morris, Barbara Werle, Frank Campanella, Edgar Stehli, Aaron Magidow, De De Young, Francoise Ruggieri, Thom Conroy, Ned Young, Kirk Duncan, William Richard Wintersole.* Dir: John Frankenheimer. Pro: Edward Lewis. Screenplay: Lewis John Carlino. (Joel–Paramount.) Rel: Floating. 100 Mins.

The Secret War of Harry Frigg
Lightly amusing comedy about a U.S. Army private, famous for his military non-conformity and his ability to break out of every jail that this attitude leads him into, suddenly promoted to General and sent to Italy to be taken P.O.W. and so help five – rather happily – incarcerated Allied Generals there to escape: a plan somewhat delayed by the beauty and availability of the lovely Contessa who owns the fine house that is their prison. Cast: *Paul Newman, Sylvia Koscina, Andrew Duggan, Tom Bosley, John Williams, Charles D. Gray, Vito Scotti, Jacques Roux, Werner Peters, James Gregory, Fabrizio Mioni, Johnny Haymer, Norman Fell, Buck Henry, Horst Ebersberg, Richard X. Slattery, George Ives.* Dir: Jack Smight. Pro: Hal E. Chester. Screenplay: P. Stone & F. Tarloff. (Albion–U.I.–Rank.) Rel: March 3. (T.) 110 Mins.

Secrets of the Nazi Criminals
A feature-length documentary film built round the Nuremberg Trial of the horrors perpetrated by the Nazis before and during the war – intended to stand as an enlightened warning to the civilised world that such things must never be allowed to happen again. Pro: Tore Sjoberg. (Eagle.) Rel: Floating.

The Serpent
Brilliantly directed and extremely well-acted Swedish film which has all the fascination of the snake which

gives the film its title, plays a part in its motivation and is also symbolic. About a group of young people, army recruits and trollops, and the orgiastic party which is the key to the action. Cast: *Christina Schollin, Harriet Anderson, Hans Ernback, Tor Isedal, Gudrun Brost, Eddie Axberg, Lars Passgard, Bjorn Gustafson, Tommy Nilsson, Morgan Anderson, Lars Edstrom, Margareta Sjodin, Signe Stade.* Dir: Hans Abramson. Story: Stig Dagerman. (Richard Schulman.) First shown at the Jacey-Tatler, Oct. 1967. 90 Mins.

Seven Golden Men
The seven of the title are a gang of bank robbers who, under cover of taking up the roadway, set out to break into the safe of Switzerland's richest bank. And it is a success of sorts – until the "honour among thieves" legend begins to wear thin! Cast: *Rossana Podesta, Philippe Leroy, Gastone Moschin, Giampiero Albertinim, Gabriele Tinti, Maurice Poli, Manuel Zarzo, Darjo de Grassi, Jose Suarez, Ennio Balbo, Alberto Bonucci.* Dir: Marco Vicario. Pro: Ugo Tucci. Screenplay: Marco Vicario. (Atlantica Cinematografica–Warner–Seven Arts.) Rel: March 24. (E.) 87 Mins.

7 Guns for the MacGregors
The fight of a family of Scots immigrants ranchers in Texas at the turn of the century against the bandits who hold the whole near-by town of San Juanito in terror. Spanish-made Western. Cast: *Robert Wood, Manny Zarzo, Nick Anderson, Paul Carter, Julio Perez Tabernero, Saturnino Cerra, Albert Waterman, Agatha Flory, Leo Anchoriz, Fernando Sancho, Perla Cristal, Georges Rigaud, Harry Cotton, Annemary Noé, Margaret Horowitz, Raphael Bardem, Molino Rojo, Cris Huerta.* Dir: Frank Grafield. Pro: Dario Sabatello. Screenplay. V. Eagle, F. Lion, D. Moreno & D. Tessari. (Italo–Spanish–Columbia.) Rel: Sept. 10. (Techniscope & T.) 90 Mins.

Seventeen
A nice addition to any collection of cinematic erotica: a Danish film about a young boy's summer holiday, during which he unsatisfactorily seduces his future wife and is seduced, far more physically enjoyably by the servant girls – and all of this is shown in titilating detail! Cast: *Ole Soltoft, Ghita Norby, Hass Christensen, Ole Monty, Bodil Steen, Susanne Heinrich, Lily Broberg, Ingolf David, Jorgen Kiil, Lise Rosendahl, Hugo Herrestrup, Annie Birgit Garde.* Dir: Anneliese Meineche. Screenplay: Bob Ramsing. (Palladium–Gala.) First shown at the Royalty, Oct. 1967. (E.) 88 Mins.

Sex from a Stranger – L'Etrangere
Enticing Marie-France Boyer as the mysterious, luscious stranger who follows literary critic Pierre Vaneck home and thereafter never leaves him for long, night or day, until the numbing twist in the end of a nicely atmosphered tale. Rest of cast: *Colette Castel, Philippe Ogouz, Pierre Massimi, Florence Briere, Jacques Marie.* Dir: Sergio Gobbi. Pro: Robert Florat. Screenplay: S. Gobbi and Jeanne Cressanges. (New Realm.) Rel: June 16. (E.) 85 Mins.

Sex Quartet – Le Fate
Delightful four-piece Italian film about four women; very amusing, with the first episode, in which *Monica Vitti* proves herself again as a vivacious and expert comedy actress, as the funniest. 1. Queen Sabina, the story of a girl chased by two amorous pickers-up who turns around and chases the third one, who's less amorous towards her, with the same intention! Cast: *Monica Vitti, Enrico Maria Salerno, Franco Balducci, Renzo Giovanpietro.* Dir: Luciano Salce. Screenplay: R. Maccari, L. Magni. 2. Queen Armenia. About a gipsy girl who seduces a doctor, but then, having won him, goes off with a van driver. Cast: *Claudia Cardinale, Gastone Moschin.* Dir: Mario Monicelli. Screenplay: T. Guerra & G. Salvioni. 3. Queen Elena. *Jean Sorel* as the young husband who finds it so easy to seduce his lovely neighbour *Raquel Welch* that he begins to wonder about his own wife! Rest of cast: *Pia Lindstrom, Massimo Fornari.* Dir: Mauro Dolognini. Screenplay: Rodolfo Sonego. 4. Queen Marta. *Alberto Sordi* as the servant who comes to accept that when his employer's wife is sober she expects impeccable employee service, but when drunk expects him to make violent love to her. Rest of cast: *Capucine, Olga Villi, Anthony Steel, Gigi Ballistra, Nino Marchetti.* Dir: Antonio Peitrangeli. Screenplay: R. Sonego. (Documento, Rome & Columbia, Paris–Gala.) First shown at Continentale, Nov. 1967. (E.) 110 Mins.

Sexy Gang
The reformation of a bad girl, friend of a crook who gives her the proceeds of a hold-up, by the subsequent love of a young artist. Cast: *Linda Vargas, Agnes Datin, Karine Ker, Sylvain Corthay, Jean-Louis Tristan.* Dir: Henry Jacques. (Inter-Production–S.F.) Rel: Floating. 88 Mins.

The Shakiest Gun in the West
Comedy Western based on the old theme of the innocent "Way Out West", this time he's a Philadelphia dentist who joins a wagon-train with the idea of pulling teeth in the New World, is married strictly for convenience by *Barbara Rhoades*, who grows to love him as his pretence of being a hero becomes a pretence no longer. Rest of cast: *Don Knotts, Jackie Coogan, Donald Barry, Ruth McDevitt, Frank McGrath, Terry Wilson, Carl Ballantine, Pat Morita, Robert Yuro, Herbert Voland, Fay DeWitt, Dub Taylor, Hope Summers, Dick Wilson, Vaughn Taylor, Ed Peck, Ed Faulkner, Arthur Space, Gregory Mullavy.* Dir: Alan Rafkin. Pro: Edward J. Montagne. Screenplay: J. Fritzell & E. Greenbaum. (U.I.–Rank.) Rel: June 2. (T.) 101 Mins.

Sherlock Holmes and the Deadly Necklace
German, English-dubbed episode in the career of the famous detective who with Dr. Watson faces up to the problem of the stolen "Cleopatra's" necklace, with the distinct suspicion that behind the crime and its aftermath is the evil hand of their old enemy Dr. Moriarty! Cast: *Christopher Lee, Senta Berger, Thorley Walters, Hans Sohnker, Hans Nielsen, Ivan Desny, Leon Askin, Wolfgang Lukschy, Edith Schultze–Westrum, Bernard Lajarrige.* Dir: Terence Fisher. (Golden Era.) Rel: Floating. 86 Mins.

The Shuttered Room
Incredible but chilling horror film about the mad old aunt shut in the attic who emerges from time to time for a murderous little outing. Cast: *Gig Young, Carol Lynley, Oliver Reed, Flora Robson, William Devlin, Bernard Kay, Judith Arthy, Robert Cawdron, Celia Hewitt.* Dir: David Greene. Pro: P. Hazelton. Screenplay: D. B. Ledrov & N. Tanchuck. (Warner.) Rel: July 9. (T.) 99 Mins.

The Slender Thread
Psychologically interesting thriller set in Seattle's Crisis Clinic, where the student volunteer on duty struggles, while the police try to track her down and save her, to keep a woman talking who has taken an overdose of sleeping tablets. Cast: *Sidney Poitier, Anne Bancroft, Telly Savalas, Steven Hill, Indus Arthur, Greg Jarvis, Robert Hoy, John Benson, Paul Newlan, Edward Asner, Jason Wingreen, Dabney Coleman, Janet Dudley, Lane Bradford, John Napier, Marjorie Nelson, N. M. Wynant.* Dir: Sydney Pollack. Pro: Stephen Alexander. Screenplay: Stirling Silliphant. (Paramount.) Rel: Floating. 98 Mins.

Smashing Time
Loosely constructed, slap-happy comedy made against a background of Swinging London, and taking a pretty disenchanted look at some of its swingingiest facets: the world of pop records and overnight stars, Carnaby Street clothes, effeminate restaurateurs, society-owned boutiques – all experienced by *Lynn Redgrave* and *Rita Tushingham* as two girls from up North who try their luck in the big city, a try not helped by all their money being pinched on arrival out of their innocently left-open bag outside King's Cross Station. Rest of cast: *Michael York, Anna Quayle, Irene Handl, Ian Carmichael, Jeremy Lloyd, Toni Palmer, Peter Jones, Arthur Mullard, George A. Cooper, Ronnie Stevens, John Clive, Murray Melvin, Mike Lennox, Bruce Lacey, Sydney Bromley, Cardew Robinson, David Lodge, Ray Mackin, Amy Dalby, The Tomorrow.* Dir: Desmond Davis. Pro: Carlo Ponti, Roy Millichip. Screenplay: George Melly. (Ponti–Paramount.) Rel: Feb. 11. (Colour.) 95 Mins.

Soledad – Bitter Fruit
French–Yugoslav–Italian co-production prize-winner which presents something of the minds of the revolutionaries and counter-revolutionaries in a South American state, where love and mistrust of comrade and lover brings tragedy for some and escape for others. Cast: *Emmanuele Riva, Beba Loncar, Laurent Terzieff, Roger Coggio, Rick Bataglia.* Dir: Jacqueline Audry. Screenplay: Colette Audry. (Contemporary.) First shown at Cameo-Poly, Sept. 1967. 93 Mins.

Some May Live
Topical story about spying in Saigon, with *Peter Cushing* the villain working for the Chinese, and *Martha Hyer* as his wife who is called upon to make

the big sacrifice. Rest of cast: *Joseph Cotten, John Ronane, David Spenser, Alec Mango, Walter Brown, Kim Smith, Burnell Tucker, Edwina Carroll, Paula Li Shiu, Keith Bonnard, Lee Peters, Carol Cleveland.* Dir: Vernon Sewell. Pro: C. Sharp & P. Snell. Screenplay: D. T. Chabtler. (Butchers.) Rel: Nov. 5. 89 Mins.

The Sorcerers
Debonair 80-year-old menace *Boris Karloff* effectively mesmerising *Ian Ogilvy* and then with his wife *Catherine Lacey* remotely controlling him on a career of theft, murder and mayhem. Rest of cast: *Elizabeth Ercy, Victor Henry, Susan George, Dani Sheridan, Ivor Dean, Peter Fraser, Meier Tzelniker, Bill Barnsley, Martin Terry, Gerald Campion, Alf Joint.* Dir: Michael Reeves. Pro: P. Curtis & T. Tenser. Screenplay: M. Reeves & Tom Baker. (Tigon.) Rel: Floating. (E.) 79 Mins.

The Sound of Music
Robert Wise's fairly straightforward screen version of the Rodgers and Hammerstein stage musical but brought into the gloriously spectacular open-air of the Austrian Alps and made extremely memorable by *Julie Andrews'* remarkable, sunny and wonderfully winning performance. She plays the postulate Nun who becomes the governess of ex-Naval Captain Von Trapp's motherless family of seven children, wins them over to her, teaches them to sing, falls in love with the captain and finally escapes with them across the mountains at the time of the Anschluss. Julie skims over the sentimentality and finally leaves you wishing the film would go on beyond the all-but three hours that it runs. Really delightful screen musical entertainment. Good performances, too, by *Peggy Wood* (the Mother Superior), *Christopher Plummer* (the Captain), *Eleanor Parker* (the glamorous Baroness) and *Richard Haydn* (the friend in need). Rest of cast: *Charmian Carr, Heather Menzies, Nicholas Hammond, Duane Chase, Angela Cartwright, Debbie Turner, Kym Karath, Anna Lee, Portia Nelson, Ben Wright, Daniel Truhitte, Norma Varden, Gil Stuart, Marni Nixon, Evadne Baker, Doris Lloyd.* Dir & Pro: R. Wise. Screenplay: E. Lehman. (Argyle–Fox). Rel: Special – Floating. (Todd-AO & D.) 172 Mins.

The Story of Israel – "Thus Spoke Theodor Herzl"
Cavalcanti's documentary about the forming of the State of Israel. Dir & Written: Cavalcanti. Pro: Y. Ephrati. (Gala.) Rel: Floating. (E.) 51 Mins.

Stranger in the House
A magnificent picture-stealing performance by *James Mason* dominates this adaptation of a Georges Simenon story about a barrister who has gone to pieces since his wife left him and is jerked back into life when he finds not only a body in the attic but that his young daughter is involved with the group who are at the centre of the crime. Rest of cast: *Geraldine Chaplin, Bobby Darin, Paul Bertoya, Ian Ogilvy, Bryan Stanyon, Pippa Steel, Clive Morton, James Hayter, Megs Jenkins, Lisa Daniely, Moira Lister, Yootha Joyce, John Henderson, Rita Webb, Danvers Walker, Julian Orchard, Ivor Dean, Marjie Lawrence, Lindy Aaron, Lucy Griffiths, Charlotte Selwyn, Melinda May, Tom Kempinski, Sheila White, Toni Palmer, Michael Standing, Anne Hart.* Dir & Screenplay: Pierre Rouve. Pro: Dimitri de Grunwald. (Grunwald–Rank.) Rel: July 2. (E.) 104 Mins.

Sudden Summer
Short travelogue sponsored by B.O.A.C. about four Middle East countries including Greece. Pro: M. Syson. (Fox.) Rel: Oct. 15.

Sullivan's Empire
Cheerful adventure melodrama about three sons tracking down their lost, presumed killed, father deep in the Amazon jungles and having to face up to hostile natives, greedy revolutionaries and other unpleasant people. Luckily they have on their side a spry, machine-gun-spraying, helicopter-flying ex-school mistress! Cast: *Martin Milner, Linden Chiles, Don Quine, Clu Gulager, Arch Johnson, Karen Jensen, Bernie Hamilton, Lee Bergere, Than Wyenn, Jeanette Nolan, Miguel de Anda, Ken Renard, Marianne Gordon, Eileen Wesson, Mark Miranda, Ruben Moreno, Nadine Nardi, Robert De Coy, Pepe Callahan, Peter Pascal.* Dir: Harvey Hart & Thomas Carr. Pro: Frank Price. Screenplay: Frank Chase. (U.I.–Rank.) Rel: Jan. 7. (Colour.) 85 Mins.

Sumuru
Sax Rohmer thriller about a sort of female Dr. Fu Manchu who's at the head of an evil world-wide organisation which plans to take over the world from the male and run it the female way! Made entirely on location in Hong Kong. In colour. Cast: *Frankie Avalon, George Nader, Shirley Eaton, Wilfrid Hyde-White, Klaus Kinski, Patti Chandler, Salli Sachse, Ursula Rank, Krista Nell, Maria Rohm, Paul Chang, Essie Huang, Jon Fong, Denise Davreux, Mary Cheng, Jill Hamilton, Lisa Gray, Christine Lok, Margaret Cheung, Louise Lee.* Dir: Lindsay Shonteff. Pro: H. A. Towers. Screenplay: Kevin Kavanagh. (Anglo–Warner–Pathe.) Rel: Dec. 3. (T & Techniscope.) 83 Mins.

The Sweet and the Bitter
Yoko Tani as the Canadian-born Japanese girl who returns to Vancouver with the object of obtaining revenge on the man she suspects of having stolen her father's fishing fleet while he was interned during the war – but finds it isn't as easy as all that! Rest of cast: *Paul Richards, Torin Thatcher, Dale Ishimoto, Jane Mallett, Teru Shimada, Sylvia Feigel, Audrey Kniveton, Sam Payne, Verlie Cooter, Peter Haworth, John Eto.* Dir, Pro & Written: James Clavell. (Monarch.) First shown at Cinephone, May, 1968.

The Swinger
Ann-Margret as the nice girl who writes naughty stories and then finds that she has to live up to the reputation of her heroines! Rest of cast: *Tony Franciosa, Robert Coote, Yvonne Romain, Horace McMahon, Nydia Westman, Craig Hill, Milton Frome, Mary Laroche, Clete Roberts, Myrna Ross, Corinne Cole, Bert Freed, Romo Vincent, Steven Geray, Larry D. Mann, Lance Le Gault, Diki Lerner, Barbara Nichols.* Dir & Pro: George Sidney. (Sidney–Paramount.) Rel: Floating. (T.) 81 Mins.

Tarzan and the Great River
Mike – Tarzan – *Henry* rushes to the aid of his professor friend *Paulo Grazindo* when the latter calls for help against the depredations of the Leopard Men, who are raiding and burning the Amazonian jungle villages. Rest of cast: *Rafer Johnson, Jan Murray, Manuel Padilla Jun., Diana Millay, Paulo Grazindo.* Dir: Robert Day. Pro: Sy Weintraub. (Paramount.) Rel: Jan. 14. (Pan & T.) 88 Mins.

Tell Me Lies.
Screen version of the Royal Shakespeare Company's stage production of the anti-American slanted "US". Cast: *Eric Allan, Mary Allen, Jeremy Anthony, Hugh Armstrong, Noel Collins, Ian Hogg, John Hussey, Glenda Jackson, Mark Jones, Marjie Lawrence, Joanne Lindsay, Leon Lissek, Robert Lloyd, Ursula Mohan, Pauline Munro, Clifford Rose, Morgan Sheppard, Hugh Sullivan, Barry Stanton, Henry Woolf, Michael Williams.* Dir & Pro: Peter Brook. (London Continental.) Rel: Floating. 117 Mins.

10.30 p.m. Summer
Jules Dassin's interpretation of Marguerite Duras's story, which she helped to script herself, about the strange tensions that develop between a man and his wife – *Peter Finch* and *Melina Mercouri* – and their mutual friend and his mistress – *Romy Schneider* – and the young wife-killer they become involved with while on holiday in Spain. Rest of cast: *Julian Mateos, Isabel Maria Perez, Neatriz Savon.* Dir: Jules Dassin. Pro: Anatole Litvak & J. Dassin. Screenplay: J. Dassin & M. Duras. (U.A.) Rel: Floating. (T.) 84 Mins.

10,000 Dollars Blood Money
One of the new-style, brutal, bloody foreign-made Westerns: about the confrontation of a kidnapper and a bounty hunter, their uneasy truce and partnership, double-cross and final show-down. Cast: *Gary Hudson, Caludio Camasco, Fernando Sancho, Lorenda Nusiak, Adriana Camasco, Pinuccio Ardia, Fidel Gonzales, Franco Lantieri.* Dir: R. Guerrieri. (Golden Era.) Rel: Floating. (T & Techniscope.) 97 Mins.

The 10th Victim
Strange story set in the 21st century when, with wars a thing of the past, the human killer instinct is satisfied by a deadly "game" in which computer selected killers stalk equally haphazardly chosen victims! Cast: *Marcello Mastroianni, Ursula Andress, Elsa Martinelli, Luce Bonifassy, Salvo Randone.* Dir: Elio Petri. Pro: Carlo Ponti. Screenplay: T. Guerra, G. Salvioni, E. Flaiano & E. Petri. (J. E. Levine–Planet.) (Colour.) Rel: Dec. 10. 92 Mins.

Terror in Tokyo
English-speaking continental spy melo about the efforts of America's Secret Agent OSS117 to discover the whereabouts of, and then destroy, a secret weapon

offered to, and turned down by the State Department, which is subsequently and most effectively used against it! Cast: *Frederick Stafford, Marina Vlady, Henri Serre*. Dir: Michael Boisrond. Screenplay: Terence Young & Pierre Foucard. (Miracle.) Rel: Sept. 24. (Scope & E.) 100 Mins.

Texas Across the River
A well made send-up of the traditional Western, with every cliché dusted off and given the free comedy treatment. Cast: *Dean Martin, Alain Delon, Joey Bishop, Rosemary Forsyth, Tina Marquand, Peter Graves, Andrew Pine, Stuart Anderson, Michael Ansara, George Wallace, Roy Barcroft, John Harmon, Dick Farnsworth, Linden Chiles*. Dir. Michael Gordon. Pro: Harry Keller. (U.I.–Rank.) Screenplay: Wells Root, Harold Greene & Ben Starr. Rel: July 9. 101 Mins.

Theatre of Death
A series of vampirish murders, a prime suspect who turns out to be himself a victim, the sinister mesmerising of a pretty young actress – all this and more seen against the grim background of Paris's "Theatre of Death". Cast: *Christopher Lee, Julian Glover, Lelia Goldoni, Jenny Till, Evelyn Laye, Ivor Dean, Joseph Furst, Betty Woolfe, Leslie Handford, Fraser Kerr, Dilys Watling, Steve Plytas, Miki Iveria, Terence Soall, Esther Anderson, Peter Cleoll, Suzanne Owens, Julie Mendez*. Dir: Samuel Gallu. Pro: M. Smedley Aston. Screenplay: E. Kasidon & R. Marshall. (Pennea–London Independent Productions.) Rel: Dec. 10. (T & Techniscope.) 90 Mins.

Thunder Alley
Love, competition and thrills on the stock-car racing circuit, where *Fabian* is the fellow whose momentary blackouts cause another driver's death and lead to a long struggle towards rehabilitation. Rest of cast: *Annette Funicello, Diane McBain, Warren Berlinger, Jan Murray, Stanley Adams, Maureen Arthur, Michael T. Mikler, Mike Bell, Kip King*. Dir: R. Rush. Pro: B. Topper. Screenplay: Sy Salkowitz. (American International–Anglo–Warner–Pathe.) Rel: April 14. (Pan & E.) 67 Mins.

Thunder of the Gods
Ann Todd's colour documentary about Greece, starting at Athens and crossing the harbour of Pireaus to Adelphi and the Oracle. Written, directed and produced, and with commentary by Miss Todd. (Warner.) Rel: Dec. 31. 30 Mins.

Thunder of the Kings
Ann Todd's documentary about ancient Egypt, with a fresh spotlight on the tombs as seen through the eyes of Miss Todd and a little boy. Some of the tombs are here photographed for the first time. Written, directed and produced and with commentary spoken by Miss Todd. (Warner.) Rel: Dec. 31. 30 Mins.

The Tiger Makes Out
Murray Schisgal's own adaptation of his successful stage comedy about a compulsive woman chaser who becomes involved with a postman's wife, a culture-vulture, who thinks she is born for better things than just being a housewife (the first time that real-life married *Eli Wallach* and *Anne Jackson* have co-starred in a film together). Rest of cast: *Bob Dishy, John Harkins, Ruth White, Roland Wood, Rae Allen, Sudie Bond, David Burns, Jack Fletcher, Bibi Osterwald, Charles Nelson, Reilly, Frances Sternhagen, Elizabeth Wilson*. Dir: Arthur Hiller. Pro: George Justin. Screenplay: M. Schisgal. (Columbia.) Rel: Feb. 18. (T.) 95 Mins.

To Sir, With Love
A sort of British, somewhat more sentimental equivalent to America's "Up the Down Staircase" with *Sidney Poitier* the new young negro teacher who within one single term by dedication and patience quite incredibly transforms a class of morons and thugs into a group of young and responsible citizens of the future! Well made, with some nice performances from Poitier and two pretty youngsters: *Judy Geeson* and *Suzy Kendall*. Rest of cast: *Christian Roberts, The "Mindbenders", "Lulu", Ann Bell, Faith Brook, Christopher Chittell, Geoffrey Bayldon, Patricia Routledge, Adrienne Posta, Edward Burnham, Rita Webb, Fiona Duncan, Fred Griffiths, Mona Bruce, Marianne Stone, Dervis Ward, Peter Attard, Sally Cann, Grahame Charles, Albert Lampert, Chitra Neogy, Elna Pearl, Stewart Bevan, Carla Challoner, Joseph Cuby, Lynn Sue Moon, Jane Peach, Gareth Robinson, Michael Des Barres, Margaret Heald, Ellison Kemp, Donita Shawe, Anthony Villaroel, Richard Willson, Sally Gosselin, Kevin Hubbard, Howard Knight, Roger Shepherd, Stephen Whittaker*. Dir, Pro & Written: James Clavell. (Columbia.) Rel: Oct. 29. (T.) 105 Mins.

Tonite Let's Make Love in London
Peter Whitehead wrote, photographed, directed, produced and edited this fidgety but quite fascinating film – in colour – about swinging, Pop, London; its art, music, dress and dollies! And what emerges from it all is the lack of any culture, the insecurity and the aimlessness of this rebellious generation. (Lorrimer.) First shown at Academy Two, Nov. 1967. 72 Mins.

Tony Rome
Neat, tough private eye thriller in the Bogart-30's tradition with *Frank Sinatra* as the 'tec of the title role involved in a most intricate web of crime springing from his ex-partner's insistence that he take up a case – which almost immediately leads to the man's death and equal lethal possibilities for Tony. Rest of cast: *Jill St. John, Richard Conte, Gena Rowlands, Simon Oakland, Jeffrey Lynn, Lloyd Bochner, Robert J. Wilke, Virginia Vincent, Joan Shawlee, Richard Krisher, Lloyd Gough, Babe Hart, Templeton Fox, Rocky Graziano, Elizabeth Fraser, Shecky Greene, Jeanne Cooper, Harry Davis, Stanley Ross, Sue Lyon*. Dir: Gordon Douglas. Pro: Aaron Rosenberg. Screenplay: R. Breen. (Arcola–Millfield/Fox.) Rel: Jan. 21. (Pan & D.) 110 Mins.

Too Many Thieves
Nicely complicated crookery about a priceless piece of Macedonian shrine treasure stolen by a quartet of thieves, who later all cheerfully double-cross and kill each other in order to raise their part of the "Take". And deeply involved is the Macedonian official whose reasons for asking attorney *Peter Falk* to try and recover the emblem are highly dubious! Rest of cast: *Britt Ekland, Joanna Barnes, Nehemiah Persoff, Pierre Olaf, David Carradine, George Coulouris, Elaine Stritch, Ludwig Donath*. Dir: Abner Biberman. Pro: R. A. Simmons. Screenplay: Geo. Bellak. (Filmways–M-G-M.) Rel: March 17. (Metrocolor.) 88 Mins.

The Tortoise and the Hare.
Half-hour film based on the old fable but with the racers now cars: an E-type and a lorry driving along the Autostrada del Sol. No dialogue: just suitable music to illustrate the contenders and some of the lovely places passed along the way. (BHE.) Rel: Feb. 11. 30 Mins.

Torture Garden
Chiller-diller about five people who go to the fair and accept macabre showman Dr. Diablo's (*Burgess Meredith*) offer to show them their – terrible, horrifying – futures. Rest of cast: *Jack Palance, Beverley Adams, Peter Cushing, Michael Bryant, Robert Hutton, John Standing, Barbara Ewing, David Baur, Michael Ripper, Nicole Shelby, Bernard Kay, John Phillips, Catherine Finn, Michael Hawkins*. Dir: Freddie Francis. Pro: Max J. Rosenberg & Milton Subotsky. Screenplay: Robert Bloch. (Amicus–Columbia.) Rel: Nov. 26. (T.) 93 Mins.

Track of Thunder
Crookery in the motor racing business with *Paul Crabtree* as the get-rich-quick operator who builds up the big race as a needle match between the two driver friends and even has them beginning to act as if he were right as they line up at the starting grid. Rest of cast: *Tom Kirk, Ray Stricklyn, H. M. Wynant, Brenda Benet, Faith Domergue, Majel Barrett, Chet Stratton, James Dobson, Sam Tarpley*. Dir: Joseph Kane. Pro: E. S. Williamson. Screenplay: M. J. Hill. (Transamerica–U.A.) Rel: May 12. (T & Techniscope.) 85 Mins.

The Tramplers
The rise and fall of ruthless dictator–cattle baron *Joseph Cotten*, who will even kill his own family in order to achieve his will, the spreading of his vast empire ever wider across Texas: and the way that son *Gordon Scott*, disgusted at his father's ways, stands up against him and smashes him. Rest of cast: *James Mitchum, Ilaria Occhini, Franco Nero, Muriel Franklin, Claudio Gora*. Dir, Pro & co-written (with Ugo Liberatore): Albert Band. (Planet.) Rel: Floating. (Colour.) 99 Mins.

Triple Cross
The Eddie Chapman Story, based on the book of that title by Frank Owen: about the real-life character, a notorious safe-cracker who the cops caught up with during his holiday in the Channel Isles and sent him to jail there. And there he was when the Germans

arrived to take over. Offering to spy for them he was parachuted into England and became a British spy. And they sent him back to work for them! Always, according to this account, Eddie served the master who offered him the cash. Incredible, holding, entertaining. Cast: *Christopher Plummer, Romy Schneider, Trevor Howard, Gert Frobe, Claudine Auger, Yul Brynner, Harry Meyen, Georges Lycan, Gil Barber, Jean-Claude Becq, Jean Claudio, Robert Favart, Bernard Fresson, Clement Harrari, Howard Vernon, Francis De Wolff, Jess Hahn.* Dir: Terence Young. Pro: Fred Feldkamp. Screenplay: Rene Hardy. (Jacques-Paul Bertrand–Cineurop–Anglo–Warner–Pathe.) Rel: Sept. 3. (T.) 126 Mins.

The Trygon Factor
Stewart Granger as the upper-class sleuth trying to get behind the "front" of the gold-melting Nuns of that English Stately Home, Emberday Hall, where masked men and murders are the order of the thrilling day! Rest of cast: *Susan Hampshire, Robert Morley, Cathleen Nesbitt, Brigitte Horney, Sophie Hardy, Eddie Arent, Diane Clare, James Culliford, Allan Cuthbertson, Colin Gordon, James Robertson Justice.* Dir: Cyril Frankel. Pro: Brian Taylor. Screenplay: Derry Quinn & Stanley Munro. (Rialto Preben Philipen–Rank.) Rel: July 2. (T.) 87 Mins.

Two for the Road
Stanley Donen's cinematic examination of love and marriage, with the story of a boorish young architect who beds and weds a young girl student, and with her finds all the friction, fury and fun of marriage; finally discovering that though it may be hell of a sort together it is a worse hell apart. Some wit, a good deal of wisdom but all spaced too far apart. An appealing performance by *Audrey Hepburn*, a less appealing, dour one by *Albert Finney*, and three delightful cameos from *William Daniels, Eleanor Bron* and *Claude Dauphin*. Rest of cast: *Nadia Gray, Georges Descrieres, Gabrielle Middleton, Jacquelien Brisset, Judy Cornwell, Irene Hilda, Dominique Joos.* Dir & Pro: S. Donen. Screenplay: Frederic Raphael. (Donen–Fox.) Rel: Oct. 15. (Pan & D.) 111 Mins.

Two Weeks in September
One of the first Anglo-French co-operative productions. Paris model *Brigitte Bardot* torn between French boy-friend *Jean Rochefort* and lover *Laurent Terzieff*, who woos her during her working stay in London and during a short holiday in Scotland. Rest of cast: *James Robertson Justice, Michael Sarne, Georgina Ward, Carole Lebel, Annie Nicolas, Murray Head.* Dir: Serge Bourguignon. Pro: Kenneth Harper & Francis Cosne. Screenplay: Pascal Jardin & S. Bourguignon. (Rank.) Rel: Nov. 5. (E & Franscope.) 95 Mins.

Ulysses
Joseph Strick's remarkable attempt to achieve the impossible and condense the vast, sprawling James Joyce account of one day in the lives of a number of people, and bring it to terms with the film: an attempt which succeeds in producing a most interesting movie, verbally rather than visually erotic and ending with the extraordinary 25-minute, sensual earthy soliloquy, of Molly Bloom as she lies in bed. Lovely performances from *Barbara Jefford* as Molly, *Milo O'Shea* as the gentle Irish Jew, Bloom, *Maurice Reeves* as the young poet, etc. Rest of cast: *T. P. McKenna, Graham Lines, Fionnuala Flanagan, Anna Manahan, Maureen Toal, Maureen Potter, Joe Lynch, Rosaleen Linehan, O. Z. Whitehead, Geoffrey Golden, Tony Doyle, Dave Kelly, Leon Collins, Des Perry, Claire Mullen, Pamela Mant.* Dir, Pro & Written (with Fred Haines): J. Strick. (Lion–Columbia.) First shown at Academy One, June 1967. 132 Mins.

Un Homm et une Femme – A Man and a Woman
Claude Lelouch's stylish and only very slightly indulgently gimmicky (in the way he uses colour and various monotone shades in his photography) story of a normal, credible love affair which develops between a racing driver whose wife has killed herself and a young continuity girl whose stuntman hubby has been killed in a film. They meet through their children being at the same Deauville boarding school and their growing affection is seen against the town's wintry background. A haunting, memorable movie and an example of the true art of the film. Beautifully acted by *Anouk Aimee* and *Jean-Louis Trintignant* and a couple of winsome youngsters (*Pierre Barouh* and *Valerie Lagrange*). Rest of cast: *Simone Paris, Antoine Sire, Souad Amidou, Yane Barry.* Dir & Story: Claude Lelouch. (Les Films–U.A.) First shown at the Curzon, Sept. 24. (E.) 105 Mins.

Up the Down Staircase
The story of a young teacher facing her first assignment in a tough, Blackboard Junglish sort of New York High School where the pupils appear to be a mixture of morons, thugs and subnormal youngsters; her involvement, defeats and small victories, snatched against a background of noise, bells, chaos and form-filling, all of which sometimes seems to leave little time for teaching. Impressively credible except for one or two obviously confected and unreal isolated incidents. Beautifully acted by *Sandy Dennis*, whose many facial and verbal mannerisms help to fill-in the highly detailed portrait. Rest of cast: *Patrick Bedford, Eileen Heckart, Ruth White, Jean Stapleton, Sorrell Booke, Roy Poole, Florence Stanley, Jeff Howard, Ellen O'Mara Jose Rodriguez, John Fantauzzi, Vinnette Carroll, Janice Mars, Loretta Leversee, Robert Levine, Elena Karem, Frances Sternhagen, Candace "Candy" Culkin, Salvatore Rasa, Lew Wallach.* Dir: Robt. Mulligan. Pro: Alan J. Pakula. Screenplay: Tad Mosel, based on the Bel Kaufman novel. (Park Place–Warner–Pathe.) Rel: Sept. 17. (T.) 123 Mins.

Up the Junction
A raw and very real picture of how the other half – that half across the river in the slums of, more particularly, Battersea – live; working in factory, fighting after the pubs shut, going off with the ton-uppers and becoming pregnant and being abortioned. All very sad and depressing and horribly convincing. Nicely acted, too; with remarkably in-key performances by *Adrienne Posta* and *Maureen Lipman* as the cockney sisters and *Dennis Waterman* as the boy who dreams of getting away from it all – and ends up in clink when he tries too hard. *Suzy Kendall* pretty in the unconvincing part of the rich little Chelsea girl who a-slumming goes and likes it! Based on the Nell Dunn novel. Rest of cast: *Michael Gothard, Liz Fraser, Hylda Baker, Alfie Bass, Linda Cole, Doreen Herrington, Jessie Robins, Barbara Archer, Ruby Head, Susan George, Sandra Williams, Michael Robbins, Aubrey Morris, Billy Murray, Michael Standing, Stephen Whittaker, Shaun Curry, Leslie Meadows, Anthony Sharman, Peter Attard, Douglas Sheldon, Queenie Watts, Olwen Griffith, Lockwood West, Michael Barrington, Mark Moss, Yvonne Manners, Harry Hutchinson, Larry Martyn, Ronald Clarke, Michael Martin, Jack Phillips, Gladys Dawson, Derek Ware, The Delacardos.* Dir: Peter Collinson. Pro: A. Havelock-Allan & John Brabourne. Screenplay: Roger Smith. (BHE–Paramount.) Rel: March 10. (Techniscope & T.) 119 Mins.

Valley of the Dolls
Melodrama about Show Business and the shocking things that go on in it! Especially how some of the young stars suffer from drug addiction, others from lovers who won't marry them, still other unfortunates from dependant relatives and illness. Some nice performances from some of the young players, especially *Barbara Parkins* and *Patty Duke*. Based on the book of the same name by Jacqueline Susann. Rest of cast: *Paul Burke, Sharon Tate, Tony Scotti, Martin Milner, Charles Drake, Alex Davion, Lee Grant, Naomi Stevens, Robert H. Harris, Jacqueline Susann, Robert Viharo, Joey Bishop, George Jessel, Susan Hayward.* Dir: Mark Robson. Pro: David Weisbart. Screenplay: Helen Deutsch, Dorothy Kingsley. (Robson/Weisbart–Fox.) Rel: Feb. 11. (Pan & D.) 123 Mins.

The Vengeance of Fu Manchu
Sax Rohmer's evil Doctor is at work again, trying to organise a world-wide crime net. Luckily there's good old Nayland Smith to thwart him once more! Cast: *Christopher Lee, Tsai Chin, Douglas Wilmer, Howard Marion-Crawford, Maria Rohm, Noel Trevarthen, Wolfgang Kieling, Susanne Roquette, Horst Frank, Peter Carsten, Mona Chong.* Dir: Jeremy Summers. Pro: H. A. Towers. Screenplay: P. Welbeck. (Anglo–Warner–Pathe.) Rel: Dec. 3. (T.) 89 Mins.

The Vengeance of She
Newcomer *Olinka Berova* as Carol, the girl who is "willed" to travel from the South of France to the hidden Middle-Eastern city of Kuma where the ruler plans to exploit her as the returned "Ayesha", to pass through the sacred flame and become his immortal Queen! Based on the Rider Haggard characters. Rest of cast: *John Richardson, Edward Judd, Colin Blakely, Jill Melford, George Sewell, Andre Morell, Noel Willman, Derek Godfrey, Daniele Noel, Gerald Lawson, Derrick Sherwin, William Lyon Brown, Charles O'Rourke, Zohra Segal, Christine Pockett, Dervis Ward.* Dir: Cliff Owen. Pro: Aida Young. Screenplay: Peter

O'Donnell. (Hammer–Assoc.–Warner-Pathe.) Rel: April 14. (T.) 101 Mins.

Virgin Youth
The story of a young man, irrationally at odds with himself and the world, being brought into contact with hard reality and forced to grow up. Cast: *Jacques Perrin, Eva Renzi*. Dir: Pierre Granier Deferre. (New Realm.) First shown at the Cameo, Victoria, May, 1968.

Virtue Runs Wild
Modest little Danish comedy about an uproarious holiday spent by three city-dwellers in a remote fishing village, all of whom benefit from their stay – especially Edward, the professor, whose sleeping with the barmaid reinstates him as master of his own, previously wife-dominated house. Cast: *John Han-Petersen, Birgitte Federspiel, Axel Strobye, Caja Heimann, Louis Miehe-Renard, Bodil Steen, Katja Miehe-Renard, Hanne Loye, Morton Grunwald, Birgit Sadolin, Carl Ottosen, Lise Thomsen, Arthur Jensen, Lily Broberg, Peter Kitter, Gunnar Lemvigh, Gabriel Axel, Ole Monty, Marchen Passer, Bjorn Puggard-Moller, Elth Pio*. Dir & Written: Sven Methling. (Saga-Bargate.) First shown at Jacey–Taler, April, 1968. (Colour.) 95 Mins.

The Visit
An adaptation of the Friedrich Dürrenmatt play which the Lunts made a success on Broadway and in Britain: basically a thesis that man is vile, illustrated by the story of a woman, now one of the wealthiest widows in the world, who comes back to the seedy, running-down central European town of her birth and offers it a million, with another million shared among the citizens, if they will legally kill her ex-lover, who made her pregnant as a young girl and by forged evidence of her loose morals, drove her out of the town to a period of prostitution in Trieste. And she watches as the town festers and the people, all of them, become corrupted and eventually contemptible as they finally trump up a case, alter the law and condemn the man to death. Well acted. Cast: *Ingrid Bergman, Anthony Quinn, Irina Demick, Paolo Stoppa, Hans-Christian Blech, Romolo Valli, Valentina Cortese, Claude Dauphin, Eduardo Cianelli, Marco Guglielmi, Lelio Luttazzi, Dante Maggio, Renzo Palmer, Fausto Tozzi, Richard Munch, Ernst Schroeder, Leonard Steckel, Jacques Dufilho*. Dir: Bernhard Wicki. Pro: J. Derode & A. Quinn. Screenplay: Ben Barzman. (Fox.) Rel: Floating. (C.) 100 Mins.

Vivre Pour Vire – Live for Life
Claude Leloch's story of a marriage into which he introduces all sorts of other themes and ideas including an obvious obsession with the Vietnam war. *Yves Montand* as the "Match" and TV ace reporter who uses the excuse of assignments to deceive his wife (*Annie Girardot*) and spend amorous weekends and is finally pried, temporarily, away from her by the advent of an American girl (*Candice Bergen*). And it all ends with the victory of marital habit as the couple get together again. Stylish, modern without being offensively so, fascinating. Rest of cast: *Irene Tunc, Anouk Ferjac*. Dir: Claude Lelouch. Pro: A. Mnouchkine & G. Dancigers. Screenplay: C. Lelouch & Pierre Ugtherhoeven. (Transamerica–U.A.) First shown at Cameo–Poly and Cameo–Victoria, March, 1968. (D.) 130 Mins.

The War Wagon
A great big, serio-comic Western about dispossessed rancher John Wayne's plan to get even with the villain who has stolen his "spread", with the buildings above and the gold below, by holding up – with the help of the gunman paid to kill him (*Kirk Douglas*) – the armoured, gatling-gunned stagecoach escorted by a whole army of gunmen in which the bad man is transferring his fortune. Entertaining, amusing and nicely acted. Rest of cast: *Howard Keel, Robert Walker, Keenan Wynn, Bruce Cabot, Valora Noland, Gene Evans, Joanna Barnes, Terry Wilson, Don Collier*. Dir: Burt Kennedy. Pro: Marvin Schwartz. Screenplay: Clair Huffaker. (Batjac–Schwartz–U.I. Rank.) Rel: Dec. 31. (T & Pan.) 101 Mins.

Waterhole 3
James Coburn as the stealer and seducer anti-hero, (a success at both) in a Western about the theft of a fortune in gold bullion and the subsequent struggle for its possession. Rest of cast: *Carroll O'Connor, Margaret Blye, Claude Akins, Timothy Carey, Joan Blondell, James Whitmore, Henry Davis, Roy Jenson*. Dir: Wm. Graham. Pro: J. Steck. Screenplay: J. T. Steck & R. R. Young. (Blake Edwards–Paramount.) Rel: Nov. 26. (T & Techniscope.) 96 Mins.

Way. . .Way Out
Jerry Lewis comedy in which as a future weatherman he's sent to the moon on his honeymoon in order to relieve the sex-starved male team on duty there. Rest of cast: *Connie Stevens, Robert Morley, Dennis Weaver, Howard Morris, Brian Keith, Dick Shawn, Anita Ekberg*. Dir: Gordon Douglas. Pro: Jerry Lewis. Screenplay. Wm. Bowers & Laslo Vadnay. (Coldwater–Fox.) Rel: Oct. 1. (Colour & C.) 106 Mins.

The Way West
Large-scale, spectacular Western based on the A. B. Guthrie (Jun.) Pulitzer prize-winning book of the same title about a wagon train struggling along the old Oregon trail in 1843. Nice to watch but with some of the story angles, and some of the characters, oddly undeveloped. Cast: *Kirk Douglas, Robert Mitchum, Richard Widmark, Lola Albright, Michael Witney, Stubby Kaye, Sally Filed, Katherine Justice, Michael McGreevey, Connie Sawyer, Harry Carey Jr., Elisabeth Fraser, William Lundigan, Anne Barton, Roy Barcroft, Eve McVeagh, Paul Lukather, Peggy Stewart, Stefan Arngrim, Jack Elam, Hal Lynch, Timothy Scott, John Mitchum, Roy Glenn, Patric Knowles, Nick Cravat, Gary Morris, Michael Lane, Eddie Little Sky, Michael Keep, Clarke Gordon, Ken Murray*. Dir: Andrew V. McLaglen. Pro: Harold Hecht. Screenplay: Ben Maddow & Mitch Lindemann. (U.A.) Rel: July 16. (Pan & Colour.) 122 Mins.

The Whisperers
Slow, deeply intuitive, brilliant study of old age and loneliness, with *Dame Edith Evans* giving a magnificen performance as the septuagenarian tottering towards senility whose smooth and dismal rhythm of life is broken first by the discovery of the stolen money her jailed son has left in her room and secondly by the temporary return of her no-good husband. A most unusual movie; written and directed with artistry and great perception by Bryan Forbes. Rest of cast: *Eric Portman, Nanette Newman, Avis Bunnage, Gerald Sim, Ronald Fraser, Leonard Rossiter, Kenneth Griffith, Harry Baird, Robert Russell, Margaret Tyzack, Clare Kelly*. Dir: B. Forbes. Pro: M. S. Laughlin & R. Shedlo. Screenplay: B. Forbes. (Seven Pines–U.A.) Rel: Sept. 24. 106 Mins.

Who Are You, Polly Magoo?
Way-out, surrealistic sort of movie about a model girl; mixing dream and fact and sometimes almost savagely cutting from one to the other. With *Dorothy McGowan* delightful in the title role, refusing to be daunted by crazy wigs and horrible fashions. Rest of cast: *Jean Rochefort, Sami Frey, Philippe Noiret, Grayson Hall*. Dir & Written: Wm. Klein. (Contemporary.) First shown at Cameo Poly, Jan., 1968. 102 Mins.

Who's Minding the Mint?
Comedy about a "money-checker" at the U.S. Mint who accidentally destroys $50,000 and then sets out with the help of an ever-increasing band of associates to print enough "genuine"-forged bills to replace them! Cast: *Jim Hutton, Dorothy Provine, Milton Berle, Joey Bishop, Bob Denver, Walter Brennan, Victor Buono, Jack Gilford, Jamie Farr, David J. Stewart, Corinne Cole, Jackie Joseph, Bryan O'Byrne, Robert Ball, Dodo Denney, Luther James, Mickey Deems, Lennie Bremen, Cordy Clark, Thom Carney, Khalil Bezaleel*. Dir: Howard Morris. Pro: Norman Maurer. Screenplay: R. S. Allen & Harvey Bullock. (Columbia.) Rel: Nov. 5. (T.) 97 Mins.

The Wild One
Though shown at a few cinemas when it first came here in 1956, this impressive, tough story of a gang of young motor-cycle thugs who descend on a small American town and terrorise it when one of their own numbers is involved in an accident of his own making, now gets its first certificate and general release. *Marlon Brando* as the inarticulate, almost sub-human leader of the mob. Rest of cast: *Mary Murphy, Robert Keith, Lee Marvin, Jay C. Flippen, Peggy Maley, Hugh Sanders, Ray Teal, John Brown, Will Wright, Robert Osterloh, Robert Bice, William Vedder, Yvonne Doughty, Keith Clarke, Gil Stratton, Jun., Darren Dublin, Johnny Tarangelo, Jerry Paris, Gene Peterson, Alvy Moore, Harry Landers, Jim Connell, Don Anderson, Angela Stevens, Bruno VeSoto, Pat O'Malley*. Dir: Laslo Benedek. Pro: Stanley Kramer. Screenplay: John Paxton. (Columbia.) Rel: April 28. 79 Mins.

Wild, Wild Planet
Italian made, English-dubbed science-fiction story set in the year 2015 when it is no longer between the nations that there is friction, but between power planets. Cast: *Lisa Gastoni, Tony Russell, Enzo*

Fiermonte, Franco Nero, Carlo Giustini. Dir: Anthony Dawson. Pro: J. Fryd & A. Margheriti. Screenplay: Ivan Reiner. (M-G-M.) Rel: Feb. 4. 85 Mins.

Will Penny
A fine, traditional Western in the "Shane" tradition; mixing today's more mature attitudes with a wonderful Bill Hart-style story. *Charlton Heston* as the all-but fifty-year-old cowboy whose taking the lonely line-rider's winter job results in him being attacked, tortured – and loved! Wonderful backgrounds, grand performances from *Heston, Joan Hackett* (as a real woman), and a number of others. Rest of cast: *Donald Pleasence, Lee Majors, Bruce Dern, Ben Johnson, Slim Pickens, Clifton James, Anthony Zerbe, Roy Jenson, G. D. Spradlin, Quentin Dean, William Schallert, Lydia Clarke, Robert Luster, Dal Jenkins, Matt Clark, Luke Askew, Anthony Costello, Gene Rutherford, Chanin Hale, Jon Francis, Stephen Edwards*, Dir & Written: Tom Gries. Pro: Fred Engel & Walter Seltzer. (Engel-Seltzer/Paramount.) Rel: Jan. 14. (T.) 108 Mins.

Winter Wonderland
Sun-fun in France's spectacular white playground. Documentary featurette. (Baim–U.A.) Rel: Oct. 22.

Witchfinder General
Bloody story of England in 1645, where against a background of the Civil War a certain sadistic magistrate rides from village to village, sorting out, trying, condemning and burning witches at three pounds a head! Cast: *Vincent Price, Ian Ogilvy, Hilary Dwyer, Rupert Davies, Robert Russell, Wilfrid Brambell, Michael Beint, Nicky Henson, John Trenaman, William Maxwell, Tony Selby, Beaufoy Milton, John Kidd, Peter Haigh, Hira Talfrey, Ann Tirard, Peter Thomas, Edward Palmer, Paul Dawkins, Michael Culver, Godfrey James, Jack Lynn, Martin Terry, Lee Peters, David Lyell, Toby Lennon, Paul Ferris, Maggie Kimberley, John Garrie, Dennis Thorne, Michael Segal, Gillian Aldham, Maggie Nolan, Tasma Brereton, Sandy Seager, Donna Reading, Sally Douglas* and *Patrick Wymark* (as Oliver Cromwell). Dir: Michael Reeves. Pro: Tony Tenser. (Tigon.) Rel: May 19. 87 Mins.

Woman Times Seven
Italian made, English-speaking seven-episode film with *Shirley MacLaine* in the leading role in each case, revealing seven facets of woman, from the girl who reads poetry while in the nude to two men to prove the superiority of the mind over body, to the woman who thinks the man following her is in love with her whereas in fact he's a detective hired by her suspicious husband! Variable in humour and effectiveness but a wonderful shop-window for Miss MacLaine's talent. Rest of cast: *Alan Arkin, Rossanno Brazzi, Michael Caine, Vittorio Gassman, Peter Sellers, Anita Ekberg.* Dir: Vittorio de Sica. Pro: Arthur Cohn. Screenplay: Cesare Zavattini. (Levine–Embassy–Fox.) Rel: June 16. (Colour.) 99 Mins.

Yoko Ono No. 4
Miss Yoko Ono's "way-out" film: 80 minutes in length, it presents close-ups of 365 walking, human bottoms, male and female, together with an amusing soundtrack of the recorded comments of the owners as they are told what is expected of them. (Connoisseur.) First shown at the Jacey–Tatler, Aug. 1967.

You Only Live Twice
One of the best of the Bond film series with James called in by M.I.5 to solve the mystery of the vanishing space-craft and so prevent the atom-bomb war that is being brought about by mutual suspicion between the Russians and Americans. And 007, with the assistance of his usual collection of girls and gimmicks, finds that it is the horrid SPECTRE people who are organising the trouble from their Japanese volcano hideaway headquarters. Some superbly filmed action sequences – as the battle between Bond in his mini-copter and four battle-copters – good performances and first-rate direction. Cast: *Sean Connery, Akiko Wakabayashi, Tetsuro Tamba, Mie Hama, Teru Shimada, Karin Dor, Lois Maxwell, Desmond Llewelyn, Charles Gray, Tsai Chin, Bernard Lee, Donald Pleasence.* Dir: Lewis Gilbert. Pro: Harry Saltzman & Albert R. Broccoli. Screenplay: Roald Dahl. (U.A.) Rel: Sept. 17. 120 Mins.

Young Dillinger
The early, violent chapters in the life of the infamous gangster: how he became Public Enemy No. 1. Related in a semi-documentary style with plenty of cold-blooded slaughter, Cast: *Nick Adams, Robert Conrad, John Ashley, Mary Ann Mobley, Victor Buono, Dan Terranova, John Hoyt, Reed Hadley, Robert Osterloh, Anthony Caruso, Art Baker, Gene Roth, Ayllene Gibbons, Frank Gerstle, Emile Meyer, Beverly Hills, Harvey Gardner, Helen Stephens, Patty Joy Harmon, Sol Gorse, Wally Rose, Walter Sande, Ted Knight, Mike Masters.* Dir: Terry O. Morse, Pro: Alfred Zimbalist. Screenplay: A. Zimbalist & A. Hoerl. (Warner–Pathe.) Rel: Jan. 21. 81 Mins.

The Young Girls of Rochefort
Jacques – "The Umbrellas of Cherbourg" – Demy's follow-up to his previous, great French musical film: the same airy-fairy little tale of love and romance, meticulously and tastefully presented, with songs and dances – and an English sound-track. Real-life sisters *Catherine Deneuve* and *Francoise Dorleac* (so tragically killed just before the film's premiere) as the sisters and the impeccable *Danielle Darrieux* as the mother who also finds lost love. Rest of cast: *George Chakiris, Grover Dale, Michel Piccoli, Gene Kelly, Jacques Perrin, Jacques Riberolles, Henri Cremieux, Patrick Jeantet, Genevieve Theinier, Pamela Hart, Leslie North, Rene Bazart.* Dir & Written: J. Demy. Pro: Mag Bodard. (Seven Arts–Gilbert–Goldschmidt–Warner-Pathe.) Rel: Floating. Shown in two versions – sub-titled and dubbed into English. (T.) 126 Mins.

Young Torless
Prize-winning German film set in a boys' boarding school prior to the Nazi era and telling the story of one of the boys who stands by until too late and watches the systematic torture and degradation of a weaker boy by two bullies. Cast: *Mathieu Carriere, Bernd Tischer, Mrian Seidowsky, Alfred Dietz, Barbara Steele, Hanne Rezzori, Herbert Asmodi, Fritz Gehlen.* Dir: Volker Schlondorff. Pro: Franz Seitz. Script: Volker Schlondorff. (Amanda in assoc. with Hunter Films.) First shown at the Cameo, Victoria, May, 1968. 85 Mins.

You're a Big Boy Now!
Comedy in the modern crazy manner, with way-out direction, musical numbers, a sketchy story and a lot of young people working very hard to put it all across with a zing! Cast: *Elizabeth Hartman, Geraldine Page, Julie Harris, Peter Kastner, Rip Torn, Michael Dunn, Tony Bill, Karen Black, Dolph Sweet, Michael O'Sullivan.* Dir & Written: Francis Ford Coppola. Pro: Phil Feldman. (Seven Arts–Warner.) Rel: July 9. (E.) 97 Mins.

Yours, Mine and Ours
"They" are the 18 children which *Henry Fonda* (10) and *Lucille Ball* (8) bring from their respective first marriages to form their new, joint alliance! The wooing, the winning and the settling down aren't all that easy, but when the respective progenies petition their parents to combine their respective family names of North and Beardsley into the one of North–Beardsley, it is obvious that calmer waters – and their nineteenth child! – are ahead. Rest of cast: *Van Johnson. Jennifer Leak, Kevin Burchett, Kimberly Beck, Mitchell Vogel, Margot Jane, Eric Shea, Gregory Atkins, Lynnell Atkins, Timothy Matthieson, Gilbert Rogers, Nancy Roth, Gary Goetzman, Suzanne Cupito, Holly O'Brien, Michele Tobin, Maralee Foster, Tracy Nelson, Stephanie Oliver, Ben Murphy.* Dir & co-written (with Mort Lachman): Melville Shavelson. Pro: Robt. F. Blumofe. (Transamerica–U.A.) Rel: June 23. (T.) 111 Mins.

INDEX

Numerals in italic represent pictorial mentions